The Clinical Treatment of Substance Abusers

THE CLINICAL TREATMENT OF SUBSTANCE ABUSERS

Leon Brill

THE FREE PRESS
A Division of Macmillan Publishing Co., Inc.
NEW YORK

Collier Macmillan Publishers
LONDON

The Free Press
A Division of Macmillan Publishing Co., Inc.
866 Third Avenue, New York, N.Y. 10022

Collier Macmillan Canada, Ltd.

Library of Congress Catalog Card Number: 81-66433

Printed in the United States of America

printing number
1 2 3 4 5 6 7 8 9 10

Library of Congress Cataloging in Publication Data

Brill, Leon.
    The clinical treatment of substance abusers.

    (Fields of practice series)
    Bibliography: p.
    Includes index.
    1. Drug abuse—Treatment—United States—Case studies.
2. Alcoholism—Treatment—United States—Case studies.
I. Title. II. Series. (DNLM: 1. Substance abuse—
Therapy. WM 270 B857t)
HV5825.B754   362.2'9   81-66433
ISBN 0-02-905160-6   .   AACR2

This book is dedicated to Dr. Harold Meiselas—colleague, friend, and mentor for almost thirty years. Dr. Meiselas pioneered in developing drug programs in New York State from the mid-1950s. He directed among the earliest programs in cyclazocine and methadone maintenance for the State Department of Mental Hygiene at Manhattan State Hospital. As Deputy Commissioner of the New York State Narcotic Addiction Control Commission (subsequently known as DACC, ODAS, and DISAS) he was associated with the most innovative and creative efforts to make the substance-abuse field truly responsive to the needs of substance abusers. This dedication is offered in the hope that it will serve as a reminder of his major contribution and the recognition due him.

Contents

Foreword

In 1978 The Free Press published the first of a series of books each of which addresses a particular theoretical approach of significance in the helping professions. Once this series was well under way it became evident that a second series was needed, one that differentially examines practice from the dimension of specific fields of practice.

Every profession has to face the complex question of specialization versus generalization. In this regard it has to come to terms with issues related to training and practice, and to make decisions about the relative emphasis given to those matters that are common to all areas of the profession's various fields of practice and those that are specific to each area.

There are of course dangers in emphasizing either extreme. If the generic is overemphasized there is a risk that important aspects of practice will be dealt with at a level of abstraction that bears little immediate relevance to what the worker actually does. If the emphasis is on the particular there is the danger of fragmentation and neglect of the need to search for commonalities and interconnections. Obviously, a balance between these two extremes is desirable.

Many of the human services, and social work in particular, have tended to overemphasize the generic to the detriment of the specific needs of clients with highly specialized needs. The majority of social work literature over the past three decades has focused either on modalities of practice as a single entity or on a specific theoretical basis of practice. This is not to say that there are not practitioners who are highly skilled in working effectively with specialized groups of clients. What is lacking is an organized compilation of the particular practice components of each of these specialized areas of practice in a way that is readily accessible to other practitioners in these areas.

Certainly within the periodical literature of social work there is a rich array of individual articles addressing specific components of practice involving work with particular client target groups. But such articles are scattered and not written from a common perspective and thus are of varying utility to practitioners.

It is the purpose of this new series to move in the direction of tapping this rich wealth of practice wisdom in a way that makes it readily available on a broad basis. To this end a series of specific fields of practice has been identified and known experts in each field have been asked to write about practice in their specialty from a common framework.

The goal of each book is to address not only the therapeutic aspects of practice in these fields but also the range of sociological, policy, administration, and research areas so as to present the reader with an overview of the specific field of practice as well as the specifics about therapy. In addition to helping the individual worker to learn more about a specific field of practice, the series as a whole, it is hoped, will provide an opportunity to make comparisons among fields of practice and thus facilitate the ongoing expansion of general knowledge.

Certainly there is growing awareness of the need for addressing the specific training and practice needs of each field of practice. Many schools of social work now arrange their curricula along the line of fields of practice. The NASW has utilized the notion of fields of practice to relate systematically to how some social workers are employed and to prescribe the roles most appropriate for them.

The fields selected for coverage in this series may or may not represent clearly defined areas of specialization in social work. Rather they are identifiable human needs or problem populations or even settings for which a discrete and identifiable cluster of attitudes, skills, and knowledge is thought to be needed in order to intervene effectively.

We are pleased to have Mr. Leon Brill as the author of the second volume in this series. Mr. Brill's impressive background as practitioner, supervisor, administrator, teacher, and author in the field of addiction makes him extraordinarily well equipped to write this book.

Mr. Brill's approach to the treatment of the client suffering from substance abuse and to his or her significant others is most humane. He constantly argues for an individualized approach to the client, adapting the treatment modality to the client's unique set of ego strengths and limitations and his unique set of significant others.

The many clinical illustrations in this volume will not only help the social worker to enhance his or her practice competence but will help workers from many other disciplines—medicine, psychiatry, education, nursing—to enrich their diagnostic acumen and their therapeutic skills.

FRANCIS J. TURNER
HERBERT S. STREAN

Preface

THIS BOOK IS INTENDED as a presentation of specific techniques for treating substance abuse, addressed to social workers, psychologists, psychiatrists, counselors, paraprofessionals, nurses, vocational rehabilitation personnel, and others in the helping professions. The book is also designed for those not directly engaged in substance abuse treatment or programming who may yet have a compelling interest in understanding what is involved, such as workers in the criminal justice system, in mental health and general medical settings, and in planning, administration, and government.

The book was initially planned to help orient social workers to the problems and issues of drug abuse treatment. As it evolved, however, it was expanded to include other treatment staff and other kinds of substance abuse, especially alcohol. Though distinctive modalities and techniques have been developed for drug abuse and alcoholism (methadone maintenance and the narcotic antagonists for drug abuse, and antabuse and the aversive modes for alcoholism), the behavioral and personality dynamics and the individual and group therapy approaches evolved for both have much in common. As the author has frequently observed, "drugs are a people thing"; we must look at the *person* rather than the substance if we are to understand the role drugs are playing in the life of any individual. The discussion therefore repeatedly touches on the dynamics and treatment of both alcoholism and drug abuse. It does not enter more fully into the chemical and medical aspects of alcoholism treatment only because this would require a separate volume for its explication.

To concretize the problems of treatment and the range of techniques required, the author sought clinical materials from five representative treatment centers in various parts of the country. The participating centers were:

1. *The Albert Einstein College of Medicine Drug Abuse Service (AECOM)*, which originated a decade ago as a unit of the Bronx Psychiatric Center and currently operates seven outpatient methadone-maintenance facilities in various parts of the Bronx, New York. Each clinic is staffed by professional and paraprofessional personnel (a social worker, an educational therapist, a vocational therapist, and a counselor) who provide treatment to substance abuse patients and their families.

The primary goal of the program is to prevent heroin abuse through the use of methadone maintenance and to help patients maintain a more stable life-style. Some of the clinics serve a predominantly middle- and lower-class Irish, Italian, and Jewish population; the others, a largely Puerto Rican and black population. In the beginning years of the program, the patients were generally highly motivated street addicts with long-standing use, and there were long waiting lists for admission. The treatment subsequently became more widely available and attracted addicts of shorter duration, with polydrug and alcohol abuse patterns, including also younger addicts who had not passed through the full cycle of addiction. This newer group had higher levels of psychopathology, and their problems of living were much more complex. Budget cuts in welfare and housing, higher unemployment, and reductions in funding for drug abuse programs complicated their situation and encumbered their treatment.

2. *The Lower Eastside Service Center* was founded by a group of community institutions in 1959 to deal with the emerging problem of drug addiction on the Lower East Side of New York City. While the initial focus was on heroin addiction, it was discovered that a broad segment of the community was actually involved in the use of multiple substances. The agency philosophy that emerged stressed the need for a variety of treatment approaches to relate to the diversity of backgrounds and problems that presented themselves. Thus, a multiservice and multimodality program was essential. Currently, the LESC offers three main modalities: a mental health clinic, methadone maintenance and other chemotherapy approaches, and a residential community. Approximately one thousand clients are served annually. Each modality has an interdisciplinary team consisting of social workers, ex-addicts, other counselors and paraprofessionals, psychiatrists, physicians, and nurses. Each modality has its own intake process but refers to the other modalities when indicated. Social workers play a role in all the modalities, but it is in the Mental Health Clinic that they have the greatest impact. The clinic offers a wide variety of services and approaches, including individual, group, and family treatment. There are also concrete services, which include assistance from Welfare, SSI, Medicaid, legal services and housing, vocational and educational coun-

seling, psychiatric evaluation, psychotropic medication, a day program for severely emotionally disabled substance abusers, a day program for older Chinese male substance abusers, a Chinese Mental Health Service, and outpostings of social workers in schools and other institutions to provide prevention, pre-intake, and consultant services. There is collaboration with probation and parole services.

3. *The University of California, Irvine, Department of Psychiatry and Human Behavior Section on Family Therapy* includes various family therapy programs for alcohol and substance abusers, directed by Dr. Edward Kaufman. The program trains family therapists, including psychiatric residents, family medicine residents, social workers, psychologists, medical students, and nurses. The focus is on families of psychotics and substance abusers. The specific alcoholism programs, including multifamily group therapy and couples group therapy are described in the chapter on family therapy.

4. *The Milwaukee County Mental Health Complex Drug Abuse Program* is a multimodality drug abuse treatment and rehabilitation program aimed primarily but not exclusively at the heroin abuser. The program uses chemotherapy in conjunction with psychotherapy, individual and group counseling emphasizing social and emotional readjustment, and vocational rehabilitation. Program components include inpatient, outpatient, and detoxification services. The multidisciplinary staff comprises physicians, registered nurses, psychiatric social workers, addiction specialists (drug counselors), and a vocational rehabilitation counselor. The goal the program strives for is the optimal biopsychosocial functioning of each client. The main indicators of progress are: freedom from illicit drug use as evidenced by frequent urine testing; a satisfactory vocational adjustment; the ability to cope with stress and crisis situations without resorting to drug abuse or other dysfunctional behavior; the development of personal relationships (family and peer group) that are satisfying and lasting; and the establishment of leisure-time activities that are not drug-related. Individual, marital, family, and group treatment methods are used, along with vocational rehabilitation and medical management to facilitate the treatment process.

5. *The University of Arkansas Graduate School of Social Work* sponsors the Arkansas Alcohol/Child Abuse Demonstration Project. The project has two main goals: to provide statistical data on alcohol-imbibing parents who abuse or neglect their adolescent children and to compare methods of effective treatment for such families. Clients are referred by community agencies such as the Juvenile Court, Adolescent Protective Services, and Arkansas Social Services. The clinical material on group couples therapy in Chapter 8 is derived from the Director's experience between December 1975 and July 1977 at the Milwaukee County Mental

Health Complex Drug Abuse Program and other alcohol and drug programs in the city, but his other contributions to this volume relate to his current experience.

The author would like to acknowledge his heavy indebtedness to the staff of these centers for agreeing to share their treatment experiences and rationales. From their different standpoints, they point up the issues encountered in treatment and the techniques, traditional and new, required to deal with those issues through individual, group, family, conjoint, and marital counseling. It will be readily apparent that there are differences and disparities in thinking and practice among them: some use the traditional psychoanalytic approach, while others are more eclectic and pragmatic, choosing from a range of options. In part, this reflects the fact that the five centers deal with different regions and client populations and employ different kinds of staff, with varying perceptions and expectations of treatment and varying levels of expertise, training, and experience. The case examples do not necessarily represent the favored approaches or biases of the author. The aim was, rather, to reflect the range and scope of modes needed to cope with the diversity of clients encountered in treatment. What emerges as surprising is the remarkable uniformity of approach and thinking evidenced on the whole.

The case illustrations and theoretical discussions of treatment issues constitute the heart of the book. While a vast bibliography has accumulated about drug and alcohol abuse generally, very little has been written about the actual techniques and approaches to be used with different drug abusers. Dr. Kaufman's recent book *Family Therapy of Drug and Alcohol Abuse*, which is frequently cited here, is a welcome exception. On the whole, more has been described for alcoholism than for drug abuse. What the present book offers is a broad and, the author believes, rational perspective on the field of substance abuse and substance abuse treatment which can serve as a beginning orientation for workers and a springboard for training and further preparation. Toward this end, additional chapters are included to serve as a matrix and context for the clinical chapters, as well as a detailed bibliography and index.

The book is divided into three sections. The four chapters in Part I offer a historical overview of the management of substance abuse in the United States since the passage of the Harrison Narcotics Act in 1914, the watershed in our handling of the heroin problem; a review of current treatment modalities and the rationales for them; a consideration of general and specific issues related to the management and treatment of substance abuse; and a discussion of drug classifications and drug terminology. A chapter on prevention is also included in this first part.

Part II offers theoretical discussions of issues in treatment and of the intake process. It also provides case illustrations of the different treatment modalities and techniques, including individual, group, couple, conjoint, and marital counseling and single and multiple family therapy. Part III deals with the "adjuncts" of treatment; that is, those crucial components of programming such as interdisciplinary collaboration, training, and supervision. The Appendixes list the principal informational resources available from the federal government and also outline the federal guidelines and criteria developed over the years for the assessment and treatment of substance abuse.

The book hardly aspires to be "definitive." In keeping with the "rational perspective" outlined for drug abuse treatment and management, it is clear that our techniques must be multifaceted if they are to begin to address the needs of the diverse population of users. The field of substance abuse is still in a state of flux, and there are too many unknowns about substance abuse to think of final answers. Workers need to develop imaginative and creative methods that fit in comfortably with their own treatment and life experiences and inclinations, personal styles, and perceptions of the needs of each client. They must, above all, avoid the previous mistake of stereotyping treatment by recognizing the complexity of substance abuse and selecting out from a range of treatment options those best suited to meet the needs of a particular client.

Acknowledgments

The author is heavily indebted to the following contributors of clinical materials for sharing their treatment experiences and rationales:

Floyd A. Aprill, Psychiatric Social Service Supervisor for the Milwaukee County Mental Health Complex Drug Abuse Program. Mr. Aprill is also Field Instructor for the University of Wisconsin-Milwaukee School of Social Welfare and program adviser for the National Drug Abuse Conference. Special thanks are due Mr. Aprill for allowing us to quote from his papers on intake and group therapy and for his private communications on these issues and the question of standards. His case studies of individual therapy, both alone and supplemented by other modes, such as relaxation and sexual therapy, represent a welcome addition to the book.

Herbert Barish, Assistant Director of the Lower Eastside Service Center, contributed two extended cases that reflect the frequent agency need for long-term involvement with chronic cases and the endless patience and endurance required to stay with the client through all his or her vicissitudes. One case was used to illustrate the need for close collaboration on the part of different staff and program components. Mr. Barish also contributed four brief case studies or vignettes, with the assistance of four members of his staff: Paul Kaiser, John Reed, Toni Fernandez, and Dan Roisman. Mr. Barish finally provided from an unpublished paper examples of some common problems encountered in treatment. He is actively associated with various social work organizations and is engaged in private practice.

From the Albert Einstein College of Medicine Drug Abuse Program, for a case discussion, my thanks are due to *Frieda Plotkin,* Director of Social Services, and her assistant *Philip Stronger.* Ms. Plotkin is responsible for the drug abuse services provided by the staff. She has a private psychotherapy practice in New York City. Mr. Stronger, a psychiatric social worker, worked as a group therapist for the New York State Drug Abuse Control Commission between 1969 and 1976 and currently has a private practice in psychotherapy.

For the section on training paraprofessionals, *Eugenia Curet* shared her experiences in the AECOM program. Ms. Curet is Supervisor of Clinical Case Management for one of the clinics. She was formerly Director of the Bachelor of Social Work Program at Universidad Mundial in Puerto Rico and consultant to the Inner-City Support Systems Project, Department of Psychiatry, at the New Jersey College of Medicine and Dentistry. Her assistant, Joanne Page, is a Master of Arts candidate at the New School of Social Research and has worked as manager of a psychiatric halfway house, case aide in a day program for schizophrenic drug abusers, and educational therapist in the AECOM program.

From the University of California at Irvine Department of Psychiatry and Human Behavior Section on Family Therapy, *Dr. Edward Kaufman* is Associate Clinical Professor of Psychiatry and Coordinator of Residency Training and Professional Education. Dr. Kaufman is also Editor-in-Chief of the *American Journal of Drug and Alcohol Abuse.* He is the author of the excellent *Family Therapy of Drug and Alcohol Abuse,* from which he graciously gave the author permission to quote and which is frequently cited in the present volume. His assistant, *Jane Roschmann,* collaborated in preparing the case material used in the chapter on family therapy.

And from the University of Arkansas School of Social Work Arkansas Alcohol/Child Abuse Project, we would like to acknowledge our thanks and indebtedness to *Dr. Jerry F. Flanzer,* who contributed material on couples therapy and also granted permission to quote from his papers on group and family-directed therapy. Dr. Flanzer is Director of the Mid-America Institute on Violence in Families. He was previously senior research consultant with the University of Wisconsin-Milwaukee Parent–Child Welfare Resource Center Project and Director of the School of Social Welfare Alcoholism Training and Research Program. The couples therapy described in Chapter 8 was performed in Milwaukee.

PART I

OVERVIEW

CHAPTER 1

Evolution of Treatment and Management Approaches

Management of the Opiate Problem: A Brief Overview

THE YEAR 1914 MARKED a turning point in the handling of the opiate problem in the United States with the passage of the Harrison Narcotics Act, which undertook to regulate the supply and distribution of heroin and effectively outlawed use of the drug (1, 2, 6, 17, 23, 25). America subsequently became obsessed with heroin use, in part because of the drug's association with crime. Since marijuana and cocaine use were believed to lead to heroin addiction, these drugs too were mistakenly classified as narcotics (cocaine is now classified as a stimulant and marijuana as a hallucinogen) and made prime targets for sanctions. For many decades there was far less awareness of the greater dangers and pervasiveness of other drugs, such as barbiturates and amphetamines, and of substances not considered drugs at all, such as alcohol and to-bacco (1, 2, 6, 9, 10, 13, 21, 23).

Though the need for treatment of dysfunctional drug abusers in the community is now widely recognized, for a long time preliminary treatment in a hospital or institution was advocated as the sole approach in every case. One of the reasons emanated from experience with the walk-in clinics established in some forty-four cities between 1919 and 1923 to deal with the problem of a restricted heroin supply following passage of the Harrison Narcotics Act (1, 9, 17, 21, 25).

3

This legislation reflected the growing opposition to the unregulated use of opiate derivates in patent medications and home remedies, which, according to some estimates, had led to the unwitting addiction of hundreds of thousands of individuals before 1914. The Harrison Act totally banned the use of heroin, and this was reinforced by subsequent Supreme Court decisions and the work of the Federal Bureau of Narcotics (1, 9, 17, 21, 23, 25).

Records of the walk-in clinics were sparse, and estimates of their effectiveness varied with the attitudes of different observers. It is now believed that at least some of these clinics, such as the ones in New York and in Shreveport, Louisiana, functioned effectively. The precise reasons why these clinics were all closed by 1924 are no longer clear, but it is believed that opposition by the American Medical Association and the police played a major role. It was the AMA view that addicts requiring treatment should first be hospitalized in a drug-free environment where rehabilitation could be pursued; only later could they safely be released to the community. This approach derived from the idea that patients needed to be "quarantined," that is, isolated as a prerequisite to treatment in order to overcome the "infection" of drug use. What the author has termed the "parole model" or institutional-aftercare model of treatment called for inpatient detoxification, the rebuilding of physical health, and the provision of vocational rehabilitation services, counseling, and social services. This phase was followed by supervised aftercare when it was felt the patient could be returned to the community. Abstinence became the primary, indeed the only worthwhile goal; no degree of rehabilitation was considered satisfactory unless the addict had totally renounced drug use and achieved a drug-free state (1, 9, 21).

Early Treatment Efforts

During the 1930s two Public Health Service Hospitals were established in Lexington, Kentucky, and in Fort Worth, Texas, based on the institutional-aftercare model of treatment. For several decades, they served as the main treatment centers for narcotic addiction in the country. They began to operate about 1939 and accepted voluntary as well as committed patients, the latter for periods of years in many cases. There had been a series of sweeping Supreme Court decisions starting in the 1920s, which defined the power of doctors with regard to the drug abuse problems of their patients. These decisions were not always clear, and doctors were discouraged from treating addicts because they feared being penalized or even jailed and deprived of their licenses to practice. The Federal Bureau of Narcotics under its Commissioner Anslinger was stringent in its attitude toward nonmedical drug use and the legislative mandates became more punitive over the years, culminating in the Boggs Law enacted in the 1950s and the "Rockefeller Legislation" in New York State in 1973. An interim period during World War II, when no heroin could be transported into the country, ended by the early 1950s. In New York, the resurgence of the heroin problem generated a local response, the establishment of the Riverside Hospital for adolescents in 1952, under the mistaken notion that this age group would be most amenable to intervention and cure. Both the Riverside Hospital and the State Department of Mental Hygiene programs initiated in 1959 adopted the institutional-aftercare model. In California a program for drug addiction was developed under the aegis of the State Department of Corrections. During the mid-1960s, institutional-aftercare programming was further expanded under the auspices of the federal government's Narcotic Addiction Rehabilitation Administration (NARA).

The 1960s also witnessed the proliferation of therapeutic communities directed by ex-addicts and modeled after Synanon in California. Their goals closely paralleled those of the institutional-aftercare paradigm, with emphasis on initial institutionalization and on total abstinence thereafter (2, 5, 8, 9, 21, 26).

The first important change in treatment philosophy occurred in 1964 with the development of chemotherapy: methadone maintenance and the narcotic antagonists (2, 5, 8, 9, 11, 21). The proponents of methadone maintenance believed that very few individuals could achieve total abstinence immediately and that many would never achieve a drug-free state. They offered the radical idea that it was acceptable for narcotic-dependent persons to be supported by a narcotic drug if this helped them to function productively in the community. This thinking coincided with developments occurring elsewhere in medicine, particularly in the treatment of psychotic patients with the major tranquilizers and the treatment of neurotic problems with the minor tranquilizers (see Chapter 3). Other modalities developed about the same time for the treatment of narcotic use included the application of nonpunitive authority concepts, which the author has termed "rational authority" (3, 5, 7, 15); religious approaches such as "Teen Challenge" (2, 8, 9, 21); residential centers and halfway houses for individuals who cannot remain in the community; and specialized day-care centers for youngsters along with special facilities for minority representatives, including women (2, 9, 15, 21).

The Multimodality Approach

It is now generally accepted that nonmedical drug users comprise a great diversity of individuals who are drug-dependent in different ways and degrees, use drugs to meet different needs, have different psychological characteristics, come from different socio-economic backgrounds, are of both sexes, and represent a wide range of ages, races, and ethnic groups. No single treatment response will work for all: we need to match a particular approach to each individual. Comprehensive programming is called for to respond to the diversity of client characteristics. The multimodality approach undertakes to provide a full range of services and to be available wherever drug users are found—for example, in health centers, industry, schools, unions, recreational centers, and hospitals. The program must allow for rapid admission of clients on either a voluntary or a compulsory basis. Services must include detoxification, emergency treatment, transitional care, and long-term ambulatory help for those individuals who can be treated in the community, as well as residential care, either professionally led or directed by ex-addicts. Ambulatory services should include day centers and clinics that offer counseling services, casework, and individual and group psychotherapy, with or without the assistance of chemotherapeutic agents such as methadone or the narcotic antagonists. There must also be a range of facilities for non–opiate users focused on the needs of the younger drug-using population as well. Drug services must be integrated into the general health and mental health services and regionally organized so that comprehensive and coordinated decentralized services are readily available in each area (2, 9, 18, 21). Emergency services should be offered not only in hospital emergency rooms but through hot lines, crash pads, information and referral centers, and the so-called free clinics, such as the one in the Haight-Ashbury section of San Francisco, which offers a wide range of services apart from drug assistance, including legal and medical assistance, help for runaways, counseling on VD and abortions, and concrete services (2, 9, 21).

The multimodality approach that gradually evolved differed vastly from what the psychoanalytic therapists had anticipated; that is, the use of traditional psychoanalytic techniques in an effort to achieve personality change and reorganization. The major modalities for narcotic addiction included chemotherapy; the use of paraprofessional aides in ex-addict-directed therapeutic communities in which professionals played little or no part at first; religious approaches; the use of coercive methods, including civil and criminal commitment through the courts; community action programs such as that of the Young Lords in the South Bronx in New York City; and programs geared to the needs of special populations of users such as the Addict Rehabilitation Center in Harlem directed to blacks and SERA and SU CASA in New York aimed at Hispanics. Although it might be concluded that the psychoanalytic model had not been at all useful in relation to drug abusers, in fact the psychoanalytic understanding of personality organization and behavioral dynamics has remained the core and foundation of treatment. There was need to reaffirm the importance of the relationship as the central core of treatment and of transference and counter-transference in dealing with clients. This was as true of individual as of group therapy (2, 4, 6, 21).

A. MAJOR MODES OF TREATMENT FOR OPIATE ABUSERS

Most of the modalities described below follow a definite prototype and have adhered closely to their model over the years. Thus, the methadone maintenance clinics have followed the Dole-Nyswander model developed at the Beth Israel–Morris Bernstein Institute in the mid-1960s, while the therapeutic communities replicated the Synanon model in California. The early prototype facilities further reinforced their model by training the leaders of new programs established in different parts of the country. The funding sources, whether city, state, or federal, dictated certain requirements and guidelines, which each program had to meet if it was to receive the funds. This too served to reinforce the model. The federal government issues a set of "Federal Funding Criteria" (see Appendix 2), which stipulate the conditions such programs must fulfill if they are to be funded. In the case of chemotherapy, the regulations regarding admission criteria, staff–patient ratios, and medical, laboratory, and other facilities were even more stringent (8, 11).

As a result, many of the methadone and therapeutic community programs resemble each other, except perhaps for differences in staff and community orientation. Dr. Bernard Primm's methadone maintenance program in the Bedford-Stuyvesant section of Brooklyn, for example, differs from other programs in its greater insistence on eventual abstinence as a goal and its focus on a predominantly black population. The therapeutic communities have moved away from the Synanon model, which seeks to hold on to its residents forever by reducing the length of stay to as little as six months in some cases, and by modifying the punitive approach of the abrasive encounter sessions, which constitute the core of the treatment effort (2, 5, 8, 21, 26). There is greater emphasis today on the use of professional personnel, modification of some of the former questionable techniques, and return to the community ("reentry").

Methadone maintenance represented an important departure from other treatment modalities in that it did not insist on total abstinence as a primary goal. On the contrary, it for the first time offered the concept that it was permissible for clients or patients to be maintained on a drug if this could be used to help them abandon the criminal life-style and move toward productive social functioning. This concept was buttressed by the experience in the 1950s and 1960s with the state hospitals' use of the major tranquilizers for psychotic patients, which permitted large numbers of chronic patients to leave the hospitals and return to the community. Dr. Dole and Dr. Nyswander, the pioneers in the field of methadone stabilization, offered the rationale that stabilization on methadone would reduce the craving for heroin and permit patients to focus on their social rehabilitation. Methadone maintenance has been described as "the substitution of one drug for another," but this ignores the central concept: methadone is used rather as a lever to help move patients toward improved social functioning and conventional patterns of living. Dole and Nyswander began by addressing the question of whether there was some medication which would permit chronic, compulsive heroin users to become law-abiding members of society. Ideally, the medication would have to be orally effective, nontoxic, and safe to give over prolonged periods. It would relieve chronic preoccupation with the use of heroin and would permit a stabilization dose not requiring frequent readjustments. Further, its duration of action would be long enough to enable all doses to be given under direct observation. More important, it had to be acceptable to patients. All these criteria were met, and the duration of action was extended by the introduction of the longer-acting (up to seventy-two hours) form known as LAAM. Methadone maintenance has also proved to be one of the most acceptable of the treatment modalities: it has served approximately ninety thousand patients nationwide and about forty thousand in and around New York City. It has also been instrumental in drawing into the treatment field for the first time large numbers of medical personnel, nurses, and other professionals and using hospitals and clinics as a base for treatment. Nevertheless, a number of issues have presented themselves, among them the illicit diversion of methadone; the fact that, though patients did not continue to abuse heroin, many continued to "chippy" with other drugs, including alcohol; and had more difficulty than anticipated getting off methadone and into an abstinent state (2, 5, 8, 9). Although great use was made of paraprofessionals in the first years of methadone maintenance, there has been recognition that many of the cases are more complicated and recalcitrant, require long periods of treatment, and often call for more professional staff, including social workers, psychiatrists, and vocational counselors. The combination of alcohol with drug abuse represents a formidable linkage that has called for more intensive treatment efforts than originally visualized.

Methadone maintenance has used a system of rewards and punishments. Patients are initially required to come in daily until they can be trusted to come in less frequently and not to divert their methadone illegally. Urinalysis is used to check that other drugs are not being used. If a patient regresses, his privileges are revoked and he reverts to coming into the clinic daily once again.

Methadone, being taken orally, helps pull addicts away from use of the needle, which was associated with the immediate "rush" of sensation following injection and the general "impulse-ridden" life-style of the addict. As mentioned, the medication is also dispensed in a legitimate agency and not hustled on the street. The staff, which includes former associates of the patient on the street, are geared to serve as role models for the patient, to draw him away from the underworld subculture and toward the values and goals of the mainstream culture. The use of the stabilizing methadone serves as a powerful lever to attract and hold for long periods patients who have been notoriously difficult to involve and retain in treatment.

Addiction needs to be viewed as a chronic-relapsing condition, hence long-term treatment will be involved in most cases of true addiction. Progress will need to be measured in relative and limited rather than absolute terms. We shall also need to differentiate among our different patients, depending on their individual strengths and weaknesses and where they stand at the time of admission into treatment. Some will indeed be able to achieve relative or total abstinence, while others may need to be maintained indefinitely on methadone. Our rationale will need to encompass the fact that for some individuals maintenance on drugs is the best or the only way they can live out their lives and function more or less autonomously in the community. The emphasis should be on whether they can function productively, rather than on their achievement of total abstinence, which may be of secondary importance.

In practice, the federal guidelines stipulate that program staff must make periodic assessments of patients' ability to achieve abstinence and must gear their treatment efforts toward that end. However, there is better understanding that patients who cannot achieve abstinence will not be dropped arbitrarily from the program, as many were in the past. If we view methadone maintenance from this standpoint, we see that it has been largely successful in its efforts to rehabilitate large numbers of heroin addicts. It has been amply documented by the Gearing studies in New York and by other studies nationally that methadone maintenance has been helpful in increasing patients' productivity and reducing their criminal activities.

There are still issues that need to be addressed, among them the fact that some 25 percent or more of the patients continue to use alcohol and other drugs for long periods and that there has been continued illicit diversion of methadone onto the streets, creating the new phenomenon known as "primary methadone abuse." Methadone has nevertheless found its place as an important modality in the multimodality approach to opiate treatment.

As indicated, one of the unanticipated problems in methadone treatment has been that of detoxifying patients and helping them get off methadone after a period of time. W. R. Martin has explained at least some of the problems involved in his papers on "protracted abstinence" (14). Martin demonstrated that a number of physiological symptoms, which are signs of stress, follow upon detoxification, complicate the patient's efforts to abstain from opiates and thus cause relapse. The current theory is that following even very slow detoxification most opioid-dependent individuals will experience a period of protracted abstinence characterized by both disturbances in mood and increases in the likelihood of relapse to opioid use. These protracted abstinence phenomena are probably superimposed on the conditioned abstinence phenomena that develop as a consequence of drug use and repeated episodes of withdrawal. There are also the previous psychological problems, which re-emerge once the defense of drug use is removed, including for many the severe depressive spectrum of mood disorders that may have antedated the drug use itself.

On the other hand, there is ample documentation that a substantial proportion of individuals who were dependent on opioids experience spontaneous remissions and changes in drug use as they grow older, a "maturing out." Other data suggest that, up to about a year, the longer an individual remains in any treatment program, the more marked and long-lasting are the changes in social adjustment or drug-using behavior. Beyond one year, however, the changes cease to grow; there appears to be an inverse relation between pretreatment social and psychological maladjustment and the duration of participation in treatment. Besides, since spontaneous remissions have been observed, it is difficult to separate treatment-induced changes from those that might have occurred without intervention (13). From this it can be inferred that most decisions about the kind of treatment to be offered must be made in the absence of a full knowledge of long-term effects. It is difficult at present to formulate optimal intervention systems. The question of training therefore becomes crucial: At present there are too few professionals with the level of training and sophistication required to consider each patient within several conceptual frameworks simultaneously and make decisions from a range of options, using multiple frameworks and procedures (13, 21).

The use of L-acetylmethadol (LAAM), a longer-acting form of methadone that permits patients to come in for their dosages only three times weekly instead of daily, has eased some of the problems of treatment, control, and diversion without any diminution of the therapeutic results. Other drugs developed recently (see Chapter 2) offer even greater therapeutic promise.

During the 1960s, high hope was held out for the *therapeutic communities directed by ex-addicts* in keeping with their so-called concept of using ex-addicts as prototypes and role models for patients in treatment. This was true in the case of the original community, Synanon, though others such as Daytop Village, Odyssey House and Phoenix House in New York City have used psychiatrists, psychologists, social workers, and other professionals as part of their staff. The original expectations of these communities were not realized fully, but they have served as an important component of multimodality programming (2, 5, 8, 9, 21). Among the criticisms frequently leveled against these facilities have been their use of abrasive and hostile "encounters" (that is, encounter groups) as their central mode of therapy; their inability to attract large numbers of clients, especially minority members, who would be willing to commit themselves to remain for one or more years in a residential setting; the mingling of young users with "hardened" older heroin addicts so that treatment often became an education and incentive toward more serious involvement with drugs and the drug life; the failure to differentiate between different categories of users, such as heroin and marijuana users; the failure to provide for careful record-keeping and for effective follow-up treatment and research; and, finally, the fact that only a small portion of the residents remained in treatment, relapsing in large numbers once they left the facility. Because these communities are strongly biased against any use of drugs, they were unable to relate to other modalities that might have picked up where they left off with patients. They were especially hostile to the use of methadone maintenance and the narcotic antagonists, which might have eased the strains of the residents' return to the community. As indicated, there has been considerable modification of the original "concept" in some cases; in addition to the employment of professionals as well as paraprofessionals, more attention has been devoted to education and training requirements, building in better record-keeping and evaluation, and developing better provision for the aftercare phase. There is still need for better differentiation among various kinds of clients, especially younger users, women, and members of minority groups (2, 5, 8, 9, 21, 26).

Perhaps the most intensive study of what takes place in therapeutic communities and how effective they are was conducted by Charles Winick (26), who investigated twenty-four communities in New York City. Dr. Winick noted a variety of such facilities, which could be differentiated by type of discipline, staff composition, length of treatment cycle, and goals. Many therapeutic communities have achieved more effective treatment approaches by concentrating on what happens at the beginning of treatment—"induction"—and at its termination—the "reentry phase." Even if a person wants to "split" from the community, he or she should have a mandatory exit interview at which staff can discuss other available activities or facilities. The "positive dropout"— the one who wishes to leave treatment before "graduation" and whose immediate goals are constructive, such as attending school—should be regarded not as a therapeutic failure but rather as someone to be helped. Therapeutic communities must accept the fact that not every drug abuser can profit from the classical long-term, high-discipline form of treatment they offer. Some can benefit from shorter-term approaches with less rigid discipline. The therapeutic communities themselves should be encouraged to explore modifications in their basic approaches. Furthermore, preparation for a career in the outside world does not receive adequate attention and time. With the likelihood that employment opportunities for ex-addict staff members will be declining, it is urgent and important for the facilities to concentrate on finding jobs, training, and placement for the graduates of their programs.

In the several years since the field work for the Winick study was completed, the number of clients receiving treatment in therapeutic communities has declined. Statewide, there were only 2,707 treatment slots in therapeutic communities in New York in 1975, with perhaps three-fourths of them occupied at any given time. There has been increased use of individual counseling by professionals such as social workers and psychologists. Some early charismatic leaders might chafe at the restrictions imposed by the funding government agencies, but they nevertheless needed to adapt to them. New emphases of the bureaucratic funding sources may have inspired new program trends. As funds became available for educational and vocational activities, such activities were given prominence in a number of the communities. Although polydrug dependence was the norm when the study was conducted, it has probably increased further since then. Since the early 1970s the therapeutic communities have been seeing more alcoholics, pill poppers, marijuana smokers, and even some non–drug abusers who had not previously been socialized into the American mainstream culture. The clients seen today are also younger.

Regarding effectiveness, Winick's study confirmed what had been known before the study: more than half the admissions drop out in the first few months, and only a very small number actually complete treatment. There has been a great deal of discussion as to what happens to the dropouts. There is a better understanding that not all who drop out should be classed as failures since they may have been "positive dropouts" who left for constructive reasons and have done well thereafter (2, 5, 9, 21, 26).

Other approaches for opiate abusers. Over the years, still other approaches were elaborated for the treatment of opiate addiction. These included religious modes such as Teen Challenge, which operates residential centers on the East and West coasts, with emphasis on religious training and evangelistic reaching out into the community for recruitment of new clients; the former Christian Damascus Church, which was geared to the needs of Puerto Rican youth in the South Bronx through a Fundamentalist Pentecostal approach, in which the leaders of the church served as loving parent figures; and the Black Muslim movement, with excessively high standards of behavior which few could maintain, so that the movement has faded out (2, 8, 21). There were also social action groups such as the Young Lords, a largely Puerto Rican group serving the South Bronx area. The Young Lords believed that social action rather than treatment was indicated to help drug abusers find a cause and reason for living as well as group supports. This group was effective in setting up its own detoxification center at the old Lincoln Hospital and has maintained it to this day at the new hospital (2, 8, 21).

Still other programs were established under public auspices, such as the New York State central agency first known as the Narcotic Addiction Control Commission (NACC), then as the Drug Abuse Control Commission (DACC), then as the Office of Drug Abuse Services (ODAS), and currently as the Division of Substance Abuse Services (DISAS). The changes in title reflect the evolution of thinking from the initial exclusive focus on narcotics to the current emphasis on other substances as well. The agency, established in 1967 by state legislation and based on the civil-commitment approach, at one time maintained some twenty-three rehabilitation centers of its own and funded a variety of private community and residential programs, including methadone maintenance. The facilities directly operated by the state agency were gradually phased out starting in the early 1970s, though DISAS, as the single state agency for the federal government and the central coordinating agency for the state, still funds the major programs in the state and exercises an overseeing and coordinating role (25, 34).

As mentioned, the author has been an advocate of still another modality or, at least, reinforcing approach, namely, "rational authority," entailing the nonpunitive use of legal authority through the courts, probation, and parole as well as the use of court diversion; that is, offering defendants caught up in the criminal justice system a choice of treatment as against incarceration (2, 5, 7, 8, 12, 15, 16, 21, 23, 24). This authority can be used as a lever to structure treatment by holding the client or patient until he or she has been enabled to make some commitment to treatment. The court diversion and the "Treatment Alternatives to Street Crime" (TASC) approaches have been extensively tested by this time and have proved their usefulness in various parts of the country.

B. SERVICES FOR NONOPIATE ABUSERS

Because of the general preoccupation with heroin, the widespread abuse of nonopiates remained largely hidden for many years. The problem was compounded because the users comprised at least two different populations: (1) those who use drugs in a legal-medical context for conventional purposes and (2) generally younger abusers, who use drugs illicitly for a variety of reasons, including sociopathic or deviant purposes. The criminal label attached to heroin addiction earlier permitted a clear demarcation between heroin addicts and conventional persons, but the distinctions between the users of other psychotropic drugs were not as clear. Until fairly recently, little thought was devoted to problems of these other drugs or to developing suitable treatment modalities for nonopiate and younger abusers. Certain questions still remain to be answered as to the kinds of facilities needed for these users and how existing techniques and approaches for heroin users should be modified to serve others, such as the polydrug users and young alcohol abusers. The facilities listed below have been developed for nonopiate and younger abusers in recent decades.

1. Crisis-intervention centers, free clinics, and crash pads. For younger users, especially those who see themselves as anti-establishment or as part of the counterculture, it has proved useful to set up centers geared to their special needs and image. Staff in these centers may have the same dress, speech, appearance, and, to some extent, even the same behavior patterns and outlook. Youngsters coming in can relate rapidly to this staff and feel accepted without extensive preliminaries and questioning. A basic service provided by these centers is crisis intervention for overdoses, detoxification, and help during "freakouts" and "bad trips" where "talking down" is indicated. These services are also offered in emergency rooms of hospitals and community clinics (21, 23).

2. Telephone hot lines. Hot lines are used extensively to provide crisis assistance. They are generally available twenty-four hours a day so that a person in distress will not need to wait. In most instances hot lines are staffed by volunteers especially trained for the purpose. Hot lines may be located almost anywhere: in hospitals, churches, stores, or private homes. Backup is provided either by additional staff at a single location or by special telephone arrangements that permit answering at more than one location. If staffing and the number of telephone lines permit more than one call at a time to be taken, it is helpful for all calls to be made through a single number.

3. Information and referral centers. Ordinarily these centers offer a place where troubled individuals can go to get information and guidance or referral to an appropriate service. They are also used to receive emergency referrals and calls. Although such places are designed for brief exchanges and the provision of information, literature, and referrals, some of them offer more extended counseling by professional staff or specially trained paraprofessionals. Such facilities have generally been located in storefronts, small loft buildings, apartments, or houses in the inner cities. In some cases, they occupy space in a larger facility such as a school, hospital, or church.

4. Counseling centers. These centers are ordinarily geared to more continuous treatment and offer more services than are available in the facilities discussed previously. Activities may include individual or group counseling; help with "concrete" problems such as housing, family assistance, vocational guidance, and job referral; welfare and legal assistance; and other services. The facility should have good liaison with cooperating agencies that can supplement its services, such as psychiatric, psychological, and medical consultation, along with additional resources for vocational guidance, training, and job placement. Optimally, counseling should involve the entire family. These centers should be conveniently located wherever there is a drug problem to ensure their accessibility to users.

5. Day centers. These centers share many of the functions of the Counseling Centers but often have a more carefully structured program since youngsters may need to spend most of the day at the center. Because treatment requires a considerable investment of time, energy, and patience on the part of the youngsters, it has been difficult for the center staff to hold them in treatment for very long. More experience and study are needed to find ways to keep youngsters from dropping out.

Chemotherapy has been used in some centers such as the one directed by Dr. Herbert Kleber in New Haven, Connecticut, where narcotic antagonists were used with narcotic abusers; or the adolescent center under Dr. Marie Nyswander in New York City, where low doses of methadone were used effectively with young heroin abusers. Because these youngsters are still involved with their families, family-focused treatment should be offered, with additional emphasis on the special education and training needs of this group.

6. Residential centers, halfway houses, and community houses. Such residences have a special role to play with youngsters who cannot remain on the street or with their families. As mentioned, youngsters should not be mingled with older adult users. Because the youngsters constitute a special group with problems and needs of their own, use should be made of whatever reinforcements come to hand, including "rational authority" if the youngster is already involved with the courts and acting out severely (2, 3, 5, 7, 9, 21, 24).

7. Medical facilities. Inpatient and outpatient detoxification facilities are needed to treat a variety of problems, such as withdrawal from heroin, barbiturates, amphetamines, and such recently troublesome drugs as the nonbarbiturate sedative-hypnotics Doriden or Quaalude and the pervasive tranquilizers, which can be addicting if grossly abused. Medical care is also needed for overdoses, abscesses, and infections such as endocarditis and hepatitis, for bad trips, panic reactions, and other contingencies. The currently much-abused drug phencycladine (PCP), also known as "angel dust" or "rocket fuel," is particularly dangerous: it may elicit psychotic-like or actual psychotic symptoms, depersonalization, and a wide range of bizarre symptoms that may be frightening to inexperienced staff. The treatment of such emergencies can be used constructively by alerting patients to the need for further help and as a basis for epidemiological studies of the drugs currently being abused in the area. In Miami, and later across the country under the National Institute on Drug Abuse's Drug Awareness Warning Network (DAWN) data collecting system, a network of emergency rooms and police and other reporting centers has been mobilized to provide a steady stream of information on what is happening in relation to drugs in different areas of the country.

C. THE COMBINED TREATMENT OF HEROIN AND ALCOHOLISM PROBLEMS

Although there has been much talk about the possibility of treating alcoholism conjointly with other drug abuse in combined settings, this has not happened in practice because of continued opposition from agencies dealing with one problem or the other. In recent years, with the proliferation of polydrug abuse, including alcohol, the separation has proved difficult to maintain. The experience of facilities such as the Eagleville Hospital in Pennsylvania, where staff has been treating abusers in joint programs for a number of years, has helped to overcome the biases of program staffs. While there is still much resistance, and the federal government maintains separate "institutes" for alcoholism and drug abuse, there have been moves to end this dichotomy in administration and treatment. The principles and techniques developed over the years for alcoholism and drug abuse, as well as for group therapy generally, can be used effectively in combined programs for alcoholism and drug abuse (2, 9, 18, 20, 21).

A study of the combined treatment of drug and alcohol abusers, cited in the *Services Research Notes* issued by NIDA's Services Research Branch in February 1977, concluded that

> ... the key question as to whether combined drug/alcohol treatment can be as effective as unitary treatment has been answered positively in a major demonstration in this area. A second issue that presents itself is the extent to which combined drug/alcohol treatment will be acceptable to the potential client population. In some large part, the acceptability of combined treatment will depend on the views the two groups of clients hold of each other and their consequent willingness to work together in treatment settings.

The *Services Research Notes* of December 1979 cites a study conducted by The Door, a combined treatment program serving rural clients in central

Florida, which confirms the previous finding that combined treatment can be effective though the results are contingent on the willingness of the clients to participate in such a program.

D. THE PLANNING PROCESS

The planning process for drug abuse treatment has become increasingly cumbersome at the state level, and undoubtedly at lower levels as well. While the objectives are laudable in themselves, it too often emerges that layer upon layer of bureaucracy has been imposed on the planning process, without effective coordination or communication between and among them. This may pose serious problems for effective planning in the future unless the situation is remedied soon.

The federal government in 1973 established the Special Action Office for Drug Abuse Prevention (SAODAP). SAODAP then required that each state set up its own "Single State Agency" (SSA) to coordinate all drug-related noncriminal activities within the state and to serve as the primary liaison with the federal government for guidelines and the routing of funds. This proved beneficial in a number of ways but created some problems of state–city liaison in states with very large cities, such as Boston or New York, where drug abuse was centered.

In 1974, under the Health Planning and Resources Development Act (P.L. 93-641), the Health Systems Agencies (HSAs) were established to review all drug abuse projects applying for federal funds and ensure that their activities were closely coordinated with those of other health activities in the state. It is apparent that when two such giant systems coexist and must collaborate to review programs and define criteria and standards, there will be problems, and this has indeed proved to be the case. Still other health care systems need to come into play, as well as the criminal justice system, the Veterans Administration, and others. Better ways need to be found to coordinate planning and communication among these systems and make sure they extend to the local regions and health areas. These activities further impact on the individual treatment programs themselves, which need to respond to a plethora of assessment forms and questionnaires and have repeatedly complained of the burden of work this places on them without the staffing complement to deal with it.

E. NIDA STUDY OF TREATMENT RESOURCES AVAILABLE
TO NONOPIATE DRUG ABUSERS

NIDA has recently sponsored a study to obtain information about the types of treatment available to persons who abuse nonopiate drugs such as barbiturates and amphetamines and to identify the critical needs of clients in such programs (22). The federal legislation that created the

Community Mental Health Centers in the early 1960s required that they provide services for drug and alcohol abusers, but this rarely happened in practice. The Domestic Council's Drug Abuse Task Force, in its *White Paper on Drug Abuse* (1975), recommended more extensive use of the CMHCs to meet the treatment needs of this group. The Drug Abuse Office and Treatment Act of 1972 and the Special Health Revenue Sharing Act of 1975 also stipulated that the CMHCs treat and rehabilitate drug abusers in their catchment areas (22).

The NIDA study examined three types of clinics: *Type I*—"free-standing" drug abuse clinics, independently and separately devoted to treating drug abusers; *Type II*—drug abuse clinics in CMHCs; and *Type III*—CMHCs without separate facilities for drug abusers. Both the samples and the number of clinics selected from different areas of the country were small, and the findings therefore need to be interpreted with caution. In the sample, the majority of clients were male, white, unmarried, young (mean age, 26.4), and unemployed. The Type I programs had young male opiate addicts with limited education and low-status jobs, many of them referred by the criminal justice system. Type II clients were more often diagnosed as having personal or emotional difficulties than Type I clients, but this may have been a function of the fact that they were being seen in CMHCs, which would be more likely to diagnose in terms of emotional disorder. The nonopiate abusers in the Type II clinics tended to be older than the Type I clients and were also better educated and with higher employment status. They were also more often self-referred. The Type III nonopiate clients tended to be the oldest, best-educated clients, with the highest unemployment status, and were more likely to be female. Many of them were self-referred. Psychosis was the most common diagnosis, followed by personality disorder or neurosis.

Planning the study proved to be difficult since very few drug treatment programs visited appeared to provide services for primary nonopiate abusers. Multiple abusers tended to be classified as primary heroin abusers, since this was better for funding purposes. Staffs in the CMHCs tended to refer drug abusers to drug clinics because they lacked the expertise to treat such clients. The diagnoses made reflected the program's orientation as much as they did the clients' actual characteristics.

Drug abuse was the most frequent primary diagnosis made for Type I clients; situational problems, drug abuse, and neurosis were diagnosed for Type II; and psychosis, personality disorders, situational problems, and neurosis for Type III programs. Regarding the types of drugs abused, Type I clients most frequently abused barbiturates and amphetamines and secondarily a variety of other drugs; Type II, barbiturates and amphetamines, but more often tranquilizers; and Type III amphetamines primarily. As to type of treatment offered, in Type I drug-free outpatient and detoxification services predominated, as did drug-free outpatient in Types II and III. Day-care was exclusive to Type III, combined with antipsychotic medications. Most patients in all program types received individual therapy (86 percent), and more than one-third were seen in group, regardless of the type of facility. Individual counseling was more frequent for depressant-abusing clients in all clinics, as it was for clients in general. Family counseling and family therapy were more often available to the Type I clients. Amphetamine abusers were also usually treated individually, though group counseling or therapy was more often available to them in the Type II clinics, which suggests that they presented more problems in treatment and needed more services, including psychological testing and detoxification. CMHC personnel had little knowledge about nonopiate abusers and were not inclined to treat them.

The NIDA study is important in that it throws light on a little-known area: our treatment of nonopiate abusers and our use of existing treatment facilities. It also points up a number of ancillary problems related to staff attitudes, lack of training, and their effects on the treatment of clients.

References

1. Brecher, E. M., and Consumer Reports Editors. *Licit and Illicit Drugs: The Consumer's Union Report on Narcotics, Stimulants, and Depressants.* Waltham, Mass.: Little, Brown, 1972.
2. Brill, L. "Drug Addiction." In *Encyclopedia of Social Work.* 17th Ed. Washington, D.C.: NASW, 1977, pp. 30–42.
3. Brill, L. "Rational Authority in Retrospect." In *Substance Abuse in the United States: Problems and Perspectives.* J. H. Lowinson and P. Ruiz, eds. Baltimore: Williams & Wilkins, 1981.
4. Brill, L. *Rehabilitation in Drug Addiction: A Report of a Five-Year Community Experiment of the New York Demonstration Center.* Mental Health Monograph #3, PHS Report #i0i3. Revised, 1964.
5. Brill, L. "Three Approaches to the Casework Treatment of Narcotics Addicts." *Social Work,* Vol. 13, No. 2, April 1968.
6. Brill, L. "The Treatment of Drug Abuse." *American Journal of Psychiatry,* 134, No. 2 (February 1977): 157–161.
7. Brill, L., and L. Lieberman. *Authority and Addiction.* Boston: Little, Brown, 1969.
8. Brill, L., and L. Lieberman. *Major Modalities in the Treatment of Drug Abuse.* New York: Behavioral Publications, 1972.
9. Brill, L., and H. Meiselas. "The Treatment of Drug Abuse: Experiences and Issues." In L. Brill and E. Harms, eds. *The Yearbook of Drug Abuse.* New York: Behavioral Publications, 1973.

10. Chafetz, M. E. *Alcohol and Health: Narcotic Knowledge.* Second Special Report to the Congress. Rockville, Md., 1974.
11. Chambers, C. D., and L. Brill. *Methadone: Experiences and Issues.* New York: Behavioral Publications, 1973.
12. Geis, C. *Not the Law's Business: Crime and Delinquency Issues.* Rockville, Md.: Center for the Study of Crime and Delinquency, # 72-9132, 1972.
13. Jaffe, J. H. "Factors in the Etiology of Drug Use and Drug Dependence. Two Models: Opiate Use and Tobacco Use." Chapter 3 in *Rehabilitation Aspects of Drug Dependence,* Arnold Schecter, ed. Cleveland: CRC Press, 1977.
14. Martin, W. R. "Pathophysiology of Narcotic Addiction: Possible Roles of Protracted Abstinence in Relapse." In *Drug Abuse: Proceedings of the International Conference.* C. J. D. Zarafonetis, ed. Philadelphia: Lea and Febiger, 1972.
15. Meiselas, H., and L. Brill. "The Role of Civil Commitment in Multimodality Programming." In *Drugs and the Criminal Justice System.* J. A. Inciardi and C. D. Chambers, eds. Beverly Hills, Calif.: Sage Publications, 1974.
16. McGlothlin, W. H.; W. Mandell; L. Brill; and C. Winick. *Civil Commitment.* Monograph prepared for NIDA. Forthcoming, 1981.
17. Musto, D. F. *The American Disease: Origins of Narcotic Control.* New Haven: Yale University Press, 1973.
18. New York State Drug Abuse Program, 1974–1975. *State Plan Update.* Albany: NYS Office of Drug Abuse Services, April 1975.
19. Nyswander, M.; C. Winick; A. Bernstein; and L. Brill. "The Treatment of Drug Addicts as Voluntary Outpatients: A Progress Report." *American Journal of Orthopsychiatry,* 28 (1958): 714–727.
20. Ottenberg, D. J. "The Evolution of Eagleville's Combined Treatment Program." Proceedings of National Drug Conference, Chicago, March 30, 1974.
21. "Program for Drug Abuse Treatment and Prevention." *In-Community Crime Prevention.* Washington, D.C.: National Advisory Commission on Criminal Justice Standards and Goals, January 1973.
22. Safer, J. M., and H. Sands. *A Comparison of Mental Health Treatment Center and Drug Abuse Treatment Center Approaches to Non-Opiate Drug Abuse.* NIDA Services Research Report, DHEW Publications No. (ADM) 79-879, 1979, Wash., D.C.
23. Schur, E. M. *Crimes Without Victims.* Englewood Cliffs, N.J.: Prentice-Hall, 1965.
24. *TASC—Treatment Alternatives to Street Crime.* Washington, D.C.: Issued by the Federal Special Action Office for Drug Abuse Prevention, 1972.
25. Terry, C. E., and M. Pellens. *The Opium Problem.* Reissue. Montclair, N.J.: Patterson Smith, 1969.
26. Winick, C. "An Empirical Assessment of Therapeutic Communities in New York City." Chapter 12 of *Yearbook of Substance Use and Abuse.* L. Brill and C. Winick, eds. New York: Human Sciences Press, 1980.

Additional References

1. Chein, I.; D. L. Gerard; R. S. Lee; et al. *The Road to H.* New York: Basic Books, 1964.

2. Dole, V. P., and M. E. Nyswander. "A Medical Treatment for Diacetyl morphine (heroin) Addiction: A Clinical Trial with Methadone Hydrochloride." *Journal of the AMA,* 193 (1965): 646 ff.

3. Duvall, H. J.; B. Z. Locke; and L. Brill. "Follow-up Study of Narcotic Drug Addicts Five Years After Hospitalization. *Public Health Reports* 73 (1963): 185–191.

4. Fenichel, O. *The Psychoanalytic Theory of Neurosis.* New York: W. W. Norton, 1945.

5. *HEW Report to the President and Congress on Drug Abuse Prevention and Treatment.* Washington, D.C., 1978.

6. New York State Drug Abuse Program, 1974–1975. *State Plan Update.* Albany: New York State Office of Drug Abuse Services, April 1975.

7. Rado, S. "The Psychoanalysis of Pharmacothymia." *Psychoanalytic Quarterly,* 2 (1933): 1–123.

8. Rasor, R. W. "The United States Public Health Service Institutional Treatment Program for Narcotic Addicts at Lexington, Ky." In L. Brill and L. Lieberman, eds., *Major Modalities in the Treatment of Drug Abuse.* New York: Behavioral Publications, 1973.

9. Service Research Notes. NIDA Services Research Branch, February 1977.

10. Simmel, E. "Alcoholism and Addiction," *Psychoanalytic Quarterly,* 17 (1948): 6–31.

CHAPTER 2

Problems and Issues in Treatment and Management

MUCH OF THE THINKING about substance abuse treatment from the 1930s to the 1950s derived from a psychoanalytic framework. Many of the conceptualizations harked back to analysts such as Ernest Simmel and Sandor Rado, who had worked with addicts, including barbiturate addicts and alcoholics, in European psychiatric hospitals. In psychoanalytic thinking, the drug addictions were linked variously with "impulse neuroses," "perversions," "compulsion neuroses," "character disorders," and, at times, the manic-depressive cycle (7, 14, 26, 30). Simmel was innovative in developing a typology of alcoholism, distinguishing among social drinkers, reactive drinkers, neurotic alcoholics, and sporadic spree abusers. In treatment, he suggested ancillary approaches such as occupational therapy in hospitals, environmental manipulation, and involvement in Alcoholics Anonymous, whose principles he found to be close to psychoanalytic thinking (30). He realized that patients could not be expected to be abstinent throughout their treatment and for this reason advocated that they be analyzed in institutions rather than treated as outpatients.

While our current approaches draw upon these early formulations, it became clear during the late 1950s and 1960s that the traditional methods of psychoanalysis were only minimally effective and that forced institutionalization was at times counterproductive. This newer thinking derived from at least three broad areas of understanding and experience: (1) issues related to addicts themselves; (2) problems emanating from the methods of psychoanalysis; and (3) issues having to do with the "state of the art"—that is, the incomplete understanding of drug abuse at the time.

Issues Related to Addicts Themselves

Many confirmed drug users were engaged in antisocial acting-out behavior as a means of coping with their underlying psychological and social problems. They were unable, for the most part, to relate to the strict structure, fixed schedules, and time-limited sessions of orthodox psychotherapy (3, 24). Their need to avoid insight and block out feeling ran counter to the processes and goals of insight therapy. The more therapists probed, the more anxiety and depression might be engendered in the patients, so that they needed to act out their tensions or drop out of therapy. Added problems were posed by the patients' inability to develop trust in authority figures, lower their defenses, and begin examining themselves more objectively.

Most addicts were also engaged in the "hustling syndrome"; that is, they resorted to illegal activities to maintain their drug habit. Their "street-junkie" life-style and the need to maintain a continuous supply of drugs engendered recurrent crises and, periodically, an acute need for help. Therapists needed to relate to them in the midst of these crises if they were to reach them at all and eventually engage them in ongoing treatment (3, 4, 6, 8, 22). The criminal definition of the heroin problem and the consequent need for addicts to resort to crime to obtain drugs involved them in the criminal justice system. Analysts were not inclined to become involved in such court situations and used this as one more reason to abstain from treating them. Further, most addicts needed whatever money they could obtain to purchase drugs and were not in a position to pay for treatment unless they were subsidized by spouses or relatives, who might then use this fact to try to influence the course of treatment. On the other hand, where patients did pay themselves with illegally obtained funds, this generated the problem of involving therapists in the patients' deviant behavior.

Only gradually was it understood that many true addictions were chronic conditions that required a very long period of intensive treatment, with relapses to be expected along the way. Because addicts already had a "pharmacological solution" to their problems in the form of their drugs, which they used to insulate themselves against any awareness of feelings, they generally did not seek help of their own accord or feel any need for it as long as their drug supply held out. In therapy, the battle lines were often drawn early between patient and therapist: the hidden agenda of the patient was to remain on drugs at all costs, while the therapist's goal was to get him or her off immediately.

Because of the addict's severe dependency needs and his frequent challenges to the therapist, treatment proved a terrible drain on the therapist's patience and endurance. It was difficult to remain objective in the face of the patient's excessive demands and continuous testing of limits. Many addicts were extremely manipulative and attempted to con the therapist as they had previously conned their parents.

Since most identified addicts in the 1950s and 1960s came from lower-class populations and minority groups, therapists found an added difficulty in relating to their special problems and needs. Classic psychoanalytic techniques, based on a middle-class European population, needed to be adapted to the sociocultural contexts of blacks, Hispanics, and lower-class white populations generally (3, 6, 14, 24, 26, 30). More than insight, addicts most frequently needed help with concrete or tangible problems such as medical care and detoxification, legal intervention in the courts, financial assistance and housing, family counseling, vocational guidance, and training or job referral. Most therapists were not equipped to offer such services. Because drug use has a physical basis and there is frequent occasion for emergency medical care, there was need for a close tie-in with hospitals and emergency rooms to deal with problems of detoxification, overdoses, hepatitis and other infections, panic reactions, and traumatic experiences. Therapists needed to build a system of cooperative relationships with a network of agencies if they were to provide the range of services required by drug abusers.

Issues Related to the Methods of Psychoanalysis

Analysts generally tended to approach users in terms of their traditional techniques and stereotypes. Most had fixed ideas about the etiology and treatment of addictions in keeping with the prevailing psychoanalytic thinking, and were reluctant to become involved with addicts because of the difficulties posed in treatment or because of their fears about being robbed, assaulted, or conned or having their other patients contaminated (3, 14, 24, 26, 30). Analysts had unreal expectations of their patients, such as that they could give up their drug use immediately while in therapy, come in at fixed times, fit into the fifty-minute sessions, and adhere to the other requirements of therapy. They were also focused on achieving personality reorganization, a goal most addicts were incapable of attaining. Nor could most addicts tolerate extensive probing into their feelings in an effort to achieve insight. For a long time, some professionals preferred to use only ex-addicts as therapists; they believed that only those who had personally experienced drug addiction were equipped to treat drug abusers. This "ex-addict mystique" has since given way to a better definition of roles for ex-addicts, not all of whom are suited to treat or to engage in prevention and education efforts (3, 4, 25).

The psychoanalytic literature tended to describe users as if they were all alike, with the same family constellations and traits universally outlined for all addicts: self-defeating impulses, weak egos, archaic superegos, oral fixations, and narcissism; poor tolerance of frustration and pain; inability to delay gratification; poor relatedness to reality and a tendency to live in fantasy; and intense anxiety and depression, which they overcame by acting out. For a long time, all narcotic addicts were diagnosed as "character disorders" (14, 27). It eventually became clear that not all drug users could be subsumed under a single diagnosis but that they rather constituted a widely diversified spectrum of personalities and diagnoses (3, 4, 21, 22, 25).

Most therapists were fixated on the psychological parameters as the primary, indeed the sole determinants of drug abuse. For a long time, there was little awareness of the sociocultural factors in drug abuse, including problems of minorities and disadvantaged populations in ghetto areas, where lack of opportunity often became the impetus for use, as well as problems of alienation among middle-class youth in suburbia and the colleges (3, 4, 11, 25, 29). Workers today stress the secondary gains of drug use in inner-city areas as well as the availability of drugs and other physiological and epidemiological factors in the generation of drug abuse. We recognize that the etiological factors are generally multifaceted and overdetermined in the Freudian sense and that the more factors we draw upon for our explanation, the better chance we have of understanding what is actually involved in any individual situation. Since most of the early therapists could not understand these factors or relate to lower-class persons, there was a tendency to avoid treating them or to recommend institutionalization or medication instead of talking to them as with their middle-class patients.

Few therapists were prepared to deal with the tangible needs of users by providing concrete services such as those social workers offer. They found it difficult to relate to the perennial crises of users, their conning, their manipulations, and their excessive demands, and had no desire to become involved in court or hospital situations. Because the demands of the users were so great, they could not be accommodated in the limited sessions offered by the therapists. Simmel was aware of these problems when he advocated the use of "aides" who could supplement the treatment of the psychiatrist (30).

Issues Related to the Prevailing "State of the Art"

The problems of treatment were compounded by the fact that there was little experience to draw upon in the 1950s. American society was obsessed with the "villain drug" heroin and was far less concerned with other drugs. The fact that heroin use was defined as a criminal problem engendered a host of additional problems and proved to be a self-fulfilling prophecy (3, 15, 21, 25, 29). The issue of suitable goals was also grossly misunderstood: therapists insisted on the patient's coming into treatment free of drugs, but total immediate abstinence was a goal most addicts could not achieve. The issue of limited or relative goals in treatment was not understood (4, 6, 21, 23, 25).

Other stereotypes abounded regarding the ability to locate, reach, involve, and help users in treatment (3, 4, 5, 6, 8, 9, 13, 21, 25). There was also a tendency to see all drug use as "bad" and to subscribe to a "domino theory" of use—that is, that any drug use would inevitably escalate to full addiction. There was little awareness that much drug use is, in fact, adaptive, helping individuals to cope with their problems of living. This became far clearer in the 1950s and 1960s, when it was learned that many persons could be helped to function better through the use of tranquilizers and antidepressants. This experience helped pave the way for the use of methadone maintenance as a treatment modality (3, 4, 12, 21, 23).

With the growing understanding that many users were "recalcitrants" who did not come willingly into treatment, there was recognition of the need for the use of authority or coercion, preferably "rational authority," as a tool for structuring treatment and engaging and holding clients (4, 5, 6, 7, 8, 9, 21, 22, 23, 25). Most therapists had not worked with authority and had strong "trained incapacities" and resistances in relation to it. They did not wish to deal with court personnel, probation, and parole and were not willing or able to work with patients who were not "motivated" or did not come into treatment voluntarily. Since up to 70 percent of offenders have at some time been involved with drugs, this constituted a serious obstacle to treatment. Because therapists saw authoritative agencies as threatening to their patients, they attempted to shield the patients from these agencies and were soon caught up in the manipulations of patients playing one against the other. It took time to understand that many users were acting out severely and could not be treated in the community but needed to be off the streets and in a residential setting. Many therapists were reluctant to use such facilities or to resort to civil commitment, even with patients who were out of control and a danger to themselves and the community (4, 5, 6, 7, 8, 9, 22, 22, 23, 25). Only with the advent of methadone maintenance did therapists acquire a strong tool that could allay the craving of the heroin users and hold them in treatment in the community over a long period of time (4, 7, 8, 9, 12, 21, 22, 25).

The state of the art did not, in sum, permit a full understanding of the basic parameters of treatment as we comprehend it today. In the following section, we shall examine the elements that helped improve our knowledge and enabled us to evolve a more rational approach to drug abuse.

A Rational Approach to Substance Abuse

Clarification of the issues outlined in the previous section made possible the evolution of an improved understanding of and more rational perspective on drug abuse. We have noted that earlier thinking tended to stereotype all drug abusers by attributing uniform, unvarying characteristics to them and prescribing a single treatment approach: the institutional-aftercare or parole model of treatment (4, 21, 22, 25).

This thinking gradually gave way to a better understanding of the diversity of drug use and drug users. It was recognized that there are varying degrees of involvement with drugs and the addiction system: some users are conventional in every respect except their drug use, while others are deeply involved in dysfunctional drug use and criminality. In recent decades, we have moved away from the exclusive preoccupation with heroin to examine the use of other drugs as well and have stopped assuming that street junkies or Bowery alcoholics constitute the entire population of users (10, 16). The fact is that the overwhelming majority of drug users are only minimally involved with drugs or else discontinue their use after only a brief period of experimentation. Until recently, the emphasis in treatment and prevention was on the substance, as if it were inherently alive and evil in itself. We have since begun to view drug abuse as a function of the person involved rather than of the substance itself. Heavy dependence on drugs depends upon the person and not on the drug. If a person is stable, he or she may engage in drug experimentation without total involvement or investment. It is the personality of the user that determines how important such drug use becomes—whether it will dominate his or her life, become an occasional recreational activity, or be dropped entirely (3, 4, 18).

Beyond this, the individual's response to a drug will be determined by such factors as the surroundings, the presence of a guide who has used the drug before, the emotional state and expectations of the subject, the prior experiences with drugs, and whether he or she has learned to experience the drug in a specific way (1, 2, 3, 4, 18). The perception of any drug tends to be highly subjective: changes in mood, behavior, and emotion can be experienced as either pleasurable or alarming, depending on the individual's psychological and social needs (1, 3, 4, 18). The effects of marijuana and the hallucinogenic drugs may range from mild to psychosis-precipitating. Drug use is also a learning experience. The user learns what sensations to anticipate and how best to respond to them. He or she can also learn to increase or decrease specific sensations and responses (1). Cultural factors play an added role in molding drug-use patterns. They tend to determine which drugs are used and preferred, how they are taken, and where they are obtained.

Subcultural groupings also introduce value systems that may lead to drug abuse. For example, individuals who grow up under conditions of socio-economic deprivation and are unable to find ways of bettering their existence may drift into criminal behavior and use. "Drift" is probably not the correct word, since criminal behavior may be the only route to upward mobility in this subculture, as described by Parsons, Merton, and Cloward and Ohlin (3). In such an environment, the role models are frequently negative, and there are many secondary gains from illicit behavior (3, 11, 15, 25, 29).

A Typology of Drug Use

Understanding the diversity of drug use is a key element in developing a rational perspective on treatment. The major categories of drug-taking behavior can be outlined as follows.

EXPERIMENTAL USE

Drugs play no special or regular role in the user's life. Use is episodic and reflects a desire to see what drugs are like or to test their effects on activities usually experienced without drugs. Use may be emulative of peer-group, parental, or other models.

SOCIAL OR RECREATIONAL USE

Drugs are associated with social or recreational activities in which the user would take part whether or not drugs were present. Little or no time and effort are devoted to seeking out the drugs. The pattern of use is occasional and situationally controlled.

THE "SEEKERS"

Drugs play a more significant role in the seeker's life. Time is devoted to making connections and obtaining drugs. The user cannot enjoy or cope with some situations without them. Use of drugs may range from irregular to regular, controlled, or heavy daily use, although the individual may still remain functional and able to meet primary social and physical needs.

SELF-MEDICATING USE

The self-medicating user generally uses legally distributed tranquilizers or stimulants. Although this type of use may have beneficial effects, it also can become a habitual way of responding to boredom, loneliness, frustration, and stress. The precise incidence of such chemical coping is not known, but data suggest that it is extensive. It is necessary to learn more about the situations and experiences that move the self-medicator to dysfunctional use. At present, it is assumed that some type of emotional difficulty underlies such use. Both self-medicators and "seekers" are attempting to deal with anxiety, depression, or other problems and often use drugs as a kind of self-therapy as well as for other reasons.

DYSFUNCTIONAL DRUG USE

Drugs have begun to dominate the life of the user in these situations. The process of obtaining and using drugs interferes with essential activities. These are ordinarily considered the "chronic cases." Street junkies and chronic alcoholics fall into this category. Dysfunctional users are driven by a compulsive need for drugs and by a craving that must be relieved at all costs. It is important not to stereotype here, for some heroin addicts remain conventional in other areas of living, and some chronic alcoholics manage to hold important positions and head families. Only some 5 percent of the alcoholic population constitute the "Skid Row" type usually conjured up when we think of chronic alcoholism (4, 10, 16, 25).

To recapitulate, a rational perspective and typology of use refute the emphasis on a stereotyped heroin addict as the prototype of all drug abusers. The rational perspective requires recognition of at least these parameters: (1) the wide diversity of the drug-using population, subsuming a full range of characteristics and diagnoses; (2) the multifaceted etiology of drug use; (3) the fact that many "true" addictions are chronic-relapsing conditions, which require long-term treatment and entail frequent relapses on the part of the client or patient; (4) the need to postulate limited or relative goals in treatment; (5) the need to focus on the person and not the substance in prevention and treatment in order to understand the role drugs are playing in his or her life; (6) the fact that much drug use is not destructive but adaptive—that is, it may be helping the individual function better and cope with his or her daily problems of living; (7) the fact that most drug use does not escalate to more dysfunctional use and full addiction; and, finally, (8) the need for a multimodal, comprehensive approach to treatment to meet the needs of the diverse individuals involved.

Summary

Recent Changes in the Drug Scene

Because the drug scene is constantly changing, treatment approaches must relate to ever new dimensions of the drug problem (4, 5, 10, 16, 20,

28, 31). The early 1970s saw the emergence of the phenomenon of poly-drug or multiple drug use and a diminution of the heroin problem in the largest cities. This was followed by an upsurge in heroin use, especially of "Mexican Brown" heroin by 1973, with further proliferation of heroin use from the larger cities to smaller cities of approximately 200,000 people. There was considerable easing of intake pressures in drug treatment programs in New York City and elsewhere in 1972 and 1973, for reasons not altogether clear. Methadone maintenance programs helped reduce the tensions ordinarily experienced in local communities, hospitals, and treatment agencies, as well as in health and welfare offices and the criminal justice system. The introduction of the longer-acting form of methadone known as L-acetylmethadol (LAAM), which could hold a patient for up to seventy-two hours, seemed to decrease the pressures further wherever it was used. Enactment of the so-called Rockefeller Legislation in 1973 drastically increased penalties for use but did not have the beneficial effects anticipated in terms of ending drug traffic, preventing drug abuse, and relieving overcrowded courts and prisons. At the same time, a change occurred in society's attitudes toward drug use, probably because some 35 million persons had by then used marijuana at least once and were changing their minds about the official approach to such use; but also because many were relying on a variety of legal drugs such as Librium and Valium as well as the antidepressants. Alcohol was finally being regarded as a drug and as a major cause for concern in view of the fact that approximately 12 million individuals were believed to be chronic alcoholics (10, 16, 19). The possibility of treating alcoholics jointly with other drug abusers was also increasingly being demonstrated in facilities such as the Eagleville Hospital and Rehabilitation Center in Pennsylvania (10, 16, 25).

Although there had been continuous questioning as to whether drug abuse treatment actually worked, HEW's 1978 Report to the President and Congress on Drug Abuse Prevention and Treatment (16) offered a strong affirmative. Reports by Sells and others, covering a range of modalities since the 1960s, similarly confirmed that treatment worked. Dr. W. H. McGlothlin, writing about the California Civil Commitment Program, indicated that civil commitment of addicts had been more effective in California than had previously been reported (20). Though heroin treatment still remained a major focus of the federal government's efforts, data as of 1979 established that the number of heroin users had declined, as had the availability of heroin. Cocaine use showed a significant increase in the eighteen-to-twenty-five age group. Although it was still being used in small amounts and only sporadically, an increase in use was predicted.

Regarding marijuana, the HEW Report of 1978 stated that daily use of marijuana among high school seniors had increased dramatically—

from 6 percent in 1975 to 11 percent in 1978. A survey on the nonmedical use of psychoactive prescription drugs revealed an increase in use, especially among young adults. Barbiturates were of particular concern because of their often dangerous effects. While overall hallucinogen use appeared to have declined, the use of phencycladine (PCP), a particularly dangerous drug, was increasing alarmingly. The survey data indicated that the percentage of twelve- to seventeen-year-olds who used PCP had almost doubled, from 3 percent in 1976 to 5.8 percent in 1977. Users among the eighteen- to twenty-five-year-olds increased from 9.5 percent to 13.9 percent in the same period. Use of the hallucinogens, especially LSD, about which there had been so much concern in the 1960s, was reported to be rising again in Northern California, according to the *New York Times* of October 21, 1979 (31).

The Eighth Annual Report to Congress in 1980 on "Marijuana and Health" from the Secretary of HEW (19) reviews recent developments in regard to marijuana research and the drug's possible health implications. It indicates that, in contrast with a decade ago, marijuana use now often begins at a much earlier age and is more likely to be frequent and regular rather than experimental. The most significant increases noted were in marijuana use by twelve- to seventeen-year-olds. Among high school seniors, daily use nearly doubled from the class of 1975 to the class of 1978, from 5.8 percent to 10.7 percent. "Street" marijuana increased markedly in potency over the past five years. Considerable progress has been made in developing simpler laboratory techniques for detecting marijuana use by examining body fluids.

The review of marijuana's effects on intellectual functioning indicates that marijuana intoxication interferes with immediate memory and a wide range of intellectual tasks in a manner that might impair classroom learning among student users. There is good evidence that marijuana interferes with driving skills and is a significant factor in erratic driving. There is also converging evidence regarding marijuana's negative effects on the pulmonary system, but less so on its impact on reproductive functioning and the body's principal defenses against disease, the immune response. The psychopathological effects have been less important, apart from panic reactions, but it is felt that the availability of much stronger varieties of cannabis may result in more serious problems than in the past. Regarding the therapeutic uses, finally, marijuana, THC, and related drugs have shown definite promise in treating the nausea and vomiting that often accompany cancer chemotherapy. A second therapeutic application that has received wide publicity is the use of THC or marijuana in reducing the vision-destroying intraocular pressure in open-angle glaucoma. Initial trials found the drug to be of varying success used alone; better results were achieved when it was used in conjunction with standard drugs (19).

New Drugs and Recent Developments

Pharmacological research has yielded some new drugs in the search for substances that can relieve pain, like narcotics, yet without the addictiveness or negative side effects of narcotics. Among these new drugs are buterphanol, marketed as Stadol; nalbuphane, marketed as Nubain; buprenorphine, trade name Temgesic; and propiram, trade name Dirame. These drugs are part of the new class of authentic opiates, the narcotic antagonists discovered in 1915 and made increasingly available in the 1950s and thereafter. The new drugs do not cause the life-threatening depression of breathing that occurs with high doses of conventional narcotics, so that an overdose would be considerably less dangerous. Further, the addiction liability is minimal, and there are no severe withdrawal symptoms if withdrawal takes place. There is some thought that Temgesic might be used as a substitute for methadone in treating heroin addiction, because it is less addictive and less toxic. Another advantage of these new drugs is that there is no appreciable decline in their pain-killing potency over time, as with the opiates, there being no detectable build-up of tolerance. A *New York Times* article dated February 2, 1980, describes buprenorphine as "a drug that has some of the pleasurable qualities of a narcotic and yet blocks heroin's effects. [It] shows promise of being both safe and effective in treating heroin addiction" (28). This article summarizes a study conducted by Nancy K. Mello and Dr. Jack H. Mendelson and reported in *Science*. The study, which involved ten men, found that heroin use had dropped sharply among those who received an 8 mg dose of the antagonist daily. The drug is described as having forty times the pain-killing potency of morphine and equally long-lasting effects. Patients reported that it did not give them any "rush," as heroin did, but that they experienced a "generalized feeling of contentment." They had only mild, almost negligible withdrawal symptoms after they stopped using the drug (28).

A major discovery, with important implications for our understanding of specialized brain and body functions and for increased knowledge of drug actions and effects, relates to the recent detection of morphine-like substances in the brain called "endorphins" and "enkephalins." These substances have been sensationalized in the press as "the brain's own narcotics." They appear to play a major role in relieving pain and stress (17) and may help to explain the effectiveness of acupuncture; this may eliminate pain by releasing the endorphins and enkephalins. There has been speculation that some individuals may have low endogenous levels of endorphins, which may then affect their behavior and mood. Such effects may also influence the likelihood of their experimenting with drugs and may predispose them to react more positively to the initial effects of opioid drugs. Though this is conjecture, it offers a promising lead for further research (17).

The foregoing reaffirms the fact that, while a great deal has been learned about drug abuse, there is much still to be learned and much that we do not yet understand, as, for example, the mechanisms of tolerance and dependence in addiction.

References

1. Becker, H. S. "Becoming a Marijuana User." *American Journal of Sociology*, 59 (1953): 235–242.
2. Brecher, E. M., and Consumer Reports Editors. *Licit and Illicit Drugs: The Consumer's Union Report on Narcotics, Stimulants and Depressants*. Waltham, Mass.: Little, Brown, 1972.
3. Brill, L. "Drug Addiction." In *Encyclopedia of Social Work*. 16th Ed. New York: NASW, 1971, 1: 24–38.
4. Brill, L. "Drug Addiction." In *Encyclopedia of Social Work*, 17th Ed. Washington D.C.: NASW, 1977, 1: 30–42.
5. Brill, L. "Rational Authority in Retrospect." In *Substance Abuse in the United States: Problems and Perspectives*. J. H. Lowinson and P. Ruiz, eds. Baltimore: Williams & Wilkins, 1981.
6. Brill, L. *Rehabilitation in Drug Addiction: A Report of a Five-Year Community Experiment of the New York Demonstration Center*. Mental Health Monograph #3, PHS #1013. Revised 1964.
7. Brill, L. "The Treatment of Drug Abuse." *American Journal of Psychiatry*, 134, No. 2 (February 1977): 157–161.
8. Brill, L. "Three Approaches to the Casework Treatment of Narcotics Addicts." *Social Work*, Vol. 13, No. 2, April 1968.
9. Brill, L., and L. Lieberman. *Major Modalities in the Treatment of Drug Abuse*. New York: Behavioral Publications, 1972.
10. Chafetz, M. E. *Alcohol and Health: Narcotics Knowledge*. Second Special Report to the Congress. Rockville, Md., 1974.
11. Chein, I.; D. L. Gerard; R. S. Lee; et al. *The Road to H*. New York: Basic Books, 1964.
12. Dole, V. P., and M. E. Nyswander. "A Medical Treatment for Diacetyl-morphine (Heroin) Addiction: A Clinical Trial with Methadone Hydrochloride." *Journal of the AMA*, 193 (1965): 646 ff.
13. Duvall, H. J.; B. Z. Locke; and L. Brill. "Follow-up Study of Narcotic Drug Addicts Five Years After Hospitalization. *Public Health Reports*, 73 (1963): 185–191.
14. Fenichel, O. *The Psychoanalytic Theory of Neurosis*. New York: W. W. Norton, 1945.
15. Geis, C. "Not the Law's Business." *Crime and Delinquency Issues*. Rockville, Md.: Center for the Study of Crime and Delinquency, # 72-9132, 1972.
16. *HEW Report to the President and Congress on Drug Abuse Prevention and Treatment*. Washington, D.C., 1978.
17. Jaffe, J. H. "Factors in the Etiology of Drug Use and Drug Dependence. Two Models: Opiate Use and Tobacco Use." Chapter 3 in *Rehabilitation Aspects of Drug Dependence*. A. Schecter, ed. Cleveland: CRC Press, 1977.

18. Lasagna, L.; J. M. Van Felsinger; and H. R. Beecher. "Drug-Induced Mood Changes in Man." *Journal of the AMA*, 157 (1955): 1006–1013.
19. *Marijuana and Health*. Eighth Annual Report to the U.S. Congress from the Secretary of Health, Education, and Welfare. DHEW Publication No. (ADM) 80-945, 1980.
20. McGlothlin, W. H.; W. Mandell; L. Brill; and C. Winick. *Civil Commitment*. Monograph prepared for NIDA, 1980.
21. Meiselas, H., and L. Brill. "The Treatment of Drug Abuse: Experiences and Issues." In *Yearbook of Drug Abuse*, L. Brill and E. Harms, eds. New York: Behavioral Publications, 1973.
22. Meiselas, H., and L. Brill. "The Role of Civil Commitment in Multimodality Programming." In *Drugs and the Criminal Justice System*, J. A. Inciardi, and C. D. Chambers, eds. Beverly Hills, Calif.: Sage Publications, 1974.
23. New York State Drug Abuse Program, 1974–1975. *State Plan Update*. Albany: NYS Office of Drug Abuse Services, April 1975.
24. Nyswander, M.; C. Winick; A. Bernstein; and L. Brill. "The Treatment of Drug Addicts as Voluntary Outpatients: A Progress Report." *American Journal of Orthopsychiatry*, 28 (1958): 714–727.
25. "Program for Drug Abuse Treatment and Prevention." In *Community Crime Prevention*. Washington, D.C.: National Advisory Commission on Criminal Justice Standards and Goals, January 1973.
26. Rado, S. "The Psychoanalysis of Pharmacothymia." *Psychoanalytic Quarterly*, 2 (1933): 1–23.
27. Reiner, B. S., and I. Kaufman. *Character Disorders in Parents of Delinquents*. New York: Family Association of America, 1958.
28. Schmeck, H. M., Jr. "Tests Show New Drug Helps Addicts Fight Heroin." *New York Times*, February 2, 1980.
29. Schur, E. *Crime Without Victims*. Englewood Cliffs, N.J.: Prentice-Hall, 1965.
30. Simmel, E. "Alcoholism and Addiction." *Psychoanalytic Quarterly*, 17 (1948): 6–31.
31. Tucker, J. B. "New Drugs Offer Help for Severe Pain," *New York Times*, October 21, 1979.

CHAPTER 3

Drug Classification and Terminology of Use

THE TROUBLESOME ISSUE of drug classification and drug terminology has constituted a stumbling block for management and treatment. There has been a serious lack of consensus and much confusion regarding the most common terms used, such as addiction, habituation, dependence, tolerance, drug abuse and misuse, and nonmedical use of drugs (6, 11). Until recently, there was an arbitrary classification of drugs into "hard drugs," by which was meant opiates and their derivatives, and "soft drugs," such as barbiturates, amphetamines, and hallucinogens, but not alcohol. This dichotomy reflected our society's varying attitudes toward drug use—sometimes hawkish, sometimes dovish—and added to the confusion of our approaches to rehabilitation, treatment, prevention, and management. Definitions could be approached from a legal, moral, medical, or social standpoint. The legal definition equated drug abuse with the mere act of using a proscribed drug or using it under proscribed conditions; the moral definition was similar, though greater emphasis was placed on the motivation or purpose for which the drug was used; the medical model opposed unsupervised use and emphasized the physical and mental consequences for the user; and the social definition stressed social responsibility and adverse effects on others (1).

Even definitions of the central term "addiction" have been controversial. Though physical dependence is most often seen as its main characteristic, this has been waived in some definitions. Loss of control or compulsion to use is the main feature in such cases. This was true of the federal government's definition in the Narcotic Addiction Rehabilitation Act of 1966, in which an addict was specified as "any individual who habitually uses any narcotic drug so as to endanger the public morals, health, safety or welfare or who is so far addicted to the use of such narcotic drugs as to have lost the power of self-control with reference to addiction." In these terms, an addict could be any frequent user who creates a moral, health, or safety problem or only a user with no control over his use. Physical dependence and withdrawal symptoms are not specified (1).

The best-known and most often quoted definition of addiction is the one proposed by the World Health Organization (WHO) in 1950 and 1957:

> Drug addiction is a state of periodic or chronic intoxication produced by the repeated consumption of a drug (natural or synthetic). Its characteristics include: (1) an overpowering desire or need (compulsion) to continue taking the drug and to obtain it by any means; (2) a tendency to increase the dose; (3) a psychic (psychological) and generally, a physical dependence on the effects of the drug; and (4) a detrimental effect on the individual and on society. [12, 13]

It can be seen that physical dependence is not actually required for addiction and is mentioned only as a possibility. The essential elements are overpowering desire, a tendency to increase the dose, and detrimental effects on society and the individual. Though this definition is still used more than any other, it has not served to clarify the confusion about terminology. In 1957 a WHO committee appended a definition of habituation as a supplement to the original definition, not a change. Drug habituation was defined as a state of periodic or chronic intoxication produced by the repeated consumption of a drug. Its characteristics included the following: (1) an overpowering desire or need (compulsion) to continue taking the drug and to obtain it by any means; (2) a tendency to increase the dose; (3) some degree of psychic dependence on the effect of the drug, but absence of physical dependence and hence of any abstinence syndrome; and (4) detrimental effects, if any, primarily on the individual. The main elements were therefore repeated consumption and an overpowering desire to consume (13).

In 1964 the difficulties in terminology were becoming increasingly apparent with the appearance of ever new agents and changing patterns of use. WHO officials therefore made a new attempt at definition, using the term "drug dependence." Drug dependence was defined as a "state of psychic or physical dependence or both on a drug arising in a person following administration of that drug on a continuous or periodic basis." The real characteristics of the dependence "vary with the agent involved"— e.g., dependence of the morphine type, the barbiturate type, or the LSD type, which are all described. To the author, this concept was even less satisfactory than the others in that it obscured the varying degrees of involvement with drugs (14, 15). I agree rather with the thinking of Jaffe: "Addiction means a behavioral pattern of compulsive drug use, characterized by overwhelming involvement with the use of a drug, the securing of its supply and a high tendency to relapse after withdrawal" (7). Though "addiction" cannot be used interchangeably with "physical dependence" in this definition, physical dependence is often a concomitant requirement. What Jaffe is saying is that it is possible to be physically dependent on drugs without being addicted and to be addicted without being physically dependent. Thus, a wounded soldier in battle might receive administrations of morphine continuously over a period of weeks to the point where he is physically addicted. He would not be an addict, however, since he would have no psychic or psychological need for the drug after he recovered and had been taken off the morphine. On the other hand, a confirmed addict, even though in jail and physically off drugs, should still be considered an addict because his need for narcotics and compulsion to use are unchanged and he would in most cases relapse to drug use as soon as he is released.

It is often assumed that narcotics have euphoric effects for all individuals and that everyone therefore has a potential for becoming a narcotic addict. That this is not the case was demonstrated by Lasagna and others in the 1950s: the majority of normal, pain-free individuals experience the effects of opiates as quite unpleasant. Furthermore, many confirmed narcotics users relate that their first experiences with opiates were not at all pleasurable; it required learning to perceive the euphoric effects in spite of the nausea and dizziness (3, 7). Such observations led workers in the field to conclude that those who persist in using opiates and who eventually become compulsive users have personality problems which antedated their use of drugs (3, 4, 7).

The term "drug abuse" emerged in the 1950s and was picked up by the President's Advisory Commission on Narcotic and Drug Abuse in the early 1960s (10). It was indicated that such abuse occurs when an individual uses drugs under the following circumstances: (1) in amounts sufficient to create a hazard to his own health or the safety of the community; (2) obtained through illicit channels; or (3) on his own initiative rather than on the basis of professional advice. Drug abuse thus includes illicit use, however infrequent or whatever the degree of harm or lack of harm. It also includes all use of alcohol, tobacco, aspirin, and so forth, unless taken under professional advice, which clearly renders this definition ludicrous and untenable. Often this definition is made to read "inconsistent with acceptable medical practice."

There is thus no generally accepted definition of "drug abuse": at times it is too wide, at times too narrow. It is generally used in its broadest sense to refer to the use, usually by self-administration, of any drug in a manner that deviates from the approved medical or social pattern within a given culture. So defined, the term rightfully includes the "misuse" of a whole spectrum of substances, ranging from agents with profound effects on the central nervous system to laxatives, headache remedies, antibiotics, and vitamins (7).

In reality, however, we are primarily concerned with the so-called psychotropic drugs, which affect mood and change behavior. Since the definition of drug abuse is largely a social one, it is not surprising that, for any particular drug, there is great variation in what is considered abuse, not only from culture to culture but also from time to time within a culture. For example, we have been far more tolerant of alcohol abuse than of narcotics or marijuana, which until recently was not even considered a drug (9). In other societies—Islamic or Mormon, for example—alcohol has been proscribed. The use of medically prescribed barbiturates to induce sleep is permissible in our society, but the self-administration of the same amount to induce euphoria is considered abuse. In most Western societies, the use of cocaine in any amount for the purpose of modifying mood is drug abuse; but in the Andes the chewing of coca leaves is practiced by 90 percent of the adult male population (3, 7). The specific drugs approved or sanctioned within any society have to do with the goals and aspirations of that society.

A difficulty in the use of drugs to alter mood is that some individuals eventually feel that the effects produced by a drug are necessary to maintain an optimal state of well-being. Such individuals are said to have a psychological dependence on the drug (habituation). There may develop a craving or compulsion to use the drug. In extreme forms, this becomes a chronic relapsing disease. Compulsive drug use is often associated with the development of tolerance and physical dependence. Tolerance develops when, after repeated administration, a given dose of a drug produces decreased effects and increasingly large doses must be administered to obtain the effects observed with the original dose. Physical dependence refers to an altered physiological state produced by the repeated administration of the drug, which necessitates continuous administration to prevent the appearance of the withdrawal or abstinence syndrome characteristic for that particular drug (3, 7).

If we are not to be caught up in the problem of terminology, it would seem best to view the entire question from the standpoint of *use* (11) and to focus on the *person* rather than the drug itself. Until very recently, we treated drugs as if they were inherently bad in themselves. It is evident that if no person were using drugs "dysfunctionally" there would be no problem. We must therefore look at the person involved to determine how and why he is using drugs, the role the drugs are playing in his life, and the extent to which he is involved. Drug use can be useful and adaptive in many instances. Most individuals can use drugs in controlled, stable ways without danger to themselves or society, and often with great benefit to both. The typology outlined helps clarify the diversity of uses of drugs and the roles they may play in different individuals' lives (4).

Drug Classifications

Drugs are generally categorized as opiates (heroin and other narcotics), barbiturates and the nonbarbiturate sedative-hypnotics ("downers"), stimulants (amphetamines and cocaine, or "uppers"), hallucinogens (LSD, mescaline, peyote, and others), inhalants (glue and other substances), and major and minor tranquilizers (Librium, Valium, and others). Under the law, these substances are also classified under various "Schedules," which detail the gravity with which they are viewed and the sanctions for their use. An effort will be made to cite the generic name, the trade or brand name and the common street names for each drug, to the extent possible (6). The drugs are not arranged in any special sequence or order.

1. The Opiates or Opioid Drugs

GENERIC NAME	COMMON, TRADE, OR BRAND NAME	STREET NAME
Opium		black stuff, hop, tar, ya-pen-yan
Morphine		hard stuff, M, Miss Emma, monkey, morf, white stuff
Meperidine	Demerol, Pethedine, Dolanthol, Dolantin	
Hydromorphone	Dilaudid	lords
Codeine		schoolboy
Paregoric		bitter, blue velvet, licorice, P.G., P.O.
Paperaverine		red water
Methadone	Dolophine, Amidone, Physeptone	dollies, meth
Heroin (diacetyl-morphine)		dope, H., Harry, horse, junk, schmeck, .shit, slag, snow
Laudanum		
Oxycodone	Percodan	

Opium and its various derivatives are obtained from the milky secretion of the opium poppy, a plant indigenous to Asia Minor. The heroin refined out of the opium is later mixed with other substances, such as quinine and/or milk sugar. Street heroin seldom contains more than 3

<u>percent narcotics</u>. The opiates are man's oldest pain reliever and are still used for this purpose. Heroin was outlawed completely in the United States by the Harrison Act but continues to be used as an analgesic in Great Britain. Codeine is an essential ingredient of cough medicines such as codeine terpinhydrate. Morphine too acts as an analgesic and causes drowsiness, mood changes, and a sense of mental clouding without the taker's going to sleep. Opiates may be smoked, "snorted" (sniffed), "skin-popped" (injected under the skin), "mainlined" (injected into the vein), or swallowed. Heroin is considered to be more powerful than morphine and codeine. Demerol continues to be the most frequently misused narcotic by physicians and nurses, perhaps because it is the most available to them. Heroin, considering its direct long-term effects on the body, does not appear to deserve its reputation as the arch-villain of drugs; the withdrawal is rarely as dramatic or life-threatening as depicted in the movies or on television, largely because the amounts obtained in street heroin are generally very small. Other drugs, such as alcohol, tobacco, barbiturates, and amphetamines, can be far more destructive to the individual than heroin, if abused. Narcotics do not in and of themselves cause the deterioration and degradation commonly attributed to them; these are, rather, a result of our social definition of the problem and a self-fulfilling prophecy, as well as a consequence of the life-style often resulting from chronic use of heroin.

The nature and severity of the withdrawal symptoms that appear when narcotic use is discontinued depend on many factors, including the particular opiate used, the total daily dosage, duration of use, and the health and personality of the addict. As indicated, most "habits" are not serious because of the small amounts of narcotics found in street heroin. In cases of severe heroin or morphine addiction, the first withdrawal signs are usually noted shortly after the time of the next scheduled dose. There is lacrimation, runny nose, yawning, and perspiration within eight to twelve hours after the last dose. About twelve to fourteen hours after the last dose, the addict may fall into a restless sleep which may last several hours. Dilated pupils, anorexia, gooseflesh, irritability, and tremor may appear, along with nausea and vomiting. There may be chilliness alternating with flushing. The gooseflesh resembles that of a plucked turkey, which gave rise to the expression "cold turkey." Abdominal cramps and pains in the bones, back muscles, and extremities are also characteristic, as are muscle spasms and kicking movements, which may be the basis for the expression "kicking the habit" (7, 8).

Abrupt withdrawal from methadone produces a syndrome which, while qualitatively similar to that of morphine, develops more slowly and is less intense and more prolonged. The addict has few or no symptoms until the third day and then complains of weakness, anxiety, insomnia, abdominal discomfort, headache, sweating, and hot and cold flashes. Even when the syndrome reaches its peak intensity, about the sixth day, vomiting and diarrhea are not prominent, and muscle aches and cramps are usually absent. In countering the withdrawal effects, the strong narcotics antagonist Naloxone reverses the respiratory depressant effects of opiates without the reinforcing or "agonistic" effects of the previously used drug, nalline. The results are prompt, and coma, should it develop, can be reversed within minutes with Naloxone. For detoxification, methadone is the drug of choice. For opiates, 10 to 20 mg. of methadone is given orally after the first appearance of withdrawal signs, and the dose is repeated, if the signs of withdrawal persist, within two to six hours (2, 8).

2. Barbiturate and Nonbarbiturate Sedative-Hypnotics

GENERIC NAME	TRADE OR BRAND NAME	STREET NAME
Barbiturates		goofballs, desatives, sleeping pills, barbs
Pentobarbitol	Nembutal	nemmies, nimbie, yellows, yellow jacket
Amobarbitol	Amytol	blues, blue birds, blue devils, blue heaven
Butobarbitol	Butisol	
Secobarbitol	Seconal, Seco-8	pink ladies, pinks, red devils, seccy, seggy
Amobarbital (amobarbital plus secobarbital)	Tuinal	Christmas tree, rainbow, tooies
Phenobarbital	Luminal, Eskabarb, Solfoton, Stental, Pentothal	phennies, purple hearts (6)

Barbiturates are the central nervous system depressants known as the downers. They serve to induce sleep or to sedate or tranquilize, and as an anticonvulsant for seizures caused by epilepsy and by other drugs. They can relieve pain. Barbiturates are arbitrarily classified in terms of the duration of their action: long-acting (luminal), short-acting to intermediate-acting (Amytal, Nembutal, Seconal), and very short-acting (Pentothal). Abusers obviously prefer the shorter-acting forms. As sedatives, barbiturates can create a sense of well-being, tranquility, and even elation. Sedation or drowsiness may last only a few hours, but distortions in the person's mood, fine motor skills, and judgmental abilities may extend for many hours. The effects can range from a sedated stage through coma to death from respiratory failure.

There are dangers in the synergistic effect of combining barbiturates with other drugs, such as alcohol and minor tranquilizers. One of the effects of barbiturates is to distort a person's sense of the passage of time as well as his memory, so that he may not remember having taken the pills and may thus add more, with possibly lethal effects (2, 6). The addictiveness of barbiturates was not adequately understood until as late as the 1960s, when the federal government finally undertook to regulate the prescription of barbiturates under the Federal Comprehensive Drug Abuse Control Acts of 1965 and 1970.

Precipitous withdrawal from the barbiturates once physical dependency has been established is extremely dangerous. Abstinence symptoms, ranging from tremulousness and irritability to seizures, delirium (d.t.'s), and death may result. Accordingly, stabilization with the drug involved or replacement by phenobarbital and gradual withdrawal are essential. Unless the individual develops more serious withdrawal symptoms such as seizures, delirium, and hallucinosis, the course is usually benign and self-limited, and full recovery is possible as early as within one week, depending on the severity of the addiction. The manifestations of withdrawal delirium associated with barbiturate dependence are identical to those of the delirium tremens associated with alcoholism. The signs and symptoms of alcohol intoxication and abstinence reactions are very similar to those with short-acting sedative-hypnotics. Treatment of alcohol intoxication and the prevention of abstinence symptoms also rest on principles of management similar to those for sedative-hypnotic drug problems. The main differences between managing alcohol withdrawal and managing withdrawal from other sedative drug problems reside in the drugs used to prevent the debilitating symptoms. Although there is cross-tolerance between barbiturates and alcohol (that is, taking one can prevent developing withdrawal symptoms for the other), most clinicians prefer one of a number of other drugs to prevent and treat withdrawal. Some advocate paraldehyde and others recommend chloral hydrate or paraldehyde. McKenna and Khantzian use chlordiazepoxide and consider it both safe and effective in preventing the alcohol abstinence syndrome (2, 8).

Nonbarbiturate sedative-hypnotics, which are newer drugs, have a potential for producing physical dependence as well as intoxication, coma, and death. They include drugs under the generic and trade names of Meprobamate (Miltown, Equanil), Glutethimide (Doridine), Ethubanate (Valmid), Ethchlorvynol (Placidyl), Methpyrylon (Loludar), chlordiazepoxide (Librium), Diazepam (Valium), and Oxazepam (Serax). Glutethimide and Methaqualone are two notorious drugs that can be very troublesome (2, 6, 8). Glutethimide has all the bad side effects of the barbiturates and additional complicating and potentially lethal properties, which make it especially hazardous. The range between the therapeutic and the lethal dose is narrower than with other sedative-hypnotics, increasing the possibility of overdose. Gastric lavage needs to be carried out within twenty-four hours after an overdose, and special care must be taken in the management of withdrawal. The benzodiazepines (Valium), especially Diazepam and Chlordiazepoxide, have become the focus of increasing concern as drugs of abuse. The combination of alcohol and Valium in toxic doses accounts for more drug problems seen in emergency rooms than any other combination of drugs, probably because Valium is the most commonly prescribed drug in the country, and most individuals are not aware of its synergistic action when combined with alcohol. For withdrawal from these drugs, the phenobarbital substitution method of detoxification works well (2, 8).

Some of the tranquilizers have been described already under the nonbarbiturate sedative-hypnotics. Here we shall undertake a further breakdown as between the minor and major tranquilizers:

GENERIC NAME	TRADE OR BRAND NAME
Minor:	
Meprobamate	Equanil, Miltown
Diphrenylmethanes	Atarax, Phober, Suauitil
Chlordiazepoxide	Librax, Librium
Diazepam	Valium
Major:	
Reserpine	Serpasil
Phenothiazines	Compazine, Pacatal, Phenesgan, Sparine, Stelazine, Thorazine

The minor tranquilizers are used to lessen anxiety, tension, and apprehension that interfere with daily functioning. The major tranquilizers are more potent and are generally used as antipsychotic drugs. They have become the main psychiatric tool for dealing with the various symptoms of psychosis such as hallucinations, delusions, overexcitement, agitation, and aggressiveness. Reserpine was the first major tranquilizer used; the phenothiazines—Compazine, Stelazine, and Thorazine—have since taken its place for psychotic patients. These drugs have helped a majority of state hospital patients find release into the community after a relatively short period of institutionalization (2, 6, 8). A serious by-product that has recently come to attention is the phenomenon of "tardive dyskinesia," a series of grotesque distortions, contortions, and tics of the body in patients who have used drugs over long periods of time.

Amphetamines, or uppers, were first developed synthetically in the United States in 1927. Though some fifty-seven different uses were stipulated for them in the 1930s and thereafter, the pendulum has swung far in the other direction, and a number of medical associations have called for their complete elimination. Others would leave room for circumscribed conditions such as narcolepsy or sleeping episodes and

3. Stimulants

GENERIC NAME	TRADE, COMMON, OR BRAND NAME	COMMON STREET NAME
		General terms: A's, copilots, ellie babies, lid poppers, pep pills, truck drivers, uppers, wake-ups
amphetamine sulphate	Benzedrine	beans, bennie, benzies, cartwheels, hearts, peachies, roses
dextroamphetamine sulphate	Dexedrine	dexies, footballs, hearts, oranges, browns
methamphetamine hydrochloride	Desoxyn, Norodin, Syndrox	bambitas, crystal, D. meth, speed, splash
methylphenidate	Ritalin }	(central nervous stimulants which differ from amphetamines chemically but resemble them in numerous pharmacological reports)
phenmetrazine	Preludin }	
benzoylmethlecgonine	Cocaine	coke, B, flake, snow, "speedball" if combined with heroin

possibly the use of Ritalin for clear cases of hyperactivity in youngsters, though this use has been questioned sharply recently. Their efficacy and safety in diminishing appetite for dieting have been attacked, but they have nevertheless been widely used and continue to be used for this purpose and as psychic energizers. The amphetamines were long considered to be nonaddicting, but in the mid-1970s Lester Grinspoon made a strong case for the likelihood that the amphetamines are indeed addicting and have a characteristic withdrawal or abstinence syndrome, different from the better-known ones of the narcotic and barbiturate addictions. Along with the psychic effects, such as depression and fatigue and at times paranoid and suicidal thoughts, there may be headaches, irritability, palpitations, dizziness, insomnia, agitation, panic, confusion, apprehension, and delirium. In addition to gross physical signs, there is a so-called "crash" following cessation of use, which entails a withdrawal picture consisting of lassitude, lethargy, sleep disturbances, and a marked depressive mood that may persist for months. Suicidal ideation and attempts are not infrequent, and staff must watch carefully for these. Hospitalization and treatment with tricyclic antidepressants are therefore recommended in withdrawal (2, 6, 8).

Amphetamine use often leads to a cycle of use consisting of an active and reactive phase. The down or coming-off phase entails the use of sedatives and barbiturates to ease the strains of a crash. The author has distinguished at least two major classes of amphetamine users: the adaptive and the escapist. The adaptive abusers are generally characterized

as using amphetamines to bolster their functioning in conventional interpersonal and social activities. In contrast, the escapist abusers take
drugs as part of their counterculture life-style. Some of these users have
been able to move to appallingly high doses of amphetamine with the
support of their group, resisting any efforts to reach them in order to
help. Treatment during withdrawal must deal with the physical as well
as psychiatric reactions, which may range from acute anxiety to a full-
blown psychosis requiring such medication as sedatives and
phenothiazines and close surveillance (2).

Cocaine is a central nervous system stimulant derived from the
leaves of the coca plant, native to the slopes of the Andes. It is most
often sniffed but it can also be injected. Its effects are strong though
short-lived. The person may feel a general sense of well-being as if he

4. Hallucinogens

GENERIC NAME	TRADE, COMMON, OR BRAND NAME	COMMON STREET NAME
D-lysergic acid diethyl-amide, LSD-25	LSD	acid, blue acid, Big D, cubes, sugar, 25
tri methoxyphenylethyl-amine	mescaline	an halonium, cactus, mesc, mescal beans, mescal buttons, P., peyote, hikori, wokowi
2,5-dimethoxy-4-methyl-amphetamine	DOM	serenity-tranquility-peace (STP)
tryptamine	Psilocybin	mushrooms
dimethyltryptamine	DMT	business-men's special
diethyltryptamine	DET	
tetrahydrocannabinol	cannabis sativa, cannabis, cannabis indica	Acapulco gold, bhang, bo, charas, ganja, grass, hash-ish, hash, hay, hemp, joint, kif, khif, loco weed, marijuana, Mary Jane, pot, reefers, roach, tea
	Atropine	
	Bufonin	
	Datura	
	Harmine	
	Ibogain	
	Kava	
	Khat	
	Morning Glory seeds	heavenly blue, pearly gates, blue star
	nutmeg	
Phencycladine	PCP	angel dust, rocket fuel

had unusual energy. Severe abuse may lead to toxic effects such as delusions, delirium, hallucinations, or convulsions. Because of the expense of cocaine, the amounts an ordinary person can use are limited. Cocaine is not addicting, which has made some individuals and even some treatment agencies respond casually to its use. There is a reevaluation of cocaine under way, with a tendency to regard it as less destructive and noxious than originally believed. Acute cocaine toxicity is seen relatively infrequently by clinicians (6, 7, 8).

The substances classed as hallucinogens have been grouped together arbitrarily, because one of their principal effects is to produce various changes in perception, mood, and thinking; a heightened awareness of self; and a confusion of boundaries. No overall term is generally adequate to describe them. In regard to LSD, for a long time the terms "psychotomimetic," meaning imitating the psychoses, and "psychedelic," meaning mind-manifesting, were used. LSD was synthesized as late as 1943 from ergot, a parasitic fungus found on wheat rye and other grasses. It is not addictive, but tolerance and reverse tolerance do occur. There are no systemized withdrawal symptoms. Individuals tolerant to LSD, mescaline, or psilocybin will be tolerant to the other two drugs as well.

LSD is odorless, colorless, and tasteless. For some years, it was used therapeutically in treating psychoses and drug and alcohol problems until the furor in the 1960s over the possibility of chromosome damage closed the gates on research except under extremely circumscribed conditions. Dependence on LSD is psychological; tolerance develops after a few days of repeated use but is usually lost in two or three days. "Flashbacks," or unexpected returns to the LSD state even though no LSD has been used, may occur weeks or months after use and can be especially frightening. The literature reports three kinds of experience under LSD: the good trip is a predominantly pleasant experience. The bad trip is a dysphoric experience characterized by anxiety, panic, feelings of persecution and depersonalization, fears of loss of ego boundaries, loss of control and time perception, and impaired performance. In an ambivalent state the subject may simultaneously experience contrasting feelings, as of heaviness and lightness, relaxation and tenseness. The bad trip has been well documented in the literature. Becker described such experiences as psychological and attributed them to the panic emerging upon experiencing a host of overwhelming sensory inputs. Learning was entailed in LSD as well as in marijuana use. The acute reactions or bad trips were of two types:

1. Psychotoxic reactions characterized by confusion and/or acute paranoia or feelings of omnipotence and invulnerability, which

might cause the user to expose himself to dangers, resulting at times in injury or death

2. Panic reactions occurring as a secondary response to the drug-induced symptoms

Fairly rapid recovery can be anticipated from these two acute states. Remission usually occurs within two or three days; recommended treatment is verbal support or "talking down" and, at times, sedation. Significant variables determining the course of any LSD trip are the personality and expectations of the subject, the presence of a dependable guide, the nature of the setting in which the drug was taken, and the age of the subject. Freedman and others felt that young users were more susceptible to dysphoric reactions. If talking down doesn't help, the AMA has recommended phenothiazines as a medication that can block the action of LSD (2).

Phencycladine or PCP is manufactured for use as a tranquilizing and anesthetic agent for primates. Otherwise known as the peace pill or elephant tranquilizer, it is also manufactured in illicit labs for street sale. Sprinkled on parsley or other herbs or mixed with marijuana, it may be smoked as a cigarette. It can also be ingested by mouth._The drug both depresses and stimulates the central nervous system, depending on the dose. Signs of use may include drowsiness, nystagmus, ataxia, agitation, excitability, and, with higher doses, respiratory depression, coma, and epileptic attacks. While most cases of acute poisoning clear up within twenty-four hours, confusion, disorientation, delusions, and hallucinations may persist for several days to several weeks. Controversy surrounds the use of medication in the treatment of the severe agitation and the concomitant psychotic symptoms, paranoid delusions, and auditory hallucinations. Until more is known about the interactions of PCP with other drugs, caution must be used in treating cases of poisoning. If diazepam is employed to decrease excitement, only small doses should be used. It is recommended that phencycladine intoxication be considered whenever an adolescent with unexplained psychosis or bizarre symptoms presents in the emergency room (8).

5. INHALANTS (TOXIC VAPORS)

Experimentation with inhalants, especially glue, among adolescents generated much alarm in the 1960s but seems to have fallen off. The vapors inhaled have included gasoline, paint thinner, naphtha, and such solvents as toluene. Glue-sniffing produced a variety of effects ranging from mild intoxication to disorientation and coma if exposure was extensive. There is conflicting information about the long-range effects of such abuse. Clinicians should obtain a careful history and conduct lab tests where indicated (8).

Comment

We have paused in this chapter to reflect on the terminology developed over the years for substance abuse and misuse and to review the rubrics under which the main groupings of substances have been classified. As indicated, there has been a serious lack of consensus and tremendous confusion regarding the most common terms used, such as addiction, habituation, drug abuse, drug misuse, and nonmedical use (11). Until recently, we had the arbitrary division of drugs into "hard" (such as opiates and their derivatives) and "soft" drugs, by which was meant others, excluding alcohol. This division reflected society's moralistic and judgmental attitudes toward the drugs. Those biases added to the problems of rehabilitating, treating, preventing, and managing drug abuse. To counter such approaches, we have espoused a "rational approach to drug abuse," which strives for greater objectivity and focuses on the person rather than the drug used or misused (5). We have nevertheless presented the basic information that persons undertaking to deal with drug abusers will need in order to understand what is involved in a particular situation. The interaction of pharmacological with physiological, psychological, and social factors renders this far from simple.

References

1. Balter, M. B. "Drug Abuse: A Conceptual Analysis and Overview of the Current Situation." Chapter 1 of *Drug Use: Epidemiological and Sociological Approaches.* E. Josephson and E. E. Carroll, eds. New York: John Wiley & Sons, 1974.
2. Brill, L. "Drug Abuse Problems: Implications for Treatment." *Abstracts for Social Workers* (NASW), Vol. 7, No. 3, Fall 1970.
3. Brill, L. "Drug Addiction." *Encyclopedia of Social Work.* 16th Ed. New York: NASW, 1971.
4. Brill, L. "Drug Addiction." *Encyclopedia of Social Work.* 17th Ed. Washington, D.C.: NASW, 1977.
5. Brill, L. "Three Approaches to the Casework Treatment of Narcotics Addicts." *Social Work,* 13, No. 2 (April 1968): 25–36.
6. Einstein, S. *Beyond Drugs.* New York: Pergamon Press, 1975.
7. Jaffe, J. H. "Drug Addiction and Drug Abuse." Chapter 16 of *The Pharmacological Basis of Therapeutics,* 3d Ed. L. S. Goodman and A. Gilman, eds. New York: Macmillan, 1965.

8. Khantzian, E. J., and G. J. McKenna. "Diagnosis and Management of Acute Drug Problems." In *The Yearbook of Substance Use and Abuse*. L. Brill and C. Winick, eds. New York: Human Sciences Press, 1980.

9. *Marijuana and Health: Eighth Report to the United States Congress*. From the Secretary of HEW, 1980. DHEW Publication No. (ADM) 80-945.

10. Rappolt, R. T. Cited in *Drug Addiction: Clinical and Socio-legal Aspects*. Vol. 2. J. M. Singh, L. H. Multer, and H. Lal, eds. Mt. Kisco, N.Y.: Futura Publishing Co., 1972.

11. Smart, R. "Addiction, Dependency, Abuse or Use: Which Are We Studying With Epidemiology?" Chapter 2 in *Drug Use: Epidemiological and Sociological Approaches*. E. Josephson and E. E. Carroll, eds. New York: John Wiley & Sons, 1974.

12. World Health Organization, Expert Committee on Mental Health, *Drugs Liable to Produce Addiction: Report on the 2nd Session of the WHO Expert Committee, 1950*. WHO Technical Report Series, Geneva, 1950.

13. World Health Organization, Expert Committee on Mental Health, *Addiction-producing Drugs: 7th Report of the WHO Expert Committee, 1957*. WHO Technical Report Series, No. 116, Geneva, 1957.

14. World Health Organization, Expert Committee on Mental Health, *Addiction-producing Drugs: 13th Report of the WHO Expert Committee, 1964*. WHO Technical Report Series, No. 273, Geneva, 1964.

15. World Health Organization, Expert Committee on Drug Dependence, *16th Report*. WHO Technical Report Series, No. 407, Geneva, 1969.

CHAPTER 4

Prevention

PREVENTION IS GENERALLY RELEGATED to a subordinate position both in discussion and in funding. The author considers it important to emphasize its crucial role by discussing it early in this book rather than as an afterthought.

It is a strange fact that, after so many years, few model prevention programs have been developed in the country. Historically, drug abuse prevention passed through several stages. Efforts at prevention through prohibition and exhortation proved ineffectual, and the heavy reliance on ex-addicts in the 1950s and 1960s yielded small results. It became evident that scare approaches were not useful as deterrents and, in fact, often had the reverse effect of turning youngsters on rather than off. Providing some individuals with drug information tended to stimulate rather than discourage (1, 2, 5, 10).

For a long time, prevention efforts were hindered by an incomplete understanding of the causes of drug dependence and the techniques needed to intervene early in the lives of youngsters to head off more serious abuse. The state of the art did not permit an explanation of why some people with social, psychological, and biochemical characteristics resembling those of addicts could use drugs without becoming addicted. Why didn't all members of inner-city minority populations or, for that matter, all alienated and anomic middle-class suburban youth become dysfunctional users? Experience enabled us to predict with some degree of certainty that there would be more heroin abuse among black inner-city groups than among white suburban residents, with the reverse holding true for the antianxiety drugs (1, 2, 5, 10). Experience permitted us to anticipate different drug abuse patterns for males and females, adolescents and adults. Thus, certain populations could be targeted for

50

certain kinds of prevention and intervention efforts, even though it was not possible to identify with certainty which individuals within each population or group would become involved with drug abuse. Black populations in inner cities have generally been reported to have a heavier involvement with heroin; the white middle classes with other drugs; the elderly with prescription and over-the-counter drugs; and women similar to the elderly. The forms of abuse are related to the specific and unique socio-economic, cultural, and psychological factors in each population. Clearly, therefore, prevention efforts must take these differences into account and must be focused on the particular problems and needs of each group.

Though the primary focus of prevention efforts has hitherto been on youth, it must be emphasized that other populations are equally vulnerable and cannot be overlooked. We must also be concerned about such groups as women, the elderly, medical drug abusers, transients and migrants, isolates living in boarding houses, persons in crisis, bar populations, college students, and others. Though we previously pursued a shotgun approach of uniform education for all groups, we now understand better the need to tailor our efforts to different targets. Some persons will be scared away from drugs by information about their harmful effects, while others may enjoy risk-taking and will be attracted by the same information. Some will be influenced only if they can be convinced that the drugs are indeed harmful; others will have such a powerful need for drugs that no information will be able to dissuade them from use. Cumulative information and experience indicate that the role of the family and maturational factors as well as prior experience with drugs are important in determining how and why individuals develop differential responses to drug use (1, 2, 4, 5, 6, 8, 10).

Two of the major groups to be concerned about are women and the elderly. The position of women in our society has increasingly been discussed as part of the "women's lib" movement in recent years. Their subordination in many areas and the boredom of their marital lives may be reasons for resorting to drug use, often of the pill-taking and over-the-counter, nonprescription drug variety, but also involving more serious drugs, including alcohol. Depression has been noted as a frequent factor in many women's lives. A review of women's use of three popular drugs—heroin, marijuana and psychotropic drugs—reveals that we have neglected to consider this subject. Although men have consistently been more involved with illegal opiate use, its use among women has increased at a greater rate than among men in the past decade. The literature suggests that the female user/addict usually comes from a blue-collar Caucasian background, lacks a high school education, and uses drugs because of social or psychological needs, as do men. In contrast to the male, she becomes involved with narcotics in her mid-twenties. Furthermore, while men outnumber women in heroin and marijuana use, the reverse is true regarding psychotropics. The kind of psychotropic drug women use varies with their age: they often begin taking amphetamines, minor tranquilizers, or antidepressants in their twenties and continue through their middle years. In their later years (sixties and on), they tend to use sedatives and barbiturates. This pattern differs from patterns among men, who usually take only stimulants in their twenties, minor tranquilizers in their middle years, and sedatives and barbiturates in later years. Prevention efforts need to focus more on women specifically, avoid stereotyping them, examine the role of men in inducting women to drug use, and develop programs specifically geared to the needs of women.

Alcoholism affects millions of women in the country today. Although it is estimated that women may account for up to 40 percent or 50 percent of the alcoholics, their problems have been ignored or lumped together with men's problems in prevention, research, and treatment. Women alcoholics represent a diverse group, differing from male alcoholics in their psychosocial and drinking characteristics. Prevention efforts should be linked to the major women's organizations, such as NOW, and encompass the federal, state, and local groups to render the problem more visible and accessible to education and prevention efforts.

The problems of the elderly are also serious from the standpoint of potential drug abuse. The customary social, financial, psychological, familial, and, of course, physical supports may be failing, and there may be a strong need to substitute other supports for them. A common problem is the use of several drugs simultaneously without understanding their proper use and the synergistic effects of their combined use. This would include legally prescribed drugs and over-the-counter drugs obtained from drugstores. Some drugs are addicting, and others have important side effects, which may exacerbate the problems of living. Alcohol abuse is a serious and often unrecognized and untreated problem. Service providers need to be aware of the multiple effects alcohol abuse has on the elderly. Four types of alcohol-related problem are often found: (1) chronic long-term alcoholism, (2) the onset of alcoholism in the later years, (3) debilitating interactive effects of alcohol use, and (4) victimization of older adults by alcoholics. Prevention and treatment are often handicapped by the failure of clinicians to understand all aspects of alcoholism and the unavailability of adequate treatment resources. Physical, mental, and social problems complicate the situation. Centers must learn to develop a diagnostic and treatment typology that involves problems with alcohol, health, and the social support system to determine the appropriate environmental and treatment resources for these patients. There is need for integrated and comprehensive treatment services to deal with all these aspects. Unfortunately, there are still few active programs in the area of specific intervention and treatment for the elderly user of psychoactive drugs. There is also need for study of the physiological and psychological changes attendant on the aging process and their relationship to drug use.

A central problem in prevention relates to a misunderstanding about the goals of prevention. In the author's view, it is not possible to stop all experimentation with drugs. In the past, most educators saw drug use as an "infection" that had to be stopped at its source. This concept is erroneous, and the attempt to prevent all experimentation is futile. Youngsters will explore new experiences for a wide range of reasons, including curiosity, peer pressure, and social-recreational needs. As mentioned, the overwhelming majority of experimenting youngsters do not move on to more serious use but either stop use entirely or continue on an irregular, controlled basis. The previous perspective on drug use hampered our prevention efforts. Our current thinking focuses on the person rather than the substance in an effort to understand the role the substance is playing in the person's life—whether for good or for bad, depending on his or her reasons for using (1, 2, 4, 5, 6, 8, 10).

Until recently, education and prevention were considered synonymous. As the author understands it, education refers primarily to providing information, which may or may not have an impact on a person's affective life, values, and attitudes. Until recently, educational efforts were focused mainly on the pharmacological effects of drugs, usually the "bad" effects, and emphasized that any use of drugs inevitably led to more serious use and addiction. Prevention is seen as the more basic approach for zeroing in on the factors that impel a person to use drugs. In the case of youngsters, this more global prevention approach focuses on the maturational needs of youngsters and is designed to help them deal more effectively with their problems of living through the development of skills and self-understanding, the ability to communicate and form satisfactory relationships with others, and the capacity to solve problems and to establish a positive self-image. Basic to all these is the elaboration of a sense of personal identity, self-esteem, and trust in authority figures and important others (1, 2, 4, 8, 9, 10). Different approaches need to be devised to meet the needs of different age groups and populations.

A widely accepted framework for thinking about prevention and intervention is the one developed by Dr. Gerald Caplan of the Harvard School of Public Health in the 1940s. Dr. Caplan postulated three stages of prevention, requiring more active intervention and treatment to head off more serious involvement or, in the tertiary stage, either to rehabilitate and cure or, at least, prevent further deterioration and breakdown as in chronic disability.

1. Primary prevention includes efforts undertaken prior to the onset

or at the very beginning of drug-abusing behavior and is particularly directed at potential risk populations.

2. Secondary prevention includes intervention efforts for incipient drug abusers before they have developed confirmed patterns of abuse. Secondary prevention activities and services call for outreach and early identification so that intervention efforts can be made in time to curb or minimize more serious or chronic use.

3. Tertiary prevention entails sustained treatment and other services to individuals whose drug abuse patterns have become severe, compulsive, and chronic and have resulted in a high degree of dysfunctional behavior. It requires efforts to cure and rehabilitate but may also call for efforts in more chronic cases to avoid more serious deterioration (3, 6).

It is worth noting that the federal government, when it established a national office for all drug abuse except alcoholism in 1973, appeared to be following the Caplan model of regarding all treatment and intervention as prevention, since the office was called the Special Action Office for Drug Abuse Prevention (SAODAP).

The techniques developed over the past decades to support these objectives include role-playing and other forms of simulation; group-oriented games; "rap" sessions, where youngsters can verbalize their concerns, as in the long-standing "Spark" program sponsored by the New York City Board of Education; value clarification; the articulation of feelings; nonverbal forms of expression; group meetings of youngsters and their parents, either separately or jointly; alternative activities such as the outings and trips of the program in Gloucester, Massachusetts; audio-visual approaches; and others (2, 4, 6, 9). There is need for better collaboration among education departments, drug programs, and community organizations to develop appropriate programs for particular target populations and to mobilize community resources and support systems to generate activities for drug abuse prevention and intervention.

A central concept advocated for drug abuse prevention has been the "Alternatives to Drug Abuse" model developed by Allen V. Cohen at the J. F. Kennedy University of California. Cohen points out that people do not stop taking drugs until and unless they have found a suitable alternative. Drug abusers often get locked into a very limited range of options, many of them antiestablishment-oriented, counterculture, and counterproductive. They refuse to accept the conventional world and so tune out and drop out. The use of alternatives is meant to help such individuals expand the base on which life decisions can be made and develop new sources of gratification through activities that are stimulating, promote maturation, and encourage effective social functioning and interaction (4). The use of such alternative outlets as sports may establish relationships with hard-to-reach populations and provide structured and unstructured activities in which clients can explore feelings and attitudes, practice new behaviors, and reduce boredom and monotony. Programs for youngsters may include yoga, martial arts, or outdoor sports, for example. The basic idea is to develop alternate life-styles and change the current way of living. Still other techniques are the provision of appropriate role models to counter the negative role models the youngsters have experienced previously. For the elderly, activities might include arts and crafts, carpentry, ceramics, music, and visiting (4).

It is apparent that Dr. Cohen's approach is important. If any criticism can be made, it might be that he has given insufficient attention to the reluctance and fears that some persons feel toward becoming involved in such alternate activities. Frequently much work needs to be done to overcome these resistances before the individual can move toward alternate activities.

It follows that helping services are an important concomitant of prevention efforts. Intervention in the early stages of drug abuse is crucial if we are to head off more serious involvement. One approach is counseling, focused on improving behavioral functioning rather than on exploring the inner life of the client, as in traditional therapy. Some situations will, of course, call for more intensive help. The interventive counseling may include individual supportive help to support the client's ego strengths and deal with essentially conscious material. The process would also use realistic reassurance and support, the "ventilation" of feelings, and the correction of reality distortions. Group counseling would aim at promoting meaningful group interactions under the direction of a skilled counselor. As in all group therapy, the groups should have their own rationale for being and should be time-limited, membership-limited, goal-oriented, and purposefully structured. Suitable referral services must be available to provide a network of continuous services in each community (1, 2, 6, 10, 11).

The core and fulcrum of all prevention efforts are the recognition that youngsters must be equipped to deal more effectively with their problems from a very early age. The burden of accomplishing this should rest primarily with the family, and this constitutes one of our basic problems: some of the most troubled and unstable children come from the most unstable and disorganized families. The psychosocial problems in what used to be termed "hard-to-reach families" appear insurmountable, so that such efforts as counseling, education, training, and treatment to bolster the home environment and improve parent–child relationships and childrearing techniques seem hopeless. Schools have attempted to take up some of the slack by establishing family-life courses and "rap" sessions as well as child and parent groups, separately or jointly. Obviously, hardly a dent has been made, and much work remains to be done before we can begin to deal effectively with the issue of prevention. We have developed exceedingly few "model programs" in the country, as mentioned, and even if we do establish such models, we still do not understand how to evaluate their effectiveness. Still, much of the brushwood has been cleared away, and we are in a better position to plan new approaches (1, 2, 5, 6, 7, 8, 9, 10).

NIDA Report on Prevention

In 1977 NIDA and other agencies issued an interagency report entitled "Recommendations for Future Federal Activities in Drug Abuse Prevention." The report outlined a variety of strategies for developing and implementing federal prevention policy (cited in 7). Among the approaches suggested for reducing "drug casualties" are limiting the variety of drugs used, reinforcing the drug-free experience, and reducing the frequency of use. Prevention activities should, in future, focus on the high social costs of drug use as well as the general drug-taking experience, with the primary goal of moderating the effects of drug-taking. Adolescent experimentation with psychoactive drugs is accepted as part of the normal maturing process. The objectives of the federal government are to reduce the number of new users (incidence) in order to delay incidence and reduce frequent or daily use.

Specifically, the following goals are recommended:

1. Reducing the percentage of frequent use of the three "gateway drugs"—tobacco, alcohol, and marijuana—by 15 percent among eight- to twenty-year-olds
2. Reducing the destructive behavior associated with alcohol and other drug abuse by 20 percent among fourteen- to twenty-year-olds as evidenced by a reduction in overdose deaths, emergency room visits, drug arrests, and other drug/alcohol-related incidents
3. Promoting restraining attitudes to the use of psychoactive substances, especially the gateway drugs, by maintaining current levels of awareness regarding the addictive nature of heroin and alcohol and raising awareness of the addictive nature of tobacco by 50 percent (7).

These new federal education and prevention objectives generally reflect a restrained approach and appear to acknowledge the benefits of moderate drug use in fostering relaxation, camaraderie, and group ceremonies as well as the fact that most users do learn limits, restraints, and responsible practices. They agree with the attitudes expressed here, that experimental and recreational use cannot be eliminated entirely and that our focus must be on destructive and dysfunctional use.

The old idea of complete abstinence from all nonmedical use has proved invalid. Education and prevention must also include the gateway drugs, for they are the first substances used by most individuals. The promotion of restrained attitudes toward drug use is a worthwhile goal, provided that distinctions are made among drugs and use patterns, as indicated. The report suggests shifting the means used to convey information: formerly it was concentrated in isolated drug courses, but it is now suggested that the information be disseminated through instruction in such courses as family development, nutrition, hygiene, safety, and interpersonal relations. Too often the message is still conveyed that *all* drugs are destructive. Perhaps the alcohol-prevention model would be useful as an approach to other drugs, since clear distinctions are drawn between responsible and destructive drinking. Strategies must be developed, also, for targeting casualties and high-risk populations and designing special programs for dealing with them (7).

References

1. Brill, L. "Drug Addiction." In *Encyclopedia of Social Work*. New York: NASW, 1971, pp. 24–38.
2. Brill, L. "Drug Addiction." In *Encyclopedia of Social Work*. Washington, D.C.: NASW, 1977, pp. 30–42.
3. Caplan, G. Principles of Preventive Psychiatry. New York: Basic Books, 1964.
4. Cohen, A. V. *Alternatives to Drug Abuse: Steps Towards Prevention*. National Clearinghouse for Drug Abuse Information Publication No. 14, Washington, D.C.: U.S. Government Printing Office, 1973.
5. DeLone, H. R. "The Ups and Downs of Drug Abuse Education." *The Saturday Review of Education*, November 11, 1972.
6. Friedman, H. R., et al. "A Comprehensive Strategy for Prevention." Report of the Strategies for Prevention Project, Narcotic Drug Research Inc. of the Drug Abuse Control Commission of New York, 1976. Unpublished monograph.
7. Liaison Task Panel on Psychoactive Drug Use/Misuse. N. Zinberg, Coordinator. Submitted to the President's Commission on Mental Health February 15, 1978. Published as Chapter 2 of the *Yearbook of Substance Use and Abuse*. L. Brill and C. Winick, eds. New York: Human Sciences Press, 1980.
8. Nowlis, H. *Drugs on the College Campus*. New York: Doubleday, Anchor, 1969.
9. Pacific Institute for Research and Evaluation: BKII. *Balancing Head and Heart: Sensible Ideas for the Prevention of Drug and Alcohol Abuse*. Walnut Creek, Calif.: Pacific Institute for Research and Evaluation, 1975.
10. "Programs for Drug Abuse Treatment and Prevention." Chapter 4 of *Community Crime Prevention*. Washington, D.C.: National Advisory Commission on Criminal Justice Standards and Goals, January 1973, pp. 85–111.
11. Smith, D. E.; D. J. Bentell; and J. L. Schwartz. *The Free Clinic: A Community Approach to Health Care and Drug Abuse*. Madison, Wisc.: Stash Publications, 1974.

PART II

THE TREATMENT OF SUBSTANCE ABUSE

CHAPTER 5

Issues in Treatment

SOME OF THE PROBLEMS and issues of treatment were touched on in previous chapters. Chapter 2 noted the major categories of problems in treatment related to the drug abusers themselves, to therapists and psychoanalytic thinking and techniques, and to "state of the art" issues. It was observed that workers tended to stereotype drug abusers as if they were all alike and to label them all character disorders, which served to discourage treatment. The description of character disorders provided by B. S. Reiner and Dr. I. Kaufman in the 1950s nevertheless dramatically caught the flavor of many of the addicts encountered in social agencies at that time:

> Persons suffering from character disorders are fixated at pregenital levels of development and express their conflicts primarily by behavioral manifestations. This behavior may include stealing, getting pregnant, getting into job difficulties or becoming involved in some social crisis. They operate at infantile levels and defeat themselves in nearly all aspects of life. Although some may have partial control, they usually are so impulse-ridden that they tend to pursue the wrong ends or else the right ends at the wrong time. There has been a tendency to regard these cases as "untreatable." [17]

Some observers, including the present author, believe that the heroin-using population of the 1950s constituted a more homogeneous group than the users of the 1960s and 1970s and that many of the characteristics described by Reiner and Kaufman were valid for this earlier group.

Findings of the New York Demonstration Center

A community study that I directed in the mid-1950s and early 1960s may have played some role in implementing the move away from the traditional psychoanalytic approaches to treatment and reinforcing the need for extensive modifications (8). The New York Demonstration Center, a five-year demonstration project, was sponsored by the National Institute of Mental Health. Its findings were reported in a Public Health Service monograph in 1963. Among the treatment changes proposed by the social work staff were these: a need to view drug addiction as a chronic relapsing condition, with limited goals the only appropriate and realistic ones; more active and directive casework, with more emphasis on reaching out; and greater flexibility in relation to appointment schedules, since addicts were so often caught up in a series of crises. It was also recommended that workers reach addicts in the midst of these crises, if they were to reach them at all, and continue working with them in the midst of their drug-using periods instead of insisting on abstinence as a condition of treatment. Instead of insight therapy, workers more often needed to provide tangible or concrete assistance for the users' immediate problems and to undertake home visits if they did not come in, with the additional goal of involving the family. Clients needed to be helped to use community resources more effectively, with special supportive assistance at the time of referral so that they would not be lost between agencies.

The report further described the need to dilute the intensity of the relationship, at least at the outset; a "preliminary treatment period" was suggested in which the client would learn to trust the agency and the worker and would be encouraged to come in on a regular basis. Caseworkers had to become aware of their own reactions and countertransferences in view of the clients' constant testing of limits and challenges to the workers. A final recommendation emphasized the need for some use of authority and compulsion as a means of structuring treatment and holding the client through his vicissitudes by a rational use of court-derived authority (8).

These recommendations were made almost two decades ago and therefore hardly represent the last word on treatment. Many have proved valid, however, and are now part of our treatment armamentarium. The report pointed up many of the issues of treatment, the characteristics of the addict population, and the special attributes needed in workers, including objectivity, endless patience, a rational perspective on the drug problem, and a firm understanding of what could and what could not be accomplished in treatment. Therapists had to be prepared to give a great deal and to expect only small returns over a long period of time. They needed to have a firm understanding of personal and family dynamics, the symbiotic relationships and interactions resulting from the victimization and "scapegoating" of the user, and the "hidden contracts" between the family members (1, 4, 5, 7, 17). Therapists who had not worked out their own feelings of rebellion against authority figures might tend to overidentify with the drug user against the family and outside agencies, especially authoritative ones such as probation and parole; conversely, they might identify with the long-suffering parents, without understanding the role they were playing in initiating and perpetuating the user's problems.

Some Treatment Issues

In brief, workers needed to become more aware of their own underlying feelings about drug abuse. They had often incorporated the prevailing feelings about drug users—such as the presumptions about their assaultiveness, criminality, and manipulativeness—and might tend to generalize that it was futile to try to treat them. They might be envious of the users' seemingly carefree existence, their lack of concern about the future, their acting-out of forbidden impulses, their dependency and, indeed, infantilism. Workers who were themselves insecure might derive feelings of power from the dependency of their clients or develop grandiose expectations of success where others had failed, reacting with rage and rejection if the clients frustrated their expectations, as they so often did. Middle-class workers failed to understand and relate to the attitudes and striving of their lower-class clients. Older workers might resent and envy the attractiveness and freedom of youthful clients who were not constrained by the usual restrictions of society and satisfied their needs without any concern for the future. Workers had to tread carefully if they were to be objective and avoid becoming judgmental, punitive, and moralistic or else overidentified with their clients and unwittingly instigative of their worst behavior (3, 8, 9).

If these caveats seem discouraging, it may be helpful to remember that all humans are more alike than different, that therapists share many of the attributes and aspirations of drug abusers and need different supports to make it in life. Many of the techniques used with other clients will be helpful for drug abusers as well, and many elements of diagnosis and treatment will be the same. As in all treatment, we need to gear the approach to the particular client, encompassing his specific problems and psychosocial needs. We must understand the role the family is playing in his abuse and the role drugs are playing in his life. At times the drug use may be all-consuming, involving the user's entire life; at other times, it may be incidental and unimportant, as in his or her occasional recreational use of marijuana or alcohol. The individual may have severe emotional problems, and the occasional drug use should not be allowed to obscure them. We noted earlier that a range of modalities has been developed for narcotic users and that each modality has something to offer certain clients. Methadone maintenance is a very strong instrumentality for engaging and holding large numbers of confirmed heroin addicts over a long period of time; therapeutic communities provide strong group and residential supports for individuals who are not sufficiently socialized or integrated to make it on the street; and the other modalities can play a role with other segments of the addict population (6, 9, 11, 14). It has proved very difficult to hold younger clients in the drug-free centers for day-long programs, and there has been much attrition in such centers. Workers need all the reinforcements they can find to hold these young users in treatment, whether in the form of chemotherapy or rational authority, as well as special training and skills development.

The problem of involving recalcitrant abusers who do not come into treatment of their own accord is very complex. Such abusers present a severe test for themselves, their families, and their communities. The concept of "rational authority" was developed in an effort to deal with this contingency (6, 8, 9, 18). In addition to parole and probation, this has more recently meant the use of court diversion approaches, whereby defendants caught up in the criminal justice system have an opportunity to opt for treatment, as against jail. In these preceedings and in the "Treatment Alternatives to Street Crime" approach, the pending charges will be dropped if the defendant successfully completes treatment (18). These approaches have yielded good results in the past decade and are now an accepted part of the treatment of offenders.

A related approach is civil commitment. There has been much controversy about the efficacy and even the morality of this approach. I am collaborating with Dr. W. H. McGlothlin of California and others in a detailed evaluation of this procedure as it has operated in California and New York under the federal government's Narcotic Addiction Rehabilitation Act, and in other parts of the world such as Canada and the Far East. The study, sponsored by NIDA, offers a rather more encouraging picture of the usefulness of the civil commitment procedure than has hitherto been presented (12). Rational authority is a technique that can be used not only for recalcitrants and offenders but for all acting-out clients; it should be studied further as a tool in treatment (6, 8, 9, 14).

The range of treatment options available to nonopiate abusers was outlined in Chapter 2. Since so many of the youngsters involved in heavy drug abuse reject their families and society, we need to find ways to counter this rejection and change their attitudes and life-styles before they become too deeply imbedded. While we have advocated the need to "get them while they are still young," the acting-out adolescents have constituted our most troublesome problem in treatment—as evidenced by the experience of the Riverside Hospital in New York in the 1950s. On the other hand, workers were surprised to learn that a very long period of involvement with drugs was not necessarily a contra-indication to treatment. Individuals with such a history had experienced a long series of "pushes and pulls" and become increasingly disenchanted with the drug life. Some had hit "rock bottom" or were close to it and felt the need for change (7). Youngsters still in the "honeymoon period" of drug use, by contrast, might be deriving satisfaction from it and not yet experiencing the negatives, so that they were far less prepared to give up their use.

Illustrations of Commonly Encountered Situations in Treatment

In considering some of the issues of treatment, it should be helpful to examine a few of the situations that commonly confront caseworkers in treatment. Herbert Barish of the Lower Eastside Service Center offers the following cases of situations or problems to illustrate what takes place in an agency and what feelings are provoked in the workers by clients (3).

EXAMPLE 1: INTIMIDATION BY CLIENT

The following case illustrates the client's need to maintain distance from the worker for fear of becoming dependent on the relationship. Since there is also an impulse to become involved, the client needs to subject the worker to severe testing to make certain that the worker will be able to tolerate and support him if he does permit himself to become engaged. This testing and challenge often become the core of treatment, assume an infinite variety of forms, and must constitute part of the worker's technique and skill if he is to deal with them effectively:

The client came in saying, "I think the only way to prove to my former wife that I love her and that she is wrong about me is to kill myself and tell her just before I do it." The social work student involved felt overwhelmed because of her inexperience; the presence of a more experienced worker in the session with her, which was intimidating; fear of saying the wrong thing and perhaps helping to precipitate the suicide; a feeling of identification with the client's depression and loneliness; and a sense of failure that the client was not really being helped. The experienced worker proved helpful since she was able to recognize what the client was really saying and to go beyond the feelings the client had provoked in her. She saw that he was trying to keep the worker at a distance and to punish her by inducing frustration, anger, and guilt. She was then able to focus on the client's need to punish and maintain distance in keeping with his previous pattern of noninvolvement (3).

EXAMPLE 2: LARCENY, ANYONE?

Clients frequently attempt to involve the worker in their illicit drug use or deviant behavior as a means of testing his honesty and reliability or of testing the worker generally, as in the first example. Such clients may offer to share stolen goods with the worker or pay for sessions with money that they announce was illicitly acquired or in other ways contaminate and enmesh the worker. In the following case example, the client tests the worker by forcing her to make a decision as to how his theft should be handled. The worker is caught in a quandary: if she overlooks the theft she becomes involved in a cover-up and indirectly condones the theft. If she reports it, she has betrayed the client and ended the relationship. Where more serious crimes have been committed such situations entail even larger decisions for the agency itself regarding the proper course of action:

This experienced worker needed help from her supervisor in relation to a situation she felt she had inadvertently helped to provoke. The client had been complaining for months that he couldn't work because he didn't have the money to buy a truck to start a small business. The client used the worker's challenge to get out of his complaining stance as an excuse to steal $10,000. The worker was confused and went through a variety of conflicting feelings. The client had managed to inveigle her into his deviant behavior and she did not know how to extricate herself: Should she try to make him return the money, overlook the theft, or report him to the police? Or should she drop him from treatment? She felt some responsibility because she had pushed him so hard. Had she perhaps conveyed a double message to him? While there was no perfect answer to this dilemma, a good starting point was the worker's careful scrutiny of her own behavior and feelings. This would be followed by her examining with the client what he was really doing and saying by his behavior, how and why he was attempting to enmesh the worker in it, and why he needed to test and challenge her in this essentially self-defeating way. How the actual theft is then dealt with needs to be resolved in terms of the needs of the client, the agency, and the community.

EXAMPLE 3: THE 4:55 CLIENT

This case situation offers a further instance of testing and challenge by clients. Clients whose lives are a series of crises inevitably catch workers up in these events. Unless the worker is experienced and skilled, he will feel inadequate and guilty because he cannot magically resolve all the client's problems. The client's extreme dependency and helplessness and the strains to which he subjects the worker will make the worker resentful and rejecting—a danger point for treatment. Coming in at inopportune times, such as five minutes before closing time, is part of the game. The worker is compelled to scramble to resolve a crisis within minutes:

Many clients love to walk in unexpectedly or else come in a day or two late for an appointment, or near closing time on Friday. They come in in crisis, without funds or housing, and on drugs. It is too late for referral to Welfare. The worker is caught between guilt at being considered a nine-to-five worker and anger at being confronted with a crisis at the last moment. He is eager to help, but is worried that he is being judged and conned by the client. Whatever the resulting action, the worker needs to sort out his own feelings and understand what the client is trying to provoke in him. He will then be freer to focus on the client's problems, needs, and methods of relating.

EXAMPLE 4: MOTIVATED CLIENT CONFRONTING AN UNMOTIVATED SOCIAL SYSTEM

A point often reiterated in this discussion has been the need for endless patience on the part of the worker. Treatment is often a long-drawn-out process, with relapses and regressions to be expected, often when the worker's hopes for a rapid cure are high. Workers must understand that progress will usually be slow and measured in small gains. If their expectations are too high, they will be caught short by the client's unexpected acting out or use of other means to frustrate their expectations:

This situation occurs frequently in treatment with many different kinds of agencies: welfare, courts, housing, vocational guidance, and employment. The worker has been making good progress with the client, who has been using drugs less and is temporarily on welfare rather than hustling, until he can find socially productive employment, and is willing to be detoxified from methadone. He is beginning to trust the worker, who is encouraging him to cope better with the outside world. The client suddenly finds that he is no longer eligible for welfare assistance on a technicality. He becomes upset, and the worker is too. The problem for her is to maintain her balance and not become discouraged herself if she is to help the client overcome his discouragement. Much patience is required through the client's acting-out at this point. The worker can be helpful if she views the situation as an experience that, if successfully overcome, will help the client build on his ability to deal with subsequent crises.

This example, of course, illustrates the use of crisis intervention as a means not only of resolving the immediate crisis but of helping the client learn how to deal with crises generally, thus building his ego strengths and preparing for future problem-solving (10, 15, 16).

EXAMPLE 5: FEÁRS OF SUCCESS: AN ACTING-OUT
SITUATION

Clients are often fearful of success, since they may have deep-rooted
feelings of inadequacy and a belief that they will not be able to sustain
any success and will sooner or later be found out as the inept people
they really are. They may also have unconscious fears about succeeding,
a belief that it is forbidden them to succeed. Freud's expression
"wrecked by success" pertains to people who cannot tolerate success
and go into a decline when confronted by achievement.

Many drug clients cannot tolerate success. Their progress in therapy
becomes a danger point that the worker must learn to watch for, because
it is so often followed by self-defeating behavior. It usually occurs when
some accomplishment is imminent, such as obtaining a high school
equivalency diploma, getting a job, or coming into property. The worker
must help the client deal with his anxiety over needing to continue to
prove himself when he has so many doubts about his adequacy:

One client was on his way to a job when he saw a jacket in an unlocked car and stole
it impulsively, even though a policeman was standing nearby. Needless to say, he
was arrested immediately. The worker, who had been hopeful about the client's
progress, felt let down. Workers need to be prepared for this type of eventuality and
to deal realistically with their own expectations. The gains made are usually limited
and slow. The worker must also help the client understand why he needed to act out
at the moment of his success.

EXAMPLE 6: THE "NOD"

In the 1950s agencies insisted that clients come in only if they were
totally abstinent, a condition few could fulfill. Agencies also dropped
clients from treatment if they relapsed. The "state of the art" did not
then permit workers and agencies to understand that such relapses were
only to be expected and that they would need to be dealing with clients
in the midst of their drug use in the course of any treatment. This does
not mean that the drug use is simply accepted:

Clients often come in high on drugs and "nod" in the course of the interview. The
worker is left feeling helpless. How should one deal with this? What is the client
attempting to communicate by his behavior, and what is he trying to provoke in the
worker? If the worker attempts simply to block out the occurrence, how will this help
both face up to what is happening in treatment?

EXAMPLE 7: "MY PAROLE OFFICER SENT ME"-

As noted earlier, many drug abusers come into treatment at the
behest of the court or a probation or parole officer. They have little

awareness of a problem and resent being referred for help. Workers need to learn how to use "rational authority" to engage and hold clients and gradually build "motivation" where none was apparent before (6, 9):

The involuntary client may maintain a strong silence and refuse to talk. It is difficult for the worker to try to open up a client who does not want to be there and may not even be aware that he has a problem. If the worker is secure enough, he may challenge the client and at least try to get at his real feelings about being there. Perhaps they can then move on from there.

EXAMPLE 8: DRUG TALK

Clients often want to talk only about drugs and their drug exploits. If the worker is a novice, he may be caught up in this ploy out of his own curiosity and overlook the fact that the client is thereby avoiding any discussion of his real problems and feelings. Some way must be found to pierce this discussion, especially in groups, where it is more apt to occur.

EXAMPLE 9: SEDUCTION OF THE WORKER

Amid the frustrations of treatment, a client will come in and tell you exactly what you want to hear. He is pleasant, agreeable and imitates your favorite jargon and clichés. He may even diagnose himself and corroborate what you have been saying and working toward. He will confirm that he has made tremendous progress and that you are the one who has helped him where others have failed.

The worker must be aware that he or she is being set up and that this is a trap. The client is not really sharing his true feelings; his underlying rage and hostility have no chance for expression. The unaware worker will experience a severe letdown once the client begins acting out again and reveals his true feelings.

EXAMPLE 10: "HOW CAN YOU HELP ME UNLESS YOU'VE BEEN WHERE I AM?"

Clients may challenge the worker by telling him that he cannot possibly understand or help them because he hasn't abused drugs himself. In the past, this became the basis for the "ex-addict mystique," the belief that only ex-addicts could help drug abusers because only they had experienced drug abuse. Workers should not allow themselves to be intimidated by such confrontations. They must remember that we are all human beings and therefore more alike than different. They can empathize with the anxiety, depression, frustration, rage, and other feelings of clients even if they haven't abused drugs themselves. At the same time, they must try to help the client explore why he is challenging the worker. This is not too different from the challenges other therapists experience when clients question their experience, credentials, and ability to help them (3).

EXAMPLE 11: THE UNEXPECTED

In working with clients at the New York Demonstration Center in the 1960s my staff and I learned that most clients did not come in on a regular basis but tended to drop in irregularly in the midst of one of their frequent crises, then disappeared, only to return again at a later date (8). The task was to accept this pattern of contact in the hope that it could gradually be transformed into regular treatment. This was also true of Mr. Barish's agency.

It often happens that the client drops out just when treatment is becoming more meaningful and the client appears to be growing more involved. The worker is sorely disappointed and makes every effort to reach out and reestablish contact, without success. After a lapse of months, the worker gets a call from the client, who asks to come in again. The worker feels exhilarated, realizing that some impact resulted from the previous contacts and that treatment can now begin again (3).

Special NIDA Study of Problems of Women

For too many years, treatment was focused on male abusers, and no separate or distinctive facilities or approaches were developed for women. It was assumed that whatever worked for men would also work for women. Only recently has it been realized that women abusers may have special needs and problems and that special centers may be required for them because of their unique life circumstances, their special position in society, and the fact that they may have additional responsibilities and concerns, such as the need to care for offspring.

A NIDA study offers the following findings and recommendations regarding female abusers (2).

1. CHARACTERISTICS.

Addicted women were found to show significantly greater psychological distress (depression, anger) and fewer personal resources and skills for coping with psychological distress or practical problem situations, such as financial needs and child care than a comparison group of nonaddicted women. They also had more physical illness and lower self-esteem than addicted men or comparison women. Addicted women were more likely to believe that people "look down" on them more than on addicted men. They rated themselves low on such masculine-associated traits as ego strength, effectiveness, and self-esteem and, at the same time, low on feminine-expressive characteristics. These sex-role conceptions also represented skill areas: women addicts felt less skilled in both male and female areas than did comparison women or addicted men.

2. FAMILY BACKGROUNDS.

Addicted women did not report that their family backgrounds were as bleak in either material or social resources as is generally depicted. They recalled their childhood and themselves as children positively. Nonetheless, they described having run away from home more often and at an earlier age than other women. They reported heavier use of alcohol by their families, which may have contributed to impulsivity and hostility. They thought of themselves in childhood as having been reasonably good, skilled, and accepted by their peers. They seem to have had problems during their high school years: becoming bored and restless, experimenting with drugs, and having trouble with the authorities. They were more likely than comparison women to have become pregnant during adolescence and to have left high school before graduation (2).

3. TREATMENT.

The NIDA study recommends the following approaches for women in treatment:

a. Build on their strengths. Educational and self-improvement programs may be helpful. Conversely, strategies that force a woman to admit only her mistakes may reinforce her low self-esteem. (In casework, this is termed ego-building and supportive therapy, emphasizing the positives and building on the client's strengths rather than resorting to uncovering techniques.)

b. Move slowly on relationship-building. Drug-dependent women report feeling lonely and isolated from meaningful relationships with others. Staff members of programs have to reach out repeatedly, since these women are used to trying to cope alone. Consistent acceptance and firm efforts to draw the client into treatment will demonstrate that the worker considers her worthy of attention. (The client is often helped to build her ego when she is very unsure about this if the worker extends himself and lets the client lean on his strength and confidence in the client.)

c. Pace and plan intervention carefully. Adequate pacing of interventions is probably the key to success. Women's higher levels of discomfort on entering treatment can work as a motivator if the program bolsters their self-esteem and does not move so quickly that the anxiety and/or depression become overwhelming. Clear and consistent explanations of what is expected and the consequences of these activities should be part of the early phases of treatment (2). (This recommendation stresses the need for good timing in treatment and cautious, slow movement to obviate precipitous confrontations or insights for which the client is not ready, which may drive her from treatment.)

Comment

In this chapter, we have considered the general issues and problems of treatment, offered a number of illustrations, and reviewed a special study of the problems and needs of women addicts, so long neglected in the drug treatment field. In the following chapter, we shall discuss the intake process, the important diagnostic and assessment component in treatment, which so often ensures that a client or patient is firmly committed to, and engaged in, treatment.

References

1. Ackerman, N. W. *Psychodynamics of Family Life*. New York: Basic Books, 1958.
2. *Addicted Women: Family Dynamics, Self-Perceptions and Support Systems*. Rockville, Md.: NIDA Monograph, 1980. Reported in *ADAMHA News*, Vol. VI, No. 7, April 4, 1980.
3. Barish, H. "The Need for Self-Understanding in the Treatment of Drug Addicts." Unpublished paper, mimeographed, September, 1972.
4. Boszormenyi-Nagy, I., and J. L. Framo, eds. *Intensive Family Therapy*. New York: Hoeber Medical Division, Harper and Row, 1965.
5. Bowen, M. "Family Concept of Schizophrenia." In D. O. Jackson, ed., *The Etiology of Schizophrenia*. New York: Basic Books, 1960.
6. Brill, L. "Rational Authority in Retrospect." In *Substance Abuse in the United States: Problems and Perspectives*. J. H. Lowinson and P. Ruiz, eds. Baltimore: Williams & Wilkins, 1981.
7. Brill, L. *The De-Addiction Process*. Springfield, Ill.: Charles C Thomas, 1972.
8. Brill, L., et al. *Rehabilitation in Drug Addiction: A Report on a Five-Year Demonstration Center*. Mental Health Monograph # 3. Washington, D.C.: PHS, NIMH, 1963.
9. Brill, L., and H. Meiselas. "The Treatment of Drug Abuse: Experiences and Issues." In *Yearbook of Drug Abuse*. L. Brill and E. Harms, eds. New York: Behavioral Publications, 1973.
10. Caplan, G. *Principles of Preventive Psychiatry*. New York: Basic Books, 1964.
11. Glasscote, R., et al. *The Treatment of Drug Abuse: Programs, Problems and Prospects*. Washington, D.C.: Joint Information Service of the American

Psychiatric Association and the National Association for Mental Health, 1972.

12. McGlothlin, W. H.; W. Mandell; L. Brill; and C. Winick. *Civil Commitment*. Monograph prepared for NIDA. Forthcoming, 1981.
13. Meiselas, H., and L. Brill. "Drug Abuse in Industry: Issues and Comments." *Industrial Medicine*, 4, No. 8 (August 1972): 10–16.
14. Meiselas, H., and L. Brill. "The Role of Civil Commitment in Multi-modality Programming." In *Drugs and Criminal Justice System*. Vol. 2. J. I. Inciardi and C. D. Chambers, eds. Beverly Hills, Calif.: Sage Publications, 1974.
15. Parad, H. J., ed. *Crisis Intervention: Selected Readings*. New York: Family Service Association of America, 1965.
16. Parad, H. J.; L. G. Selby; and J. Quinlan. "Crisis Intervention with Families and Groups." In *Theories of Social Work with Groups*. R. W. Roberts and N. Northen, eds. New York: Columbia University Press, 1976.
17. Reiner, B. S., and I. Kaufman. *Character Disorders in Parents of Delinquents*. New York: Family Association of America, 1958.
18. *Treatment Alternatives to Street Crime*. Reprint. Washington, D.C.: Special Action Office for Drug Abuse Prevention, 1972.

CHAPTER 6

The Intake Process

IT IS DURING THE INTAKE PHASE that a client's perception of the agency's ambience and its ability to help him is formed, and his willingness to proceed further in treatment reinforced. To the extent that the client helps determine the conditions of his treatment, to that extent will his treatment be actualized and affirmed. For many years, social agencies felt it necessary to obtain a "complete" psychosocial history before making a decision to accept or reject a client. In some cases, the process entailed a series of visits over a period of weeks or even months. It was soon discovered that this procedure would not work for drug abusers, who came in with very mixed feelings and were often caught up in a crisis or a host of other pressures, including current drug use. Their intolerance of delay and red tape created a problem for the agency, which wished to screen applicants more carefully and admit only those it thought it could help. Different modalities devised different approaches to deal with this issue: ex-addict-directed therapeutic communities in the 1950s and early 1960s made use of day centers known as "pressure cookers," which sifted out those who could not withstand the strains and stresses of encounter therapy and residential living (5, 10). The chemotherapy programs needed to comply with strict federal and state guidelines and regulations regarding patient admissions, optimal program sizes, and staff-patient ratios; space, medical, laboratory, and security requirements; length of treatment, the goals to be sought; counseling approaches; and other factors affecting intake and treatment (5, 6, 10). A study by the New York City Human Resources Administration in the early 1970s found that approximately 30 percent of the applicants on the methadone waiting list disappeared and were not available for admission by the time they were finally reached after many months of waiting.

Programs developed innovative ways to deal with this dilemma. The

74

Morris Bernstein Institute of the Beth Israel Hospital complex in New York, for example, tried to find the optimal balance between obtaining sufficient data to satisfy the requirements and criteria of acceptance and taking on patients as rapidly as possible in order to avoid losing them in the process. The Milwaukee program described later in this chapter similarly found ways to expedite the intake process, as did others around the country (2, 10, 11).

In any case, it is apparent that the notion that a "complete" psychosocial history and diagnosis can be obtained in one or even several interviews is questionable. It would be more useful in practice to see assessment as a continuous process throughout treatment, to be reformulated periodically as we learn more about the client and bring other members of the family into treatment. From this standpoint, one could say that all diagnosis is treatment and all treatment is diagnosis: the way we approach the client from the outset, the ambience of the agency, the issues we seem concerned about, the way we view the client's problems, our objectivity and willingness to listen and accept, the extent to which we involve the client in the "treatment contract" and allow him to help determine and define the conditions of treatment, and the presence or absence of minority staff—all these factors will enter the client's own "diagnosis" as to whether he can be helped by the agency (4, 9).

In programs with admission criteria requiring immediate total abstinence and regular appointments, it was found that very few clients could meet these standards. It was also found somewhat later that many clients would not come into any traditional program with the Establishment look, but gravitated instead to free clinics, drop-in centers, crash pads, and information and referral centers where staff came from similar backgrounds and had the same dress, speech, and, in some cases, attitudes as the clients (10). Indeed, the counselors might even be former friends who had shared their drug life and were now ex-addict aides who served as role models and bridges into the agency and treatment. After trust was established, these clients could be engaged more firmly in the program and moved along to more intensive help. In many clinics, paraprofessional or indigenous workers were the first to deal with the clients, moving them on quickly to more professional help where this was indicated. There was need for more flexible clinics and for revision of the traditional "Establishment" centers if they were to become more acceptable to patients.

It has been learned that the focus in intake should be on the here-and-now rather than on the past, though there is a need to elicit a certain amount of historical information in order to understand how the client got from there to here and, indeed, to meet the criteria of acceptance for chemotherapy programs. It is essential that we understand the role drugs are playing in the life of the client—whether they are indeed the

primary problem or are merely ancillary to other social and psychological problems. Until fairly recently, agency workers were so caught up in
their concern about drug use that they allowed it to obscure their understanding of a client's real difficulties. A youngster found to be experimenting with marijuana, for example, might have been treated by some
workers as if he were a confirmed dysfunctional drug abuser, in disre-
gard of the reality that he had serious emotional or social problems,
which were the proper focus of help—or, conversely, that he had no
problem, including no drug problem, and required no help. We must
learn to individualize treatment and use the intake process to make a
truly "differential diagnosis" that distinguishes our client from all other
clients and points up his unique problems and needs. The client must be
an active participant in this process since the extent to which he is
involved will determine the effectiveness of the future course of treatment. The counselor must be well trained and "eclectic"—that is, aware
of a wide range of options from which he can choose to meet the particular needs of the client (5, 10).

Examples of Intake Procedures Used in Different Settings

THE LOWER EASTSIDE SERVICE CENTER

The LESC Mental Health Clinic uses a novel approach for intake,
integrating a therapeutic community concept through the use of "orientation groups" (3). Most of the clients referred are asked to participate in
one of these "OG's," which meet daily for an hour, for one to three
weeks, depending on the client's needs. Each client first has a brief
prescreening interview to obtain basic information and a general evaluation of his suitability for the OG. Clients who appear to be prepsychotic,
schizophrenic, or fearful of participating in groups are not admitted to
the OG but are scheduled for individual intake appointments. If a client
sent to the OG is later found unsuitable, the group leaders arrange an
individual interview. The purposes of the OG are to assess client
motivation, examine the defenses that prevent the real problems from
emerging, orient clients to the Mental Health Clinic approach, and generally prepare them for admission to treatment. Clients in the group
confront each other and examine their manipulative behavior and the
real reasons they are coming in. Clients who are not motivated generally
drop out before the more extensive intake interview. The OG is led by
an ex-addict and a social worker with an MSW degree.

At the intake interview a brief psychosocial history is obtained, and
the social worker attempts to clarify for the client the real reasons he is

here. A psychodynamic assessment is made, and a treatment plan is recommended. The client continues in the OG until his case can be presented to the Intake Review Team, which consists of the entire clinic staff meeting on a weekly basis. The psychiatrist then formulates a treatment plan based on all the information available (individual and group therapy, vocational rehabilitation and employment referral, work shop training, medical and psychiatric services, chemotherapy, and residential living). Treatment may range from one to five sessions weekly. Any client found not suitable for the Mental Health Clinic may be referred to another modality within the agency or to another agency.

THE MILWAUKEE COUNTY MENTAL HEALTH COMPLEX DRUG ABUSE PROGRAM

The methadone maintenance program at the Milwaukee County MHC has been implemented by modifying the intake process from delayed treatment to same-day service. The directors believe that engaging the client during the intake process and the beginning phase of treatment is essential for client retention and successful treatment.

A responsive intake procedure that minimizes obstacles in treatment and meets the client where he not only facilitates engagement of the client, but conveys a message to the community of addicts which implies that help is available immediately. Conversely, a cumbersome, drawn-out intake procedure with a waiting period before treatment conveys a message that immediate help is not available. [1]

Prospective clients quickly learn this via the informal communication network of addicts and are thereby frequently discouraged from seeking treatment. In programs using a drawn-out admission procedure, large numbers of poorly motivated or ambivalent clients may therefore be screened out by their knowledge that treatment will be delayed. This type of program will probably have a lower intake volume, but it is predicted that it will have a higher client retention rate than a more accessible program in that clients who are not screened out by prolonged intake procedures will have higher initial motivation. The responsibility of the drug counselor actively to engage less motivated clients will thus be greater in a more open program.

These results were observed in the Milwaukee program. Statistics and staff reactions confirmed the hypothesis that intake process (via the message to the community) was a determining factor in whether the drug abuse program had an opportunity to engage certain potential clients in the total number of applicants applying for treatment. In the quarter immediately following implementation of same-day service, intake volume increased 300 percent and net client admissions increased 1,000 percent over the previous quarter. The intake process thus became a determining factor in whether certain individuals chose to seek assistance from the drug abuse program or select another course of action. Further, significant numbers of applicants judged to have poor motivation, who usually drop out of treatment, remained in treatment and were doing well in their rehabilitation. Where a program has sufficient resources and wishes to reach out to new clients, a more responsive intake procedure that meets the clients where they are, with minimal delays and obstacles to treatment, can further that goal.

Developing Effective Criteria and Standards

Over the years, the federal government has expended much money and energy in developing effective standards, guidelines, and criteria for assessment and treatment. Appendix 2, A through F, from the "Federal Funding Criteria," with which all programs hoping to obtain full or partial federal funding must comply; the "Standards for Drug Abuse Treatment and Rehabilitation Programs" elaborated by the Joint Commission on Accreditation of Hospitals under the aegis of the National Institute of Mental Health, and the revised "Consolidated Standards" of the same Commission, spell out these efforts to define and refine these standards as a means of improving programs and paving the way for accreditation and licensure of programs and staff.

The social work field has long been cognizant of the importance of the initial diagnostic process in treatment (7, 8). For many years, the traditional psychosocial assessment format consisted of: (1) identifying information; (2) referral source and nature of the problem onset; (3) precipitating and sustaining factors; and (4) evaluation. An effort was made to balance the social service data base and the psychosocial assessment. The social work profile used at the Milwaukee County MHC represents a cross between the conventional social history (social service data base) and the leaner psychosocial evaluation (social service diagnostic statement).

In the Milwaukee program, new clients are interviewed by a psychiatric social worker for additional information within a week after their admission to the program. The worker collects and examines the facts and circumstances of the individual's drug abuse and associated environmental and psychosocial problems, including any interpersonal, psychological, psychiatric, educational, vocational, legal, leisure-time, housing, financial, or life-style problems. This entails obtaining a drug abuse history, social assessment, psychological history, activities assessment, legal assessment, and preliminary vocational assessment. It also requires the identification and review of environmental or psycho-social factors sustaining or reinforcing dysfunctional behavior or patterns of substance abuse. Within two weeks of admission, this information must be documented with corroboration from other sources in the "Initial Social Work Profile." The profile is divided into two sections: the "social history," which includes data-base information, and the "assessment," which presents the social worker's assessment of the data base, appraisal of the nature of the patient's drug abuse and associated problems and his inner and outward functioning and resources (strengths and limitations) in relation to the helping means of the Drug Abuse program and other community resources. Within this general format, the worker has professional discretion regarding the manner in which to present the required information. In cases where the diagnostic evaluation and Initial Social Work Profile cannot be completed within the designated time frame, the reasons for noncompliance and a plan of correction must be entered into the client's clinical record (1).

Case Illustration of Intake Process

The following Profile provides an example of the Milwaukee agency's intake formulations:

IDENTIFYING INFORMATION, REFERRAL, AND NATURE OF THE PROBLEM

John Doe, a thirty-one-year-old divorced white male, was self-referred to the Drug Abuse Program following the death of a close friend due to an accidental overdose. The intake screening indicates that he is addicted to narcotics as evidenced by acute and chronic venipuncture tracks, positive urine drug screen, and a narcan-induced opiate withdrawal state. The patient relates a five-year history of narcotic dependency as well as alcoholism and polydrug abuse dating to preadolescence. The patient scored in the moderately depressed range on a modified Beck depression scale and appears clinically depressed. A history of somatic complaints, depression, and anxiety predates substance abuse and is identified as early as age ten.

FAMILY HISTORY (FAMILY OF ORIGIN)

Mr. Doe is the younger of two children born to an upper-middle-class family. His sister, eight years older, maintained an emotional distance from him. He describes her as a "super coper" who always did well in everything. She married at eighteen and has been estranged from the family since then. Her husband is described as an alcoholic. The family was highly matriarchal, with a passive, silent, inadequate father and a very dominant mother. The parents readily supplied Mr. Doe with material support but lacked emotional warmth and spontaneity. He describes the family as "nonverbal, noncommunicative" and as suppressing anything unpleasant. As long as he can remember, he was angry with his parents for the emasculated role cast upon the father. He himself was obsessed with not being passive and dominated like the father.

PSYCHOLOGICAL AND SUBSTANCE ABUSE HISTORY (INCLUDING TREATMENT HISTORY)

As a child, Mr. Doe was tense, irritable, and plagued by feelings of worthlessness and hopelessness. At the age of ten, he began to exhibit symptoms of acute anxiety and developed a "hyperventilation syndrome" and chronic headaches. At thirteen, he started to abuse alcohol because "drinking made me feel more aggressive and less passive—made me forget my doubts and lessened my depression and anxiety." In his teen years, his use of alcohol was reinforced by his peer group, which regarded consumption of large volumes of alcohol as "in." His drinking brought him recognition and status. It enabled him to be friends with the popular boys and to have dates with the good-looking girls. At the same time, it helped alleviate his somatic complaints, cope with his emotional problems, and "get back at my parents." When he graduated from alcohol to polydrug abuse, he received the same payoffs for his drug-taking behavior. Throughout his childhood and adolescence, he relied heavily on chemical solutions to life problems. Despite this handicap, he was able to graduate from high school and enter college.

While in college, he referred himself to the university Mental Hygiene Clinic in an effort to relieve his depression and alter his life-style. He was seen for approximately one year in a combination of dynamically oriented uncovering therapy and behavior-modification treatment. After a short honeymoon of initial improvement in treatment, he deteriorated and started drinking heavily and using central nervous system depressant drugs. He began missing therapy sessions and eventually terminated treatment. Shortly after failing in business (see "Educational/Vocational History") at the age of twenty-six, Mr. Doe began experimenting with illegal narcotics. He found opiate use to be an extremely potent method of obliterating emotional distress and soon turned to narcotics as his drug of choice. Within six months, he was "strung out" and deeply immersed in the "ripping and running" of the addiction life-style. Drug use continued unabated in this manner for the next five years. Four weeks prior to his application for treatment, his best and apparently only remaining close friend died of a drug overdose. This loss greatly disturbed him and precipitated the current treatment referral. This was Mr. Doe's first treatment episode in an alcohol or drug abuse program. He indicates that since his friend's death he has been anxious, tense, and unable to sleep at night. He feels lonely, depressed, and sad.

EDUCATIONAL/VOCATIONAL HISTORY

Mr. Doe is a high school graduate who completed the first two years of college at the state university. He majored in psychology and art. After dropping out of college, he found employment as a life insurance agent. He was never successful in this position and was terminated after a year because of poor job performance and difficulty getting along with his superiors. When he attempted to obtain similar employment with other life insurance agencies, he discovered that he had been blackballed by his former employer. He attempted to establish his own business at twenty-six, but failed. He made no further efforts to secure regular employment and now works as an occasional day laborer. He does not have any clear vocational objectives at this time and seems to lack confidence that he could succeed in any meaningful vocation. He has expressed an interest in eventually returning to school to complete his bachelor's degree.

MARITAL HISTORY

While in college, Mr. Doe met a young nursing student whom he married after a brief courtship. Although he now describes his ex-wife as an extremely domineering, harsh, and abrasive woman, he states that he was not aware of these personality characteristics prior to their marriage. The marriage, which was childless, lasted five years and ended in divorce five years prior to his application for treatment. The marital relationship was characterized by a high degree of discord and frequent loud and often violent fights. The fights were typically over trivia and never resolved anything. They would be followed by rapid reconciliations and an equally rapid resumption of hostilities. According to Mr. Doe, his wife knew his "belt line" and consistently tried to provoke him to the point of losing control. She especially liked to put him down and embarrass him in front of his parents and friends. She was an extremely aggressive woman who would continuously barrage her husband with both physical and emotional assaults. She enmeshed her parents in the marital dynamics and frequently invoked their assistance in verbally and physically ganging up on him. Despite his negative description of their marriage, Mr. Doe still hopes to be reconciled some day with his ex-wife.

HOUSING/FINANCIAL/LEGAL CONSIDERATIONS

Mr. Doe is currently unemployed and is financially dependent upon his parents, with whom he lives. He has financed his addiction by extensive borrowing, first from commercial financial institutions, then from friends and family. He is $20,000 in debt, not including the money he owes his parents. He also owes back alimony and is faced with legal action, including possible incarceration for failure to comply with court-ordered payments to his ex-wife. Mr. Doe feels completely alone and lacking the support of interpersonal relationships of any kind. He has never been involved with the criminal justice system.

PEER-GROUP FUNCTIONING

Regarding the lack of friends, Mr. Doe states that most of his former friends are uncomfortable with him because of his drug background and therefore avoid him.

The few straight friends who still relate to him are involved with their own families and jobs and spend little time with him, while the majority of his drug-abusing friends are either dead or in jail.

RECREATION AND LEISURE-TIME ACTIVITIES

Mr. Doe has no non-drug-related social or recreational activities. He states that when he is not engaged in drug-seeking behavior he sits around the house bored. Prior to his current social isolation and heavy involvement in an addiction life-style, he enjoyed reading, painting, and listening to classical music.

ASSESSMENT

Mr. Doe presents the picture of a bright, verbal young man with considerable potential, but with multiple psychosocial problems and limited support systems. His primary problems lie in the emotional and interpersonal areas. There is a great deal of interpersonal pathology, which has sustained and reinforced both emotional problems and continued drug-abusing behavior. His emotionally barren early family life resulted in a deprivation of basic dependency needs and unresolved hostility toward his parents. He has never related satisfactorily to his father, whom he resents for not providing an appropriate masculine role model. He equates concrete achievements and aggressiveness with an appropriate masculine role. Much of his behavior is seen as attempts to establish a masculine identity, by being aggressive rather than passive and dominated like his father, and to cope with his lack of success in this area through illicit drug use.

When he was dating, he never liked any shy, passive woman who would allow him to have his own way. Instead, he gravitated to dominant, aggressive women like his mother. He went into his marriage with his eyes closed and was not consciously aware that his ex-wife was a domineering person. He is now aware of many similarities between his wife and his mother. By "marrying my mother," he placed himself in the same dominated position as his father, but in this case it was more extreme. He was no match for his ex-wife and in confrontation was almost completely emasculated by her. In a very real sense, his marriage represented the fulfillment of the worst fantasies and fears of his early childhood. Despite this, he is ready for a reconciliation if his ex-wife will have him back. His dating and marital history illustrate how his perception and judgment were deeply affected by neurotic needs and deeply engrained ego defense mechanisms. His emotional problems include poor self-concept, guilt over his lack of success in life, depression, anxiety, and a recurring pattern of substance abuse to cope with stress and emotional problems. Intrapsychic and interpersonal pathology have been closely intertwined. Mr. Doe's lack of success in interpersonal relationships has reinforced his depression and poor self-concept. This has, in turn, reinforced tendencies to seek out interpersonal relationships in which he will be emotionally abused. His role confusion and compulsion to prove himself a real man have dominated his adopted patterns of behavior.

As indicated, he lacks emotional support from important others and feels very isolated socially. He has never had a positive relationship with his family of origin, and the relationship with the ex-wife is seen more as a masochistic venture than as a meaningful interpersonal relationship. His relationship with the parents is strained, and he does not have a supportive peer group of any kind. The psychological history and clinical evaluation suggest the probability of a "primary affective disorder." Mr. Doe scored in the moderately depressed range on a modified Beck depression scale and appears clinically depressed. His symptoms include dysphoric mood, loss of interest and pleasure in activities, lack of energy/fatigue, poor appetite, insomnia, preoccupation with physical health, feelings of worthlessness and self-reproach, hopelessness, irritability, and anxiety. His psychological history documents problems with anxiety and depression predating substance abuse. His long history of involvement with alcohol and drugs would appear to represent an attempt to cope with stress and alleviate the emotional problems previously enumerated. He is currently unemployed, as mentioned, and has no prospects since he has been blackballed in his employment field. Although he has the potential for college-level work and has expressed an interest in returning to school even though his psychosocial problems may interfere with his school performance, he has not yet made any move to reapply.

TREATMENT

Given the scope of Mr. Doe's problems, it was decided that treatment must be multidimensional and include the following:

1. _Intensive psychotherapy_ to resolve intrapsychic and interpersonal problems, improve emotional and social competencies, and achieve abstinence from illicit drug abuse. Therapy should be educational as well as ameliorative in focus and should seek to develop appropriate nonchemical coping mechanisms as well as to facilitate emotional and intellectual insights into the nature of the current difficulties. The client is seen as a good candidate for traditional psychotherapy: He has above-average intelligence, good verbal skills, sensitivity, and the capacity for insight and has responded well to exploration of problem areas by the social worker. Mr. Doe demonstrates a beginning capacity to utilize the therapeutic relationship for the purpose of problem-solving and change. His current level of psychic distress is sufficiently high to motivate him to follow through with a therapeutic treatment regime.

2. _Counseling and social services_ to strengthen the patient's limited support systems. This would include family therapy to maximize emotional support from the family of origin, group therapy for peer support, and activity therapy to develop appropriate leisure-time activities.

3. _Training in progressive relaxation_ and/or other behavior-modification techniques for coping with tensions and anxieties of daily living. Progressive relaxation training would provide a useful adjunct to insight development and problem-focused treatment by facilitating the development of an active coping skill for alleviating acute anxiety and achieving some degree of symptomatic relief. This would enhance Mr. Doe's sense of mastery and control and give him an early success experience in what would undoubtedly be a long-term process.

4. _Vocational rehabilitation_ to clarify vocational objectives and institute an appropriate educational or job development program.

5. _Methadone maintenance_ to alleviate illicit narcotic use.

6. _Psychiatric evaluation/consultation_ to assess the possible need for medical management of depression.

Although the two agencies described in this chapter have tried to find innovative ways to deal with the problem of accumulating sufficient information as rapidly as possible in order to engage and hold the patient successfully, the actual data content and assessments are traditional in that they represent an attempt to find an optimal balance between the information base and the assessment as a preliminary to treatment. Because of the special problems noted in the case of drug abusers, the information and assessment need to be obtained and made as rapidly as possible, with the proviso that information relating to length of drug use, involvement with other drug programs, and so forth, is required in order to satisfy the federal and state criteria for admission to a methadone program. The case studies presented in the next chapter will further illustrate the kinds of situations that come up at intake.

References

1. Aprill, F. A. "Initial Social Work Profile"- Private communication to author, May 1980.
2. Aprill, F. A. Some thoughts on the intake process. Private communication to author, March 1980.
3. Barish, H. Intake process of the Lower Eastside Service Center, Private communication to the author, October 1979.
4. Brill, L. _The De-Addiction Process: Studies in the De-Addiction of Confirmed Heroin Addicts._ Springfield, Ill.: Charles C. Thomas, 1972.
5. Brill, L., and H. Meiselas. "The Treatment of Drug Abuse: Experiences and Issues." In L. Brill and E. Harms, eds., _The Yearbook of Drug Abuse._ New York: Behavioral Publications, 1973.
6. Chambers, C. D., and L. Brill. _Methadone: Experiences and Issues._ New York: Behavioral Publications, 1972.
7. Hamilton, G. _Theory and Practice of Social Case Work._ New York: School of Social Work, Columbia University Press, 1940.
8. Hollis, F. _Casework: A Psychosocial Therapy._ New York: Random House, 1964.
9. Jaffe, J. H., and L. Brill. "Cyclazocine: A Long-Acting Narcotic Antagonist—Its voluntary Acceptance as a Treatment Modality by Narcotic Abusers." _International Journal of the Addictions,_ 1, No. 1 (1966): 99–123.
10. "Programs for Drug Abuse Treatment and Prevention." Chapter 4 of _Community Crime Prevention._ Washington, D.C.: National Advisory Commission for Criminal Justice Standards and Goals, January 23, 1973.

11. Wiesen, R. C., and F. A. Aprill. "Intake Message to the Community: A Report on the Implementation of Same-Day Service in a Methadone Maintenance Program—Its Effect on Intake Volume and Implications for Treatment." Mimeo version. Milwaukee County Mental Health Center Drug Abuse Program, n.d.

CHAPTER 7

Individual Therapy

ON THE BASIS OF OUR PRELIMINARY CONSIDERATION, in the previous chapters, of the issues that helped shape current approaches to the drug problem, we can now proceed to examine the various modes of treatment developed for drug abusers and their families. The brief case studies presented in this chapter by representatives of the Milwaukee County Mental Health Complex Drug Abuse Program, the Lower Eastside Service Center, and the Albert Einstein College of Medicine Drug Abuse Program reflect the eclectic and pragmatic approaches of these centers since they draw upon a wide variety of techniques, including more recent ones such as relaxation therapy and sex therapy. The presentation by Frieda Plotkin of the Albert Einstein College of Medicine reveals her psychoanalytic training and thinking in respect to terminology, modes of approach, and diagnostic formulations.

The Milwaukee County MHC Drug Abuse Program

The following seven case presentations and discussions illustrate the range of problems encountered in a more or less typical drug treatment agency. A constant concern in all these cases is the need to differentiate between the patients' presenting problems and the underlying biopsychosocial factors that precipitate, sustain, or reinforce dysfunctional behavior. According to Floyd Aprill, Supervisor of the program, individualized treatment planning based on careful differential diagnosis is the key to successful drug abuse treatment (1). The most frequent error of inexperienced clinicians involves mistakes in client evaluation or treatment planning. Two factors that contribute to this problem are focusing on the presenting symptoms to the exclusion of underlying causation and indiscriminately utilizing treatment techniques without determining their appropriateness. Workers need to develop their diagnostic as well as their treatment skills.

CASE 1, OTIS JOHNSON: RESISTANCE TO TREATMENT

This case illustrates the ambivalence every patient brings into treatment, which must be dealt with if the patient is to be retained in treatment. Patients will engage in distance-creating maneuvers in order to protect themselves from involvement and avoid getting close to and trusting another person. They will engage in various forms of testing and challenging behavior in order to gauge the worker's ability to withstand their problems and dependency.

Otis Johnson, a thirty-one-year-old black male, was self-referred to the methadone maintenance program for drug abuse treatment. Mr. Johnson had demonstrated a repeated pattern of failing to engage in treatment and had prematurely terminated previous treatment episodes "against medical advice" (AMA). He had spent his early years in the urban ghetto of a large Eastern metropolis. The youngest of six children born to alcoholic parents, he came to live with relatives in the Midwest at the age of thirteen, following the death of his parents. At nineteen, he married a woman who was pregnant with his child and started using heroin. The Johnsons had four children by the time they agreed to separate after a ten-year marriage. A high school graduate with technical skills, Otis had maintained more or less steady employment as a machinist.

Otis had a history of ten previous admissions for drug abuse treatment in a succession of facilities, including several drug-free outpatient programs, an inpatient detoxification program, and an outpatient methadone maintenance clinic. His pattern was to come in for a few days and then sign out or simply disappear. None of the previous treatment experiences had been completed successfully. During previous episodes, he tended to minimize or deny the presence of psychosocial problems. Individual counseling was focused on helping Otis recognize and work through his ambivalent feelings toward treatment. The counselor helped him become aware that he both wanted help and was afraid to risk himself by fully acknowledging his problems and committing himself to treatment. Treatment represented an approach-avoidance conflict.

As counseling progressed, it became apparent that Otis had tremendous feelings of inadequacy and insecurity, which were threatening for him to dwell upon. These feelings, which intensified when he asked for help, had simply overwhelmed him during previous treatment and had precipitated premature terminations of treatment. As he came to acknowledge and work through these feelings, he overcame his resistance to therapy and was able to engage himself more fully in the ongoing process.

The case illustrates a common problem of therapy: the conflicted feelings regarding treatment and change that a client brings into treatment with him. This ambivalence must be resolved if the client is to be retained in treatment. Too often, this approach-avoidance conflict has been dismissed as "poor patient motivation".

CASE 2, FRAN DUNN: FEAR OF SUCCESS

This case illustrates the fear of success and failure that many drug-abusing clients bring into treatment with them. The precipitation of pseudo-withdrawal symptoms was an interesting by-product of this conflict. Because of the agency's eclectic approach, it was able to bring to bear the technique of relaxation therapy, which alleviated the client's fears and stress and allayed the withdrawal symptoms.

Fran Dunn, a forty-three-year-old divorced black male, had been a methadone maintenance client for seven years when he developed a pseudo-withdrawal syndrome, consisting of tremors, profuse sweating, restlessness, lacrimation, nasal congestion, uncontrollable yawning, feelings of change in temperature, muscle aches, and stomach pains. Mr. Dunn had only a grade school education but was extremely ambitious and hard-driving. He had a history of chronic headaches since his youth and tended to keep his feelings to himself, believing that "a man has to work out his own problems." Failing to succeed according to his expectations, he became addicted to narcotics at the age of twenty-one. He had his first treatment episode at thirty-six. He initially attempted an inpatient detoxification regimen, which he drove himself to complete as rapidly as possible. He soon relapsed to heroin use and reapplied for treatment. Once again, he forced himself to complete a rapid detoxification, and once again he relapsed. He immediately reapplied for treatment but this time requested and was accepted for methadone maintenance. After stabilizing on the maximum dose of the clinic, which was 80 mg. per day, he demonstrated rapid rehabilitative gains. He abandoned heroin use almost immediately and found employment as a construction worker. He proved himself conscientious both on and off the job. He enjoyed working beyond the required schedule and often worked up to sixty hours a week.

During the next seven years, Mr. Dunn maintained an excellent work adjustment and completely avoided illicit drug use. Most of the time, he remained at his maximum dose and demonstrated a great fear of going on any lower dose, although this was suggested many times. Otherwise, he presented no special treatment problems.

At this time, he began complaining of withdrawal symptoms. After a medical examination had eliminated the possibility that there was a physical reason for the symptoms, counseling was focused upon exploring environmental/psychosocial factors that might have precipitated them. The counselor learned that Mr. Dunn had been promoted to the position of foreman three weeks prior to the onset of the symptoms. He initially denied any connection but gradually began to acknowledge feelings of anxiety and fear of failure. The counselor addressed Mr. Dunn's unrealistic fear of failure and helped him realize that he had the competence to handle his new position and the related stresses satisfactorily. At the same time Mr. Dunn was instructed in the techniques of progressive relaxation so that he could actively manage realistic stress developing from his more demanding position. As he actively dealt with the stresses through on-the-job, goal-directed behaviors, his pseudo-withdrawal symptoms abated. In the two years since this breakthrough, he has become more relaxed on the job and less compulsive regarding overtime and has felt more accepted on the company leadership team. At the same time he has confronted his long-standing fear of reducing his methadone level and successfully cut his dosage level in half. He is now stabilized on 40 mg. of methadone per day and is anticipating further dosage reductions in future.

Pseudo-withdrawal syndromes are relatively common among methadone maintenance patients and may occur in spite of high maintenance doses. The syndrome is usually associated with psychological stress and is thought to represent a "learned depressive or anxiety equivalent." Patients usually report feelings of anxiety or depression and have limited insight into the relationship between current life problems and the pseudo-withdrawal syndrome. The counselor needs to explore the life problems that may be precipitating the syndrome and develop goal-directed methods of problem resolution (nonchemical and nonphysiological methods of stress management).

CASE 3, DEBRA SCOTT: DEPRESSION AS A CENTRAL FEATURE IN TREATMENT

Many clients engage in drug-taking in an effort to medicate themselves to combat depression. There is a need for intensive psychotherapy as well as drug management to cope with the resulting drug problem, in this case severe amphetamine abuse.

Debra Scott, a thirty-year-old married white female in methadone maintenance treatment for fourteen months, demonstrated a chronic pattern of heavy amphetamine abuse. Secondary problems attributable to her drug use were abscesses, extreme weight loss, malnutrition, disturbed mental state, and neglect of homemaker and child-care responsibilities.

Debra grew up in a large Midwestern city, the oldest of three children born to a lower-middle-class family. Her mother died when she was three years old and her father when she was sixteen. Debra was not close to her siblings and had few close associates or friends. She graduated from high school, secured employment as a secretary, and was leading an uneventful life when, at the age of twenty-one, her right arm was permanently disabled as a result of a skiing accident. Following the accident, she started to abuse amphetamines. At twenty-six she began to use heroin and soon became dependent on narcotics, mainly heroin and street methadone. At twenty-nine Debra, who then had married and become pregnant, applied for drug treatment. She was placed on ambulatory methadone maintenance and counseling. Although she quickly stabilized on low-dose methadone and ceased all use of illicit narcotics, her amphetamine use continued unabated.

Several months after entering treatment, Debra gave birth. She had difficulty adjusting to motherhood and lacked adequate mothering skills. Her crippled arm made even simple child-care tasks formidable. In spite of intensive individual counseling by her drug counselor and child-care education by a visiting nurse, Debra's condition deteriorated markedly. At seven months post partum, the visiting nurse reported Debra to the child protection services, noting that the apartment needed cleaning and that Debra was frequently intoxicated and unable to care for the child. She also felt that the child was not developing normally as a result of lack of stimulation. At the same time, the drug treatment staff noted that Debra had numerous abscesses resulting from chronic intravenous amphetamine use. There was also hair and weight loss, a disturbed sleep pattern, and a lack of appetite. By this time Debra weighed only 68 pounds and had begun to exhibit blatant symptoms of disturbed mental status. She experienced both auditory and visual hallucinations and paranoid ideation. Since she was unable to care for herself or her family, she reluctantly entered the hospital for isolation from drugs and stabilization of her physical and mental condition. After a ten-day stay, she signed out of the hospital against medical advice and resumed ambulatory treatment.

The staff felt that Debra's chronic amphetamine use was an attempt at self-medication for an underlying depression. They decided to institute a program of medical management using tricyclate antidepressants. During the first three months of this treatment Debra stabilized her physical and emotional condition, gained 40 pounds, and discontinued her use of amphetamines. The concomitant problems of abscesses, hallucinations, and paranoid ideation cleared up with the cessation of the amphetamine abuse. At the same time the child protective services inspected the home, found everything in order, and closed their case. Debra began to play a more active role with her child and, with the help of her counselor and a nurse, undertook to improve her mothering skills. During the next year her treatment was focused on continuing the methadone maintenance and medical management of her depression, supplemented by individual counseling aimed at improving her level of self-esteem and developing appropriate leisure-time activities. She is now physically and socially active and uses her leisure time appropriately. In spite of her physical handicap, she has developed good child-care skills, and her son is developing normally. She is beginning to take pride in her ability as a mother and has established a caring relationship with her son and husband. She has been stabilized on low-dose methadone and has not abused illicit narcotics, amphetamines, or other drugs in over a year.

Depression is frequently associated with narcotic dependency. The diagnosis of a primary affective disorder is usually complicated by the masking effects of the addiction and the drug-taking behavior. Drug-taking may often be an attempt at self-medication, as in the case of Debra. Anxiety and depression, loss of libido, flattened affect, lack of energy, loss of appetite, sleep disturbance, and somatic complaints may mistakenly be attributed to the presence or absence of drugs. Depressed patients may be more aware of their anxiety than of their depression and may be resistant to antidepressant therapy. Patients with primary affective disorders may require psychotherapy and medical management in addition to the drug abuse treatment.

CASE 4, JOHN SMITH: NEED FOR SEPARATION

This case points up the need for separation and individuation of drug abusers from their families. Because such separation is so difficult to achieve, there is a need for family-oriented therapy to work at the problem from both ends. Such an approach allows us to understand the family dynamics that first created the problem and affords clues as to the best means for resolving it.

John Smith, a twenty-six-year-old single black male, had made little progress over a protracted period of time in numerous treatment programs, encompassing many modalities. The first year of his current methadone maintenance treatment episode was characterized by a similar lack of progress. Although he was receiving blocking doses of methadone and intensive individual counseling, John continued to use narcotics on a regular basis and consistently undermined and sabotaged the vocational-planning process.

John was the oldest of four children born to a working-class couple. His early family life was dominated by a dependent and manipulative mother who was herself a narcotics addict. The mother had numerous legitimate and pseudo-legitimate medical problems, which provided easy access to a seemingly endless supply of physician-prescribed pharmaceutical narcotics as well as a convenient method for manipulating the family members.

At the age of twelve John had started to abuse drugs by taking pharmaceutical narcotics, which were readily available in the home. His drug-taking and consequent addiction were regarded as normative behavior and were accepted by the parents. The abuse pattern was repeated by each of the siblings as they reached the age of puberty. At an early age, John also began truanting from school, often to stay home to care for his sick mother. After dropping out of school, John failed to establish a satisfactory vocational adjustment. Whenever he found a good job, he typically quit or was fired because of poor attendance or inability to get along with his co-workers and superiors. He continued to reside with his parents and failed to develop any interests outside the home. He maintained his narcotic addiction by tapping his mother's supply. The pattern was broken periodically by his numerous unsuccessful treatment episodes and occasional incarcerations.

In time the entire family applied and was accepted for methadone treatment. The initial treatment focus was on individual rather than family-unit treatment. It soon became apparent that this was the major reason for John's lack of progress. Although chronologically an adult, John had never been permitted to undergo the normal separation-individuation process and establish an autonomous identity apart from the family. Whenever he attempted to establish some degree of independence—as by getting a job or developing interests outside the home—the mother would feel threatened and use her pseudo-health problems to manipulate John into abandoning his drive for autonomy and staying home to care for her. By these tactics and by providing him with an unlimited supply of narcotics, she had been able to keep him dependent on her, sabotaging all treatment efforts to help him separate himself.

The staff felt that it was essential to institute a concomitant program of conjoint family therapy. A special treatment team, comprising a psychiatrist, psychiatric social worker, nurse, and vocational counselor, were assigned to initiate this program. The team approach was to pierce the family system to facilitate the family's acceptance of separate individual as well as family identities. Only when this was accomplished would John's parents permit their children to differentiate themselves from the family and establish autonomous identities. Thus, the focus of treatment was shifted from John's symptoms to the core problem of a pathological family which inhibited the children's normal development and growth.

CASE 5, JOE ANDREWS: "IMPORTANT OTHERS" AND OUTSIDE AGENCIES UNDERMINING TREATMENT

In such cases as the one following, it becomes especially important to involve outside forces in the treatment process.

Joe Andrews, a married white male, was twenty-five when he applied for treatment. The only child of a working-class couple, Joe dropped out of high school in the eleventh grade and married shortly thereafter. At the time he applied for treatment, Joe, his wife, and their five children were subsisting on welfare since he had never held a steady job. His pattern of illicit drug use had begun at the age of fifteen, when he started using marijuana on a regular basis. Always somewhat tense and uncomfortable in personal situations, Joe discovered that marijuana lessened his anxiety and made him feel more secure. He experimented with the use of barbiturates and LSD at seventeen (at the same time that he was dropping out of school and getting married) but did not continue long-term use of these drugs. He started using heroin at the age of twenty to cope with the pressures of everyday life and quickly became addicted. After five years in the "street life," he applied for treatment. There had been no previous drug abuse or psychiatric treatment episodes.

Although the intake workup revealed that Joe had only a slight to moderate narcotic dependency, he complained that his methadone was not holding him and asked for rapid increases in his dosage. He wanted to "get to the highest dose" as if that would magically take care of his problems. Even at high levels (80 mg.) of methadone, he had sporadic dirty urines (evidence of illicit drug use) and only made gestures at finding employment and following through with the Division of Vocational Rehabilitation referral he had requested. Six months after entering treatment, he joined a fundamentalist religious sect that was strongly antimethadone. At their insistence, he began requesting decreases in his dosage and in six months successfully cut down to 40 mg. During this time his urinalyses were all satisfactory, and he was beginning to follow through with vocational planning. When he went below 40 mg., he began to show symptoms of tension and anxiety as well as a resumption of illicit opiate use. At the urging of the staff, he aborted his detoxification at this point and stabilized on 40 mg. of methadone. At that dosage level his anxiety diminished, and he was able to discontinue illicit drug use.

When the church associates learned that he had stopped detoxing, they placed increased pressure on him to get off methadone and started ostracizing him socially. Under this pressure, Joe attempted detoxification several times over the next few months, against medical advice. These premature detoxifications all ended in failure. Joe decided that he would continue to detox "no matter what." A year after entering treatment, he made the final effort to detoxify. After three months he had decreased his dosage to 20 mg. By this time he had abandoned his efforts to find employment or pursue vocational objectives. He used illicit opiates sporadically and exhibited high levels of anxiety and depression. He began hallucinating that there were snipers on the roof out to kill him and his family. He began to talk of suicide and turned on the gas in his home. He attacked his wife. The police were called, and he was taken to a hospital as a psychiatric emergency. In the hospital he appeared in acute distress, agitated, and very frightened. He experienced auditory and visual hallucinations and paranoid delusional material. Although many of his acute symptoms abated after a few days, he signed himself out against medical advice.

Joe returned to the methadone program, where he was treated with psychotropic medication and individual counseling. He appeared lucid and said that he felt well after being out of the hospital. During the hospitalization his wife and five children had left him, but he was hopeful that they would return. One month after his departure from the hospital, he had a second acute psychotic episode and physically assaulted his wife. After this incident, he was arrested and lost to treatment because of his incarceration.

The case illustrates the potentially devastating effect "important others" can have on the treatment process. Initially, Joe's church group gave him a positive identity and the emotional support and motivation he needed to accomplish a constructive life-style change. Unfortunately, his continued acceptance by this group was made conditional upon his accomplishing their objective of becoming totally and immediately drug-free. Although Joe made several valiant efforts to comply, he repeatedly failed to achieve this objective. His rejection by his religious peers and his consequent loss of self-esteem and threatened loss of identity proved so devastating that he was unable to cope with the reality and escaped into mental illness.

CASE 6; MICHAEL TURNER: USE OF LEISURE TIME

This case illustrates a common problem that was endemic in methadone clinics for many years. Patients who did not know how to use their leisure time clung to the methadone clinic and hovered about the grounds after they had received their medication. Too often, they entered into "negative contracts" with other patients and got into trouble. It was unfortunate that the clinics did not have sufficient staff or did not realize the nature of the problem and attempt to make positive use of the fact that patients were clinging to the clinics by involving them in additional constructive activities. It also demonstrates the need for long-term help frequently.

Michael Turner, a forty-six-year-old divorced white male in methadone treatment for a protracted period of time, sabotaged attempts at job placement or vocational training, continuously loitering about the clinic and abusing depressant drugs. He was the oldest of three children born to a working-class family. As an adolescent, he became involved with a delinquent peer group who introduced him to criminal behavior and narcotic drugs. For the next two decades, he maintained a more or less heavy involvement with drugs. He was incarcerated several times, but returned to narcotic drugs after each incarceration. A high school dropout, Michael had been periodically employed at marginal, low-paying jobs. He married at the age of twenty-one, was separated from his wife on and off, and eventually divorced her. At the age of forty he was referred by his probation officer to a methadone maintenance program. At the time he applied for treatment, he was employed and heavily involved in an addictive life-style. He presented the picture of a person with low self-esteem, poor self-concept, low stress/frustration tolerance, little impulse control, and insecurity in interpersonal relationships.

Treatment consisted of methadone maintenance, vocational rehabilitation, and individual counseling focused on developing insight into feelings about the "self"; developing non-drug-related leisure-time and social activities; building increased stress tolerance; and improving self-concept. Initially Michael made slow progress in treatment. He had great difficulty modifying his addictive life-style, resisted vocational counseling, and failed to retain even menial jobs. Although he was no longer abusing narcotics, he demonstrated a chronic pattern with depressant drugs, primarily barbiturates, which necessitated intermittent hospitalizations for detoxification and drying out. After several months of treatment, he began to disengage himself from the addiction life-style. He replaced his dependence on the drug subculture with a dependence on the subculture of the methadone clinic. Still insecure, lonely, and lacking self-confidence, he hung about the clinic for socialization and companionship. He became involved with a clique of patients with similar needs.

During the next three years, he continued to sabotage attempts at job placement or vocational training and continued to loiter about the clinic and periodically abuse depressants in order to manage stress. The frequency of this depressant drug use gradually declined as he developed alternate methods for coping with stress and gained insight into his feelings and their connection with his drug-taking behavior. After three years of treatment he felt secure enough to begin to disengage himself from the clinic subculture. He developed enough confidence to risk integration into straight society by complying with a vocational rehabilitation regimen without sabotaging the program. He received counseling in stress management and work adjustment training. After a year of this, he was placed in a position with a large manufacturing firm where he established a satisfactory work record. He has been able to give up the clinic subculture, feels more secure in interpersonal situations, and has developed non-drug-related leisure-time activities. He can now deal with stress and no longer has need to resort to using depressant drugs to alleviate anxiety.

Michael's case illustrates the need for long-term treatment for the successful rehabilitation of patients who lack significant internal or external resources and need to undergo a gradual process of growth, maturation, and reeducation before they can make positive life-style changes. Michael's treatment was not characterized by a single dramatic breakthrough but consisted rather of a slow, gradual process of growth characterized by three steps forward, two steps backward, and one step forward again. As he went through this process, he gradually developed improved ego strengths and made the transition from the drug subculture to the clinic subculture and then to straight society. For patients like Michael, there is no shortcut to the long-term and gradual process of maturation facilitated by intensive and extensive treatment.

CASE 7, FRED JONES: CLOSE COLLABORATION BETWEEN DRUG AGENCY AND EMPLOYER

I have written in detail about the need of the client to find his way back to the world of work (3). Mr. Aprill's case illustrates this point.

Fred Jones, a twenty-eight-year-old single white male, was self-referred to the methadone maintenance program. An addict since the age of nineteen, he had had three previous treatment experiences. On each occasion he relapsed to heroin shortly after discontinuing methadone treatment. Soon after his reinstatement to methadone maintenance, he found employment in the public works department of a nearby municipality. He reported difficulties in adjusting to his new job, particularly in relating to his co-workers, who, he felt, were ostracizing him and regarded him as an outsider. His strategy for coping with this interpersonal situation was to act out via absenteeism and drug use. When he was threatened with loss of employment, he revealed his drug problem and treatment status to the employer. At Fred's request, the counselor contacted the employer in an effort to negotiate mutually agreeable conditions under which Fred could retain his employment while working on his problems of illicit drug use and work adjustment. The counselor made a clear presentation on drug abuse and the facts of treatment. The dual focus of the presentation was to demystify the drug abuse by exploring the employer's fears and beliefs about it, and to acknowledge the employer's needs and assure him that there would be sufficient program follow-up and contact and that his goals—satisfactory attendance and a good work adjustment—would be implemented by the treatment program. The plan was accepted by the employer as a condition of the patient's continued employment. A continuing interaction was established among the employer, the patient, and the program.

The primary treatment focus for Fred centered on his perceptions of the work situation, feelings toward co-workers, and means of handling interpersonal stress. It should be noted that Fred's interpersonal anxiety and fear of relating to straight co-workers colored his perception of them and of the actual work situation. This set up a self-fulfilling prophecy whereby his actions caused him to be objectively viewed as an outsider. As he worked through his feelings, he came to perceive the work situation as less threatening and became more comfortable in relating to his co-workers. Concomitant with this, he was gradually accepted by the co-workers, and his absenteeism and drug use abated. Over the next two years he maintained a satisfactory work adjustment and in time developed close personal relationships with some of his co-workers. He was then able to withdraw from methadone and was discharged as a clinical success.

Fred is typical of many drug users who have difficulty integrating themselves into straight society. The case also illustrates the need for client advocacy and for treatment staff to obtain the goodwill and cooperation of employers and other significant support systems. As a byproduct of the open communication and mutual understanding established with the employer, a permanent linkage was effected, which subsequently facilitated the referral of other drug-impaired employees for job placement.

The Lower Eastside Service Center

The following case examples from the LESC illustrate the kinds of intervention provided at this center, a multimodality agency that includes residential and day centers and a methadone maintenance clinic.

CASE 1, JOAN JONES: SOCIAL WORKER HELPS SUICIDAL
PATIENT TO ESTABLISH CONTROLS

The first case entails the very difficult problem of working with a suicidal patient. Unless the worker is very experienced and secure in his own skills, he may precipitate the client into worse behavior or misinterpret the meaning of suicidal "gestures," which should never be taken lightly.

Joan is a thirty-year-old white woman who has been in treatment for three years and is currently drug-free. She has been diagnosed as a borderline personality with areas of high functioning despite a fundamental lack of ego integration. She was able to return to school and complete two years of college with an A average and to rear an emotionally stable daughter even though she experienced continual dissociative reactions of depersonalization. She was able to accomplish this by repression and isolation of affect.

Joan was reared by a rigid, distant, but consistent mother and a warmer but alcoholic and probably psychopathic father, who disappeared for long periods. In addition, she was the object of sadistic sexual acting-out by an older sister for several years. It was during these experiences that she first felt the depersonalization, which was a welcome relief from pain and humiliation. Though it enabled her to avoid ego fragmentation, it forced her to relinquish much of her affective life.

At the point when she entered treatment, she was acutely suicidal, having made at least six "gestures" during the two previous years. These occurred without any recognition by her of depression. Early in treatment, following another suicidal attempt, the social worker recognized her inability to control her behavior through ventilation of feeling. The worker made it clear that she would be constantly available to her but told her not to make any further attempts if she wished to remain in treatment. (The worker was thereby indirectly giving Joan permission to live without dealing with the underlying guilt and rage, which were inaccessible.) In her statement, the worker made clear her concern and emotional availability (unlike the mother) and her commitment not to abandon Joan (unlike the father). This fostered the development of an early therapeutic alliance through the "lending" of an observing and supporting ego which was not available within Joan.*

The social worker was very experienced and attempted to use herself to provide support and controls against Joan's suicidal gestures. The intervention was successful: such risk-taking as telling a patient directly to desist from destructive behavior is often necessary to break through massive acting-out and defensive behavior. The social worker must be very well attuned to the patient to make sure that she is not precipitating worse behavior in reaction (2).

CASE 2, JOHN CHU: DEALING WITH SOCIOCULTURAL FACTORS IN A CHINESE PATIENT WITH AMBIVALENCE ABOUT TREATMENT

This case illustrates the special social and cultural problems presented by different clients, in this case a Chinese male. The worker needs to be attuned to such factors and able to distinguish between the true role they are playing and the client's use of them to resist treatment.

---

*"We have noted that depression, whether hysterical or affective, is a common central symptom among drug-abusing patients; and suicidal gestures and attempts are not infrequent. Drugs often serve to mask depression. When the therapist can get a patient to a drug-free state, he or she will be confronted with the major underlying pathology."— Herbert Barish, Assistant Director of LESC.

Once the worker has made this differentiation in his mind, he must still decide how to intervene—as in a case where the cultural background may dictate suppression of feeling and therapy requires that the feeling be ventilated.

The patient is a twenty-seven-year-old Chinese-American man who lives with his parents and works as a bookkeeper. He first began using heroin when he was twenty, smoking it daily, then cleaned up and began using methadone on the street. He has no history of treatment and has never been detoxified. He has no record of arrest, nor is there any history of mental illness or medical problems. He is single and comes from a large family.

When he requested admission into the methadone program, he was interviewed and given an appointment for a physical because he didn't have any track marks (evidence of injection of heroin with a needle), and it was not clear that he was a confirmed heroin addict. He failed to keep two appointments to see the doctor and subsequently showed much ambivalence regarding admission to the methadone program. He returned again to talk with the social worker about his problems. He seemed preoccupied with the fact that he always returned to drugs and couldn't understand why he couldn't control himself. He had been made to feel that he was "no good" by his parents and siblings. He felt he hadn't accomplished anything and was indeed the worst one in the family. No other member of the family had a drug problem. He felt terribly guilty and out of control. Despite the fact that he didn't really want to get high, he couldn't overcome the urge. The Chinese believe that drug abuse can be discontinued by the exercise of will power and that self-control determines the outcome of human behavior. They do not credit feelings, thoughts, or emotions as having a role to play in this problem. John therefore felt that there was something in him which caused his inability to give up drugs.

The social worker's task was to get around the cultural resistance and help the client understand that he had become involved with drugs because of his feelings, poor self-image, and the like. John denied this interpretation and cited the rationalization that his friends were also using drugs. Yet he was obsessed with the fact that he had to keep using them. The social worker tried to get him to think about how feelings influenced actions. What had happened to him when he first got into drugs? The client said he had been "uncertain" at that time because of a new job, which bored him. He admitted "feeling bad." The social worker got him to make connections between "feeling bad" and using drugs. He said that when he felt bad, he would buy methadone from the first person he met. He was aware of his impulsiveness here, since he didn't wait for someone he could trust. Other examples were cited, and eventually he was able to relate drugs to various feelings of being "down," "feeling bad," being uncertain and anxious.

The LESC has serviced the older drug-abusing Chinese population for many years. The past year saw the influx of some younger male Chinese substance abusers. Most of the other Chinese males had had their thirty- to forty-year history of heroin and opium addiction replaced by methadone and received social services provided by a Chinese staff member. These older men could not become involved in insightful forms of treatment, because their traditional cultural beliefs were at odds with American mental health concepts. This cultural influence also affected many of the younger men, but not to the same degree. Nevertheless, these cultural beliefs must be taken into account if the worker is to establish a therapeutic relationship. The patient must learn that feelings do exist and are important, to counteract the fatalistic belief that it is only will power that matters—as well as the subsidiary belief that once you are addicted, you will always be addicted. The social worker made a good beginning by first understanding the cultural variables yet persisting in helping the patient understand the feelings involved and beginning to counteract the cultural blockings.

CASE 3, SAM PERKINS: USE OF CONCRETE AND SUPPORTIVE SERVICES FOR A SCHIZOPHRENIC PATIENT

The following situation illustrates the role of the worker in crisis intervention, which entails helping the client to confront a crisis and, additionally, learn from the crisis so that he is better equipped to deal with crises in future. At such times, it is important for the worker to maintain his own objectivity so that the patient can lean on it and be helped to maintain his balance. In this case, the supportive services the social worker provided also helped turn the crisis into a learning experience for the patient.

Sam Perkins, a thirty-seven-year-old white male, was involved in both the Mental Health Clinic and the methadone maintenance treatment unit. He subjected other staff to abuse and threats but did not do this with the primary social worker. The social worker was able to remain supportive yet neutral by providing concrete services at a crucial and upsetting time for the patient. He had been in the methadone program for three years but had previously been in other methadone programs for a total of ten years. The diagnosis was "paranoid schizophrenic, drug-dependent individual." The social worker saw the patient twice weekly in the MHC, with the treatment centering on living needs such as unemployment, Medicaid, and housing. The worker helped him find housing, get unemployment benefits, and pursue the question of Medicaid.

The first traumatic situation Sam brought in after he started individual therapy related to a notice of pending termination he had received from the methadone program. It was fairly certain that he would need to leave the program and that his appeal would not be fruitful.* Sam accused the staff of being after him and said other

---

*It should be pointed out that such notices of termination can occur for a number of reasons: the patient may have consistently violated the rules of the program despite repeated warnings; he may have engaged in assaultive behavior against a staff member or another patient; and so on.

patients had done worse things than he had. The social worker allowed him to articulate these feelings for a time but tried to help him focus on the realities and find a new program that would accept him.

At the time of his appeal, Sam became more frustrated, abusive, and anxious. He came to the agency in a rage when he learned he had lost his appeal. Once again, he was allowed to ventilate his rage. The worker again attempted to help him focus on the reality that he needed to find another program and, as before, offered him her full help in doing so. Sam was able to acknowledge that his fear was interfering with his ability to ask for what he wanted. He was encouraged to say very plainly what it was he now wanted and needed. Together, the worker and patient instituted a program search and were successful in finding another program. The patient then asked the worker to accompany him to the new program because he was afraid to go alone, and she agreed. On the appointed day, both went to the program, and the patient was accepted there.

CASE 4, FRANK MARTIN: USE OF JOINT THERAPY TO RESOLVE A MOTHER–SON SYMBIOSIS

This case is focused on the mother–son relationship, very commonly observed to be symbiotic in addiction. It underlines the need to work with other members of the family if the "identified person," the drug abuser, is to be helped to individuate himself and work out his problems. Here, the social worker noticed a special kind of communication between the two and by focusing on it was able to open up some crucial areas of interaction between the mother and son.

Frank Martin is a twenty-eight-year-old white male of Italian background, living with his widowed mother. He has been an assistant cook. He had periodically used tuinols (barbiturates) and recently started again. He was therefore asked by the social worker to attend regular counseling sessions and to bring his mother in for the therapy as well. In one of the joint sessions, Mrs. Martin ordered her son to remove his hat. When the social worker wondered how Frank felt about this, he responded by defending his mother's action. The social worker asked whether the mother did other things like this and Frank mentioned several other instances of control. He was thoughtful for a while, then said that his mother treated him like a baby.

During the session, it was noticed that Frank and his mother often ended their remarks with "You know what I mean." There appeared to be a lot of hidden assumptions in their conversation. The social worker picked up on the phrase each time it was uttered, explaining that she did not know what was meant and asking each to explain how he or she meant it. What was it they were really saying to each other? As a result of this clarification, Frank was able to say that he was constantly being infantilized and made to feel dependent. He was also able to express resentment about his mother's almost total control of his life, including even the "scheduling" of his tuinol intake. (He explained that his mother held the pills for him and controlled the timing and amount of his intake.) The three then entered into a contract in which the mother would stop her involvement in his drug intake and Frank would try to take greater responsibility for his own life.

Albert Einstein College of Medicine Methadone Maintenance Program

PSYCHOTHERAPY OF A TWENTY-YEAR-OLD METHADONE PATIENT

Presentation of the following case is intermingled with a running commentary on the treatment. This case reflects a Freudian approach in its diagnostic approach and terminology.

The patient, Ms. Gordon, came to treatment as a twenty-year-old single female. She was abusing heroin and amphetamines and had been arrested but not convicted for selling narcotics. She had no prior involvement with drug treatment programs. She seemed to be a dependent, angry, and often out-of-control person. In appearance, she was a stocky little girl with short hair. She was then living with a very maternal, protective female with whom she was involved in a lesbian relationship with primarily maternal qualities.

Background. Ms. Gordon was institutionalized at the age of two, when her mother abandoned her. Her father was unavailable during most of her childhood since he was intermittently drunk and emotionally uninvolved with her. She was educated in a series of parochial and training schools.

When she joined the methadone clinic, she became deeply involved in program activities, which included daily group and individual treatment. She attended regularly and would walk through the clinic looking into the offices until she found her therapist. If she did not see her, she would stand in the hall crying out "Rosalyn" until the therapist appeared. Her involvement was then structured better so that she would have an opportunity to meet her therapist immediately upon arriving each day.

It is important to note that for us as practitioners (Ms. Plotkin and staff), treatment had started with the recognition that Ms. Gordon's behavior had significant psychological meaning. We therefore needed to respond as straightforwardly as possible to that meaning. The worker has another choice, which is to connect the patient's manifest feeling-state with her drug use. We chose not to take this approach, feeling that only substantial characterological change would allow not only drug-free functioning but also the development of a whole human being. As Wurmser states, "Compulsive drug use is merely one symptom among others, the expression of an underlying disturbance, not the illness itself" (4). It is the illness that we treat. Rather than focus exclusively on the destructiveness of the drug-taking behavior, we chose to focus on developmental issues. Treatment of the patient is combined with supportive and insight approaches (3).

The first issue was the establishment of a relationship with the therapist and the therapist's overt activity in the case. The second involved recognizing in the patient problems of infantile dependency and intolerable abandonment anxiety, poor impulse control, aggressiveness, drug use as a defense against her affect, alternations between super-dependency and rage over the program structure (i.e., the ungratifying parent-figures), and constant violent attempts to prove that she was basically a worthless and unlovable human being. The first year and a half of treatment entailed the establishment of a close, active and supportive relationship, which attempted to repair and approximate the absent mother–child soothing dyad. Two years into treatment, a male co-therapist was introduced, because it was felt to be important to provide a male and female object to work out her conflicts. It was also hoped that the introduction of the male therapist would help the patient move from the overly dependent, clinging relationship she had established with the female therapist. This provided a framework in which the patient could work out problems of object-splitting. Along these lines, Ms. Gordon would address the female therapist and ignore the male therapist. When she was asked why she did this, she responded that the male therapist didn't care about her. On one occasion, the following dialogue ensued:

> Th: How come you aren't talking to Matt?
> Pt: I don't know.
> Th: You always seem to talk to me, leaving Matt out.
> Pt: (To female therapist) He doesn't know me as well as you do.
> Th: You seem to want to block him out.
> Pt: Well, he doesn't give a fuck about me.
> Th: It's like you're saying all men are like your father, and you can't trust them to care. But Matt isn't your father.
> Pt: Oh!

This is one instance of her attempt to split the therapists and the attempt to counter it. For Ms. Gordon, the world was divided into good mothers and bad fathers. She also displaced her aggression onto the male therapist while preserving the female therapist as the good object. She generally engaged in primitive splitting of all good and all bad self-images and object images. It was soon discovered that there was within her a deep level with a deprived, hungry infant at the mercy of tension that stems from oral-aggressive conflict. As noted previously, Ms. Gordon also had problems with impulse control. Examples of this include instances when we tried to set limits. At such times, we attempted to teach her to think things through before acting. We spoke of her tendency to put things into action before thinking, often destructively. Countertransference issues arose here in trying to set limits and dealing with

Ms. Gordon's unneutralized aggression. If she went ungratified for any length of time, she would scream:

Pt: If you don't give me what I want, I'll throw the chair upside down!
Th: You are neither big enough nor powerful enough.

By thus confronting her primitive fantasy of omnipotence, we attempted to work through some of the infantile grandiosity that she also powerfully turned against herself, thinking she was very bad. Part of the therapy entails providing a corrective emotional experience as well as an interpretive one. At one point, for example, Ms. Gordon asked, "Do you like me?" The therapists felt that for this patient, who had just taken what was for her a considerable risk, it would not be wise to remain silent or reflect the question back to her. Instead, we responded that she was very likable and we enjoyed working with her; further, that she had been working hard to resolve her difficulties. We continued to maintain the relationship with her despite the promotion of one of the therapists to an administrative position and transfer of the other to a different clinic. We continued to reassure the patient that we were still available to her despite her repeated attempts to prove herself undesirable. When she told the male therapist that she wanted a new therapist because she didn't like him, he responded that she could see as many people as she wished, but that he liked her and would continue to be her therapist.

In examining this case, we see that the focus was on helping Ms. Gordon control herself; attempting to work through the splitting, terrifying fantasies of being abandoned, of losing control and going insane; and dealing with repetitive violent attempts on her part to get the therapists to allow primitive, dependent behavior. As Ms. G became better able to tolerate these and other frightening feelings and to feel more secure in the relationships, she was able to reduce her methadone dosage.

The question of the worker's security is an important one if one is to work with addicts: One has to differentiate between active heroin abusers who are substantially out of control; methadone patients who seek stability through this mode of treatment; and those special methadone patients who seek and need psychotherapy. It has been our experience that, in spite of the deprivations and narcissistic rage, violence or acting-out of anger on the therapist is rare. This is true despite everyday threats. Most significantly, some therapists repeatedly run into such difficulties while others never do. There are some dangers and many provocations, since the work is clearly with people who have borderline control. This needs to be anticipated and worked with in the same way that social workers have been working with other situations. It is also felt that, as methadone is decreased below 25 mg. and the tranquilizing effect is reduced, one will see a substantial resurgence of long-suppressed pathological material. In Ms. Gordon, feelings of rage, embarrassment, and almost paranoid shyness surfaced with decreased methadone dosages. The more she was able to tolerate her feelings and express them effectively, the more able she came to tolerate lower doses of methadone (4).

The foregoing cases were cited to illustrate the range of problems and situations that occur in different drug abuse agencies. As we saw, there is no single way to deal effectively with all these situations: We do not have, if we ever shall have, a unified system of principles and techniques with which to approach treatment. The field of drug abuse is in a constant state of flux. There are too many things we do not yet understand about drug abuse itself, and there are too many things not yet understood about treatment for us to hope for a "science" of treatment. As mentioned earlier, the worker must be eclectic, choosing from a range of techniques and options the ones best suited to help a particular client or patient with his problems. There can be no talk of standardization of treatment.

In the following chapter, we shall continue our exploration of kinds of problems and techniques for treating them by examining a series of cases treated by individual therapy in conjunction with supplementary modes of treatment, involving such other methods as relaxation and sexual therapy as well as group modes.

References

1. Aprill, F. A. Case studies of patients treated at the Milwaukee County Mental Health Center Drug Abuse Program. Private communication to author, 1980.
2. Barish, H. Case studies of patients treated at the Lower Eastside Service Center. Private communication to author, 1979.
3. Meiselas, H., and L. Brill. "Drug Abuse in Industry: Issues and Comments." *Industrial Medicine,* 4 No. 8 (August 1972): 10–16.
4. Plotkin, F., et al. Psychotherapy of a twenty-year-old methadone patient. Private communication to author, 1979.

CHAPTER 8

Individual Treatment in Conjunction with Other Modes

THIS CHAPTER CONTINUES THE discussion in Chapter 7 by illustrating the use of individual therapy in conjunction with other modes of treatment. In fact, we already began this discussion in Case 4 from the LESC (pp. 100–101), which included the patient's mother in treatment. Here we shall first present five more cases from the Milwaukee County Mental Health Center and then conclude this chapter with a more detailed long-term case from the Lower Eastside Service Center.

Case Illustrations from the Milwaukee County Mental Health Center Drug Abuse Program

CASE 1, CHARLES GREEN: CRISIS INTERVENTION THROUGH INTENSIVE INDIVIDUAL THERAPY REINFORCED BY CONJOINT MARITAL THERAPY

In this situation, the wife was used as an active therapeutic ally to reinforce the client's treatment and counter his deep-seated feelings of worthlessness.

Charles Green, a thirty-one-year-old white male, had been on a methadone maintenance program for three and a half years when he developed a problem with depression and abuse of depressant drugs. He had consistently maintained a stable psycho-

social and behavioral adjustment prior to this setback. Upon admission to the program, Charles had presented the profile of an individual with considerable ego strength (internal resources) and good external supports (environmental resources). He was bright, verbal, and highly motivated for treatment. He was employed full time as an electrician and had no financial or legal problems. He had a close positive relationship with his family of origin and with his fiancée, a very intelligent and competent professional woman who had never abused chemical substances. After stabilizing on methadone, Charles rapidly abandoned illicit drug use. During the first three years of treatment, he maintained full-time employment, a relatively good psychosocial adjustment, and drug-free status.

Soon after his thirtieth birthday, Charles and his fiancée were married. At the same time, he began a self-imposed detoxification from methadone. While he was in the process of withdrawing from methadone, two events occurred that were to prove extremely stressful for him. Within the space of a few weeks, he was laid off from his job and his parents were killed in an automobile accident. Despite these losses, he attempted to continue detoxification. When it finally became apparent to him that he could not complete his detoxification on schedule, he was overwhelmed by feelings of guilt and failure and fearful that his wife would desert him. He developed insomnia, feelings of depression, high levels of subjective distress, and cravings to use drugs to escape. He turned to the use of depressants to allay his psychic pain

An extensive therapeutic program consisting of twice-weekly individual and conjoint marital counseling was instituted to address the crisis. The goals of the therapeutic regime were (1) to facilitate his recognition and working-through of realistic feelings of loss over the death of his parents; (2) to develop and strengthen nonchemical methods of managing the stress such as progressive relaxation techniques; (3) to facilitate the couple's development of shared nonchemical "highs" based on mutually enjoyable pursuits such as camping, bowling, and socialization with close friends; and (4) confront unrealistic beliefs contributing to his depression and negative feelings about himself.

Clinically, the confrontation of Charles's false belief system proved to be the most critical issue. Charles regarded drug-taking as a moral rather than a functional issue. He consequently believed that his abuse of depressant drugs and his continued need for methadone made him a bad person and a failure unworthy of his wife's love. Feelings of guilt, failure, and depression resulted. He came to perceive correctly, after much confrontation by his therapist and the wife (who proved to be a major therapeutic ally), that his wife's love was not contingent upon his being off methadone and that his acceptance by his wife was not related to achievement of a drug-free state. He stopped condemning and punishing himself for not completing his detoxification and accepted the continued need for methadone treatment. At the same time, he abandoned his efforts to find an escape through intoxication. His subjective feelings of distress and depression subsided to an asymptomatic level.

The Greens continued weekly conjoint counseling for two years after this crisis situation. They came to establish a much closer and stronger relationship than before their ordeal. They could now share many pleasurable life activities and learned to enjoy life and each other. Charles's response repertoire was expanded to include a variety of nonchemical methods for stress management. Overall, he achieved a much stronger psychosocial adjustment than before the crisis. Paradoxically, after he came to accept the continued need for methadone no longer related to feelings of low self-worth or acceptance by his wife, he succeeded in completing his detoxification and was discharged from treatment.

Although Charles, an individual with considerable internal strengths and a good support system, was able to make excellent behavioral changes and establish a stable psychosocial adjustment through methadone treatment, he still retained some negative feelings about himself. These did not significantly jeopardize his adjustment as long as everything was going well for him. When a combination of events—marriage, loss of job, and death of his parents—coincided with his failure to detoxify from methadone, a crisis was precipitated and his stability was undermined. Crisis intervention followed by intensive individual and conjoint marital therapy enabled him to establish a level of psychosocial adjustment higher than before his crisis. It should be noted that Charles was satisfied with his precrisis level of adjustment and probably would never have been motivated to progress farther were it not for the crisis. Although there was a temporary (six-month) period of deterioration, the net effect was to foster a healthier and happier individual. Although each crisis engenders the risk of a negative resolution, there is also the potential that, with proper therapeutic intervention, the crisis can be utilized as an opportunity for client growth and self-actualization (1).

CASE 2; JODY HALL: ANXIETY GENERATES INCREASED DRUG-TAKING AND PSEUDO-SOMATIC COMPLAINTS

Marital counseling was used effectively to help resolve an unviable relationship with this patient's husband.

Jody Hall, a thirty-two-year-old white female, had maintained a satisfactory adjustment for two years while on methadone maintenance. Shortly after reconciling with her estranged husband, she developed multiple somatic complaints (insomnia, loss of appetite, headaches) and pseudo-withdrawal symptoms (restlessness, lacrimation and nasal congestion, yawning, sweating, feelings of change in temperature, stomach pains, and muscle ache). She began to abuse depressant drugs, particularly Valium.

Jody was the only child of an upper-middle-class couple. Her father was a prominent attorney in the small town where she was raised. Before Jody used drugs, she had been a very anxious and insecure girl, with exaggerated dependency needs and subject to prolonged periods of depression. She began to experiment with drugs in her early twenties and found that opiates and downers reduced her anxiety and enabled her to feel normal. While in college she became deeply involved with a drug-using peer group and developed a physical dependence on narcotics. At the same time, she married a man who was both an alcoholic and a drug abuser. After ten years of this life-style, she separated from her husband and applied for drug abuse treatment. She was placed on a methadone maintenance treatment regimen, which enabled her to establish and maintain a stable illicit-drug-free adjustment.

When her husband entered treatment at the same facility, she felt obliged to attempt a reconciliation. Although they genuinely cared for each other, neither knew how to communicate or demonstrate feelings. Beyond this, a great deal of hurt and resentment had built up over the years. When Mr. Hall continued to maintain a near-constant state of inebriation despite drug and alcohol treatment, Jody felt responsible for his failure. She became anxious and depressed and returned to her old pattern of using drugs to relieve her distress. Treatment consisted of individual psychotherapy focused on Jody's feelings of guilt and responsibility for her husband's failure and marital counseling stressing communication training. As Jody worked through her guilt feelings and allowed her husband to accept responsibility for his own behavior, her level of psychic distress diminished, and her somatic complaints were reduced to an asymptomatic level. She abandoned her use of depressant drugs as a coping mechanism.

As a result of the marital counseling, the Halls determined that they did not have a sufficient basis for continuing a lifelong relationship and agreed to separate permanently. Although separated, the Halls learned to communicate effectively and no longer harbored negative feelings toward each other. Each felt free to develop in his or her own way without remaining a prisoner of the past.

The case illustrates how anxiety and negative emotions stemming from a stressful relationship were translated into somatic and pseudo-withdrawal symptoms and precipitated a return to previously abandoned patterns of drug-taking behavior as a means of alleviating psychic distress.

CASE 3, ROGER BLACK: PROBLEMS FOR WHICH WORKING CONJOINTLY WITH COUPLES BECOMES ESSENTIAL

If one member of a couple does well, the other may feel threatened and may act out and help pull down the partner. Working conjointly allows us to encompass both ends of the spectrum and to deal with the negative interactions. In this case the therapy helped dissolve a negative relationship so that the members were free to seek out more constructive unions.

Roger Black, a twenty-six-year-old single white male, had enrolled in a methadone treatment program four months previously but had a poor pattern of clinic attendance and continued heroin abuse in spite of blocking doses of methadone. At the time he applied for treatment, he had a ten-year addiction history and had been incarcerated several times for drug-related offenses. For about eighteen months prior to his application for treatment, he had lived with a young woman who was also addicted to narcotics.

At first he attempted an ambulatory detoxification regimen. This program proved ineffective because of a continued pattern of illicit drug use. His clinic attendance was sporadic, and by the end of the first month he had stopped coming completely. One month later he reapplied for treatment and was accepted for methadone maintenance. Although blocking doses of methadone were prescribed, Roger used heroin regularly over the next two months. He was also observed on several occasions trying to give altered urine samples. When confronted with his continuing use of opiates, Roger could offer no explanation other than a continued craving for narcotics. Upon exploring the factors that might have contributed to his narcotic craving and drug-seeking behavior, it was discovered that his girlfriend was still using actively and that heroin was freely available in their home.

During the following months, Roger and his girlfriend received both individual and conjoint couple counseling. Once both partners were in treatment, they found that they were able to reinforce each other in changing their drug-centered life-styles and refraining from narcotic drug use. Roger's illicit drug use soon abated, and his clinic attendance and cooperation with treatment staff improved dramatically. Over the next three years, Roger and his partner maintained an illicit-drug-free status while actively participating in a counseling program, which facilitated their growth as individuals and their reintegration into straight society. As Roger and his partner experienced positive success experiences by accomplishing their life goals and objectives, they became more confident of their own abilities and gradually grew away from each other. Although their relationship is now terminated, they remain friends and occasionally see each other. Each has developed a positive relationship with a new "significant other." After a three-and-a-half-year course of treatment, Roger successfully withdrew from methadone and was discharged as a success.

CASE 4, JACKIE JACKSON: PROBLEMS OF ALCOHOLISM IN A METHADONE CLINIC PATIENT

This problem has been discovered in up to 30 percent of the methadone patients across the country. Although patients with such problems were initially dropped from the programs, in time attempts were made to treat the alcoholism problem as well, and special services were therefore built into some clinics to accomplish this. The patient in this case also had a destructive relationship with her husband, and marital counseling and assertiveness training were called into play to help the patient with this relationship.

Jackie Jackson, a twenty-six-year-old married black female with a dual problem of alcoholism and drug abuse, was in the second trimester of pregnancy when drug program outreach efforts succeeded in enrolling her in treatment. She was the youngest of three daughters born to a working-class family. Her parents were divorced when she was three years old, and she was reared by her mother. As a child, Jackie was not particularly close to her family; she was an insecure, lonely girl who had difficulty making friends. When she was seventeen she became pregnant and married the father of her child. Her husband was an egocentric, immature young man with extremely limited ego strengths and strong sociopathic personality characteristics. Mr. Jackson was heavily involved in criminal behavior and the addictive life and was both an alcoholic and a heroin addict. After her marriage Jackie was introduced to alcohol and narcotics by her husband.

Her married life was the life of a fugitive, constantly relocating from state to state to avoid members of the drug community who had been alienated by her husband and posed a serious threat to his life and physical safety. She had no friends or outside interests and was abused physically and emotionally by her husband. She coped with these problems by remaining in an almost constant state of inebriation via alcohol and narcotics. When not intoxicated, she was often depressed and had suicidal ideation and behavior. During the nine years she lived this way, she made several attempts to get treatment. Each time she failed to follow through when she was forced to pack in the middle of the night and flee with her husband to safer surroundings.

At the time of her application for treatment, Jackie was twenty-six years old and five months pregnant. She was placed in an outpatient treatment regimen consisting of methadone maintenance and individual counseling and was also referred for prenatal care. Her husband, who was already in treatment, continued to receive methadone maintenance and individual counseling.

During the first few months of treatment, Jackie made very little progress. She and her husband continued their previous destructive life-style and reinforced each other's use of alcohol and other drugs. Conjoint marital counseling was added to the treatment plan to help break through their interpersonal negative integration. Mr. Jackson heavily resisted the marital counseling. Three months later Jackie gave birth to a premature infant, who died shortly thereafter as a result of the effects of "fetal alcohol syndrome." One month later her husband announced that they were going to move to another state in order to avoid members of the addict community who were out to kill him.

After much soul-searching Jackie decided not to accompany her husband in his self-imposed exile as she had done formerly. Instead, she and her children remained in town, and she continued in methadone treatment. This was a crucial decision and breakthrough for Jackie: although she had received much abuse at her husband's hands, he was the only significant adult person in her life, and it took a great deal of courage to risk facing life without him. In the following months Jackie was helped in treatment to work through a normal grief process over the loss of her child and the separation from her husband. In addition to individual counseling twice weekly, she was enrolled in a weekly women's assertiveness group. She was also persuaded to participate in antabuse treatment. Without her husband's destructive behavior, Jackie began to respond to treatment and was able to reduce her alcohol and drug abuse to an asymptomatic level. Over the next four years her treatment was focused on improving her self-concept and facilitating emotional growth and development. Though she had several setbacks, she managed to establish a reasonably stable psychosocial adjustment with the support of ongoing methadone maintenance, antabuse treatment, and individual counseling.

CASE 5, JOE GARCIA: LOSS OF LIBIDO AND FAILURE IN SEXUAL PERFORMANCE

When this problem occurs in a methadone clinic, it presents special difficulties of diagnosis; there is need to distinguish between the possible effects of the methadone and the effects of psychological and marital problems. In this case, marital counseling and sex education proved useful in dealing with these problems.

Joe Garcia, a thirty-year-old married Hispanic male, had been in methadone mainte-nance treatment for eighteen months when he complained of a lack of libido and sexual performance problems. The youngest of three children born to a middle-class family, Joe grew up in a small Southern community. He graduated from high school and completed one year of community college when he was drafted into the army. While assigned to combat duty in Southeast Asia, he used but did not become addicted to narcotics. Upon separation from the service, he moved to the Midwest, married, and found employment as an insurance salesman. At the age of twenty-four he was temporarily incapacitated by an automobile accident. Pharmaceutical nar-cotics were prescribed for pain control, and he continued to use them after the original analgesic need was no longer present. As he became more involved in com-pulsive drug use, he was fired from his job and was divorced from his wife. For two years he forged prescriptions for pharmaceutical narcotics, then elected to apply for methadone treatment.

After being stabilized on 80 mg., he made several rapid behavioral changes. He ceased illicit narcotics, returned to work for his former employer, and developed a non-drug-related peer group and appropriate leisure-time activities. A year after entering treatment he married a straight woman he had known for several years.

In an effort to ensure the quick establishment of a family, Mrs. Garcia began to monitor and chart her body temperature so that she and her husband could have coitus during her most fertile times. As these efforts proved unsuccessful, Joe increas-ingly began to suffer from a lack of libido and had difficulty having an erection. After several months of sexual adjustment problems, Joe brought this matter to the atten-tion of his counselor. Loss of libido and difficulty in getting and maintaining an erection are commonly reported side effects of methadone. These effects are gener-ally dose-related and normally subside as a patient lowers his methadone dose and/or remains on a maintenance dose for an extended period of time. In this case Joe had been stabilized on 80 mg. of methadone for more than a year prior to the onset of his sexual adjustment problems. Before his marriage, he had maintained a normal sexual adjustment in spite of a relatively high daily dose of methadone. It was therefore felt that his sexual adjustment problem had both psychosocial and physiological components.

A time-limited program of conjoint marital counseling and sex education was instituted. Sessions had an educational focus and included didactic presentations and discussions to help the Garcias become aware of both the effects of methadone on sexual functioning and the inhibitory effect of anxiety and negative emotion on sexual feelings. (The worker has found the audio cassette "Daily Living: Coping with Tension and Anxiety—A Modern Sexual Outlook" by Arnold Lazarus a useful didactic presentation for patients with sexual adjustment problems.) The concept of performance anxiety as it pertained to the Garcias was presented and explored. It was particularly emphasized that Mr. Garcia did not have to perform with his penis on every occasion and that it was not only all right but, indeed, highly desirable for them to relax and enjoy themselves together in noncoital forms of sexual interaction. They were urged to turn in their thermometer, relax, enjoy foreplay, and play without attempting coitus.

The suggestion against attempting coitus placed the Garcias in a position of being able to abandon their coital performance anxiety. They were to follow the therapeutic instructions and also had permission not to perform. As they became more relaxed in their sexual encounters, spontaneity and enjoyment returned to their sexual relationship. Joe experienced an increase in libido and an increasing ability to sustain an erection. Within a month, they were able to enjoy both foreplay and coitus. The Garcias learned that they must learn to stop trying to force sex before they could alleviate their performance anxiety and enjoy sex.

Case Illustrations from Milwaukee County Drug Abuse Program and Lower Eastside Service Center—Summary

The following key or index to case illustrations was prepared to facilitate the review of the brief cases summarized in Chapters 7 and 8. Mr. Aprill provided the index for the cases submitted by him, and the author added the data for those presented by Mr. Barish and his staff.

INDIVIDUAL THERAPY	PROBLEMS ENCOUNTERED/RESPONSE
1. Joan Jones	• suicidal "gestures" • lack of ego integration in borderline personality; isolation of affect and repression, depersonalization • need for therapist to impose controls, with risk-taking intervention
2. John Chu	• special sociocultural problems in Chinese male • repression of feelings; role in generating addiction • ambivalence about treatment

INDIVIDUAL THERAPY	PROBLEMS ENCOUNTERED/RESPONSE
3. Sam Perkins	• need for crisis intervention; use of crisis intervention to achieve better ego integration • worker's use of self to provide support to patient • use of concrete services to patient • paranoid schizophrenia diagnosis
4. Otis Johnson	• failure to engage in treatment • ambivalence/approach-avoidance conflict
5. Frank Doe	• pseudo-withdrawal syndrome
6. Debra Scott	• primary affective disorders/masked depression
7. John Smith	• pathological family of origin • effects of illicit drug use/addiction life-style • chronic unemployment • family unit treatment
8. Joe Andrews	• importance of support systems, significant others • effects on treatment and patient's self-concept • premature detoxification • acute psychotic episode
9. Michael Turner	• addiction life-style • chronic unemployment • transition from drug subculture to clinic subculture to straight society • importance of long-term treatment for facilitating client growth and maturation
10. Fred Jones	• work adjustment problems • interpersonal anxiety • reintegrating into straight society • role of client advocacy

INDIVIDUAL THERAPY SUPPLEMENTED BY OTHER MODES	PROBLEMS ENCOUNTERED/RESPONSE
11. Frank Martini	• mother-son symbiosis • use of joint therapy as technique • infantilization of patient • encouragement by worker for Frank to move toward greater independence of mother
12. Charles Green	• relapse to CNS depressant drug use under stress • grief reaction/situational adjustment reaction • crisis intervention • progressive relaxation training
13. Jody Hall	• relapse to CNS depressant drug use under stress • somatic complaints • marital problems, effect on psychic distress
14. Roger Black	• drug-abusing spouse, effects on him
15. Jackie Jackson	• sociopathic spouse, effects of • alcoholism/fetal alcohol syndrome • battered wife syndrome
16. Joe Garcia	• sexual adjustment problem

Case Illustration from the Lower Eastside Service Center

The following case and the case presented in the chapter on interdisciplinary collaboration, pages 157–67, were prepared by Herbert Barish. Both provide examples of the long-term efforts required to deal with chronically addicted patients. As mentioned, endless endurance and patience are needed to tolerate the constant ups and downs and to measure the results in small gains and limited goals rather than in sweeping, dramatic recoveries and great leaps forward. The course of treatment is plodding and slow, with much acting-out, regression, and relapses along the way. Just as the worker must learn to endure this painfully slow pace and long-drawn-out treatment, the reader will need to be patient in following the progress of the case reported here. It was nevertheless included because it was believed to be typical of the many cases actually being seen in drug abuse programs. In this case, as in the one presented later, group was used at different times as well as individual therapy. Also provided was supplementary treatment such as relaxation therapy and sex therapy, and additional reinforcements such as the use of controls through probation and welfare.

INTAKE PROCESS

Mrs. A., a thirty-six-year-old black woman, had been referred to the LESC by the Welfare Department, which requires that person with a current or even previous drug problem, must be involved in a drug treatment program. The initial reason for referral is frequently because of external pressure or a concrete problem. Staff must accept this type of motivation and attempt to establish beginning connections during the intake process to engage the client in treatment. In the screening interview Mrs. A. presented herself as drug-free and as an ex-addict though it later emerged that she was still using cocaine and marijuana. (Clients often understate the extent of their drug use until subsequent treatment makes them more open.) There was a history of psychiatric hospitalization. Her request was for help in finding a job. She had a good history of fairly continuous employment during the previous four years. The pre-screening interviewer recommended that Mrs. A. have an intake appointment without being referred to the Orientation Group, the usual procedure, because of her psychiatric history and current drug status. Mrs. A. admitted that she felt conflicted about many problems in her life and felt inadequate to understand and confront them. She appeared to be an attractive woman, intelligent, cooperative, and verbal, but with much underlying anger and agitation.

PSYCHOSOCIAL HISTORY

Mrs. A. was born in an Eastern state, the third of four children. Her father was a traveling salesman, and her mother a domestic worker. The younger of her two brothers had conventional employment, but the older brother, to whom she felt closest, was serving a long prison sentence for selling narcotics. Her younger sister was the favorite child.

Mrs. A. loved her father but rarely saw him since he was so frequently away from home. She thought the mother was abusive of the father. She was often in trouble in school, truant, and involved in gang fights. At twelve she was held by the police for being out at night. She had her first sexual experience at that age and was pregnant at thirteen. Her mother subsequently cared for the baby. At fifteen she was arrested for prostitution and sent away as an "incorrigible" to the State Industrial School for Girls. At sixteen she attempted to break out of the school and stabbed three matrons. She was sent to a psychiatric hospital for evaluation and was declared legally sane, with a psychiatric diagnosis of "dyssocial reaction in a sociopathic character disorder." The report also indicated that she made a "narcissistic, impulsive, self-gratifying adjustment to life, with little capacity to postpone pressure or exercise judgment regarding her impulsive behavior." She had fantasies about marrying a white man. After three weeks at the hospital she was discharged, returned to the court, and sent to the state reformatory at the age of seventeen. She remained there for two years.

She began using heroin when she left the reformatory. Soon thereafter she married and moved to another city with her husband. She was arrested several times for drug use and prostitution. Her husband was imprisoned when she was twenty-one and she returned to live with her mother. She became involved with the drug culture, remarried, and lived with her second husband for eight years. Her parents were divorced by this time, and each had remarried. Her mother had numerous lovers, which Mrs. A. resented. At the age of thirty-three she decided to stop using drugs and did so by resorting to street methadone. She got her first legal job as a saleswoman and began to make friends with non-drug-users. She entered a methadone maintenance program. (It is generally difficult to get a coherent picture during the intake interview, and the information will probably have to be amended as treatment gets under way. Since there is so much turmoil in the lives of the clients, it is difficult to pin down motivations and make causal connections; this will come later in therapy. Every effort must be made to use whatever levers are at hand to hold the client in treatment and develop strategies for dealing with the problems presented.)

It emerged that at the time of intake Mrs. A. was married to a third husband, who was dating other women. This precipitated assaultive behavior on her part so that they needed to separate. He wished to return to her in spite of her violent behavior. The intake worker felt that Mrs. A. had good motivation and a capacity for insight and should be given maximum service. She was assigned to individual therapy once weekly and group therapy in a women's group once weekly. The social worker was to pursue the issue of vocational placement.

COURSE OF TREATMENT

First two months. Mrs. A.'s attendance was sporadic, and lateness was common. She would come in for a few weeks, then stay away for several weeks. Early treatment was focused on her resistance to becoming involved. Each time she failed to appear, a letter was sent assuring her that the worker cared about her. It appeared that Mrs. A. was engaging in this behavior to challenge the clinic to close her case. The social worker was very persistent, pursuing her when she missed appointments and expressing her concern. (This kind of testing and challenge is very frequent and is part of the resistance, an attempt to learn whether the client can indeed be tolerated in all her "badness." It is easy for the worker to get caught up in her own feelings of countertransference and to react, which would mean falling into the trap set by the client.) At times Mrs. A. also behaved in a very dependent fashion, attempting to get the worker to tell her what to do. The worker confronted this and challenged Mrs. A. to follow through on her own initiative once she understood what it was she really wanted for herself. Mrs. A.'s common-law husband tried to sabotage treatment by discouraging her from keeping her appointments. The worker urged Mrs. A. to confront her husband on this issue rather than act it out. The husband refused to be involved in treatment himself. (It is common for family members to attempt to sabotage treatment by downgrading it, not getting involved, seducing the client to stay away, creating turmoil and crises, and withholding funds if fees are involved.)

Remainder of first year of treatment. After seven months Mrs. A. was still continuing her pattern of erratic attendance, but she was in fact becoming more involved. Though she had attended the group sessions when she first started, she stopped because she became angry with the group leader, a woman. Her fear of acting-out violently in the group was worked out in individual therapy. She obtained her high school equivalency degree and applied to the mini-college on the premises of the agency. Her educational goals were the most conflict-free area of her functioning.

A crisis ensued when her husband was arrested for drugs. She got involved in a battle with drug dealers, but no one was seriously hurt. Despite all this, she was keeping her appointments and relating better, displaying concern about the chaos of her life. When her husband returned from jail, she refused to allow him into the apartment. She was assaulted by her husband and wondered why women were allowed to be beaten by their men. (The consistent approach of the social worker in showing her concern and offering support proved helpful; still the worker also consistently asked the client to take responsibility for her own life and behavior, and this allowed Mrs. A. to remain in treatment.)

Second year of treatment. A new crisis occurred when the social worker left the agency and was replaced by a new worker. Mrs. A. was able to weather this change since she was feeling far better about herself. A male worker was chosen this time under the supposition that such a change in therapist would be helpful. It nevertheless took many months before Mrs. A. was able to respond to the new worker. She worked on and off, being helped with supplemental welfare assistance. She attended the mini-college and did well in her studies. Therapy was focused on her underlying rage, on developing insight into how she was influenced in her growing-up years, and on working on her relationship with her new boyfriend and his child. There was also focus on reducing her chronic depression and dealing constructively with her problems.

Third Year of Treatment. Mrs. A. acted out badly when her worker went on vacation. When he returned, the worker voiced his frustration that she should still be acting out at this late date. This confrontation and voicing of the worker's real feelings proved very useful in allowing Mrs. A. to see the worker as another human being and not superhuman. Mrs. A. became more trusting than before and shared more material about her current and past relationships. This led to more expression of feelings of deprivation, and connections were made with the depression, which was still evident. Mrs. A. recognized that she could give to herself and need not wait expectantly for outside supplies of symbolic love, which, if they were not forthcoming, contributed to her depression. She finally graduated from the college with a BA. She had received one year's credit for life experience (which was also salutory in terms of helping her to accept her prior life experience as well as contributing to the degree). She is still continuing therapy and is planning to apply for admission to a school of social work. She has a more stable relationship with her boyfriend (2).

This chapter and the previous one were designed to demonstrate treatment by individual counseling, at times supplemented by methadone maintenance, the use of relaxation and sex therapy, and other methods. The use of compulsion through the courts and probation and parole systems was also undertaken, though not elaborated on here. Also shown was the use of individual therapy in conjunction with supplementary modes where "important others" needed to be involved if the drug abuser was to be treated effectively. In the following chapters, we shall be discussing the use of various forms of group therapy: conjoint and couples or marital therapy, family therapy, group, and multiple family therapy.

References

1. Aprill, F. A. Case studies of patients from the Milwaukee County Mental Health Center Drug Abuse Program. Private communication to author, 1980.
2. Barish, H. Case studies of patients from the Lower Eastside Service Center. Private communication with author, 1979.

CHAPTER 9

Group Therapy

SINCE THE 1950s THERAPISTS have complained about the severe difficulties inherent in working with groups of drug abusers. This was true of Zucker, Laskowitz, Kaplan, and others (3, 10, 11). Therapists did not know how to use group methods to control the negativism and acting-out behavior of drug-abusing clients or how to deal with their constant challenges and testing behavior, perennial crises and regressions, mistrust of authority, and loyalty to their street contacts and contracts (7, 8, 10). Group therapy was first undertaken in such institutional settings as the Public Health Service hospitals at Lexington, Kentucky, and Fort Worth, Texas (14), and at the Riverside Hospital in New York City operated by probation and parole systems. In New York, California, and Pennsylvania probation and parole officers attempted to use their legal controls to structure treatment (3, 4). The establishment of ex-addict-directed therapeutic communities such as Synanon in California and Daytop Village and Phoenix House in New York saw the initiation of the abrasive encounter groups in which the ventilation of hostile feelings became the focal point of treatment (3, 4).

The author's experience in conducting groups of cyclazocine and methadone patients at the Albert Einstein College of Medicine and Lincoln Hospital in the South Bronx pointed up these difficulties (3, 4, 8). Patients invariably brought their street attitudes into treatment, and their stance in group was often negative and challenging. Members of the groups were caught between the need to maintain their street code and the need to be honest in treatment. The street code was never to inform on other members, and this code needed to be broken. Some members attempted to use the group to make contacts for drugs or other illicit behavior. If a member began chippying (using) again, it was difficult for other members to remain abstinent or to raise the issue in the group. In an effort to counter this, at the beginning of treatment the

118

therapist established a "treatment contract" for group behavior along the lines of Karl Menninger's model, defining the conditions and goals of treatment. Members were told that they must ignore the street code, which could only lead to destruction of the group and relapse or worse for them. They must report on the behavior of the others if the therapy was to have any value. They were not to engage in any pushing within the group or any other action that would undermine the group. Members who relapsed were removed from the group and seen individually until they could be reinstated.

To counter the negativism that frequently took over, the groups were "loaded" with aides who could defeat such attitudes and provide strong supports for more positive activities. Use was made of ex-addicts, former members of groups, who had done well, indigenous personnel from the area, medical students, and others. In methadone, the group had a very powerful reinforcer; it relieved the drug craving, even though it did not always prevent chippying with other drugs and alcohol. To a lesser extent this was also true of cyclazocine. The groups also served as a screening device for the cyclazocine patients: those who could not make it on cyclazocine were shifted to methadone.

There was need to focus discussion away from "drug talk" and dwell on the real problems. Use was also made of wives' groups to examine the other side of the patients' problems, the negative interactions within the couple that recapitulated the patients' earlier problems with their parents. These sessions were conducted behind a one-way screen to help the staff of the Lincoln Hospital Mental Health Clinic learn about drug abuse and about therapy with acting-out patients (3, 8). In time the wives were able to examine their own feelings and understand their own role in the frequently destructive interplay with their spouses. When this occurred, it posed a new problem for the patients: Their spouses began moving away from them and asserting their independence. Most of the wives were riddled with feelings of inferiority and found some security in the relationship with an addict spouse.

Though it was the earlier bias not to mix different kinds of substance abusers in a single group, the emergence of polydrug abuse in the 1960s, with users mixing alcohol with a variety of other drugs, led to programs combining treatment of these different users at facilities such as the one at Eagleville, Pennsylvania. What has emerged clearly in the past few years is the need to tailor groups more strictly to the needs of particular patients rather than to use a uniform approach to all groups. The author has found it possible and useful to combine young alcohol abusers with other drug abusers on the basis of common psychosocial and demographic characteristics rather than on the basis of the kind of substance used. Such an approach is advocated by J. P. Flanzer and F. A. Aprill, following the model developed by E. McBroom for outpatient group therapy in 1972 (6, 7, 12). Like McBroom, they delineate four levels of socialization of clients requiring four distinct kinds of group in treatment.

Flanzer-McBroom Model for Group Treatment of Drug Abusers

Clients who are socialized in the drug culture. This type of drug addict has learned behaviors suitable for the drug subculture primarily for reasons of group identification. He has assumed roles not acceptable to the rest of society and has not learned conventionally acceptable behavior. For example, the drug culture teaches drug users not to trust, to be wary of authority, to seek immediate gratification, and to avoid intimate relationships. This results in sociopathic-appearing but not true sociopathic personality. Involvement in the drug culture may be traced to sociological instead of psychological causes.* It is necessary to add, however, that here too the effects of the drug life would be bound to have effects on the person and personality as well, in time.

Clients who are inadequately socialized into society's values. This type of client has not had the opportunities to learn from adequate models, which normally occurs early in life. There is some capacity for current learning. Such clients become involved in drug abuse to compensate for feelings of inadequacy, to meet oral dependency needs, to relieve stress, to hide difficulties in interpersonal relationships, and so on. This is the bread-and-butter group of most treatment efforts. Such clients are frequently misdiagnosed as "character disorders," which precludes their being accepted into treatment: Character disorders are considered not treatable, "unworkable," or undesirable because they constitute a chronic, long-term, and recalcitrant group in treatment. Careful observation of such pseudo-sociopathic drug abusers often reveals psychotic and psychoneurotic problems (7).

Clients who are unsocialized in conventional values. Some clients have been severely neglected and deprived as children and have consequently internalized few social values. Lacking basic trust, they represent true sociopathic individuals, pathogenic criminals. They are often destructive to themselves and to others, have not internalized social norms, and project their difficulties onto the external environment.

Clients who are presocialized; lack of socialization. These clients realize that they are in trouble with their drug problem but have not yet suc-

---

*This category appears to be the same as the one delineated by Dr. Chein in *The Road to H.* Here users looked like true addicts in that their life-styles approximated those of addicts, but differed in that they lacked the "craving" of true addicts.

cumbed to the drug culture. They have achieved some socialization in cultural values, but not enough to withstand drug temptations. Their prognosis is good, since they have ego and environmental strengths. They can best be served in drug-free modalities.

Treatment

The treatment of the four groups needs to be varied according to each group's characteristics.

Clients who are socialized in the drug culture have roles that are adequate for the drug community but inadequate for societal integration. They have not yet resorted to criminal behavior to support their addiction. Many of them have maintained productive marital and familial relationships and have not experienced a marked deterioration of that level of coping. Treatment is in two phases: a clear focus on rehabilitation, and reconstruction of the family and peer-group relationships damaged by the addictive life-style. The treatment is multifamily group counseling, educative in orientation. Much time is spent on the conscious level, with direct interpretation, reasoning, and the explanation of behavior to demonstrate to the abuser the irresponsible and self-defeating aspects of his actions. In the second phase treatment focuses on the reintegration of the patient into the community, discussing fears and anxieties about reentry. Heterogeneous growth groups, including straight clients as well as drug abusers, can be used to provide a safe milieu for risk-taking.

Clients who are inadequately socialized need to develop competence and mastery over their impulses and reinforce their ego strengths in general. Social group work and group psychotherapy, with their focus on building ego strength in interaction with group members, are the treatments of choice for inadequately socialized drug addicts. In addition, the educational and integrative types of groups outlined for the drug-culture patients can be useful.

Clients who are unsocialized are characterized by a sociopathic personality. It is suggested that a highly structured milieu or therapeutic community focusing on personality reorganization and behavioral change is the treatment of choice. On an outpatient basis, group therapy using a behavioral model may be the most viable approach. After sociopathic individuals have gained the necessary nurturing and internalization of self, which often develop through these group modes, they can undertake psychotherapeutic groups.

Clients who are presocialized are those who realize that they are in serious trouble with their drug problem but have not yet succumbed to the drug culture. As indicated, their prognosis is excellent. Following short-term detoxification, if they are physically dependent, they can best be served in drug-free treatment modalities. They do not belong in a methadone maintenance program, for such a move might accelerate their contact with the drug culture.

In planning treatment generally for the four groups, the composition of the groups is of paramount importance. Group dynamics theories suggest the need for groupings within a relatively narrow socioeconomic and age range and of a size between eight and eighteen to maximize social-interaction benefits. An essential aspect is homogeneity in the nature of the problem or underlying psychopathology. Heterogeneity exposes the patient to other individuals in the group who will not fulfill his interpersonal needs but will rather frustrate him and make him aware of his different conflict areas and suggest alternative interpersonal modes of behavior. The homogeneous group becomes cohesive more quickly and offers immediate support to the members. Better attendance, less conflict, and greater symptom relief result. However, the homogeneous groups tend to remain on a superficial level and to be an ineffective medium for the building of character structure. There is a danger of negative reinforcement and repetition of street games. It is difficult to do deep therapy with such groups and to avoid deep therapy with the heterogeneous groups. Thus, the homogeneous educative and behavioral-model group are preferable for drug abusers. Social groups, work groups and psychotherapy and psychoanalytically oriented groups should be heterogeneous. Reality factors such as time and expense, therapist training and experience, and agency policy regarding the acceptance of drug abuse clients may often dictate homogeneous drug abuse groups.

Careful consideration must be given the design of drug abuse programs offering group therapy. The therapy must be geared to the needs of particular patients rather than attempting to apply one group treatment modality to all. Flanzer and April were therefore careful to propose specific treatment strategies based on a careful differential diagnosis and to use the foregoing model to suggest how this could best be accomplished (7).

The Abrahms "Cognitive-Behavioral Model"

Abrahms's model is radically different from Flanzer's and postulates very different objectives (1). The model derives from the behavioral school based on the work of Wolpe and Lazarus, Miller, and others (13, 16).

To explain his model, Abrahms cites his study in which fourteen methadone maintenance patients participated in a ten-week program comparing the effectiveness of a cognitive-behavioral group and the usual discussion-type group in developing adaptive behavioral skills and improved self-evaluation. Abrahms felt that "the development of personal resources, internalization of coping strategies and the deemphasis on external mechanisms of problem-solving and reinforcement such as that provided by chemical abuse might psychologically inoculate the opioid-addicted individual against routine stresses of the drug-free life" (1). The purpose of the experimental group was to develop adaptive behaviors and attitudes competitive with drug abuse and to ameliorate skill deficits. The therapeutic behavioral program was highly structured, consisting of deep muscular relaxation training, with imagined and actual approaches to conflict situations (2); identification and practice of verbal and nonverbal components of assertiveness, including appropriate and effective expression of personal needs; identification and engagement in pleasant events; and isolation and graduated rehearsal of small units of behavior leading to goal attainment. Patients simulated such highly anxiety-arousing situations as job interviews and drug-refusal interactions with drug addicts. They rehearsed appropriate responses, observed themselves on videotape, and discussed underlying cognitions related to these events. Additional cognitive components included identifying and disputing irrational assumptions and covert sensitizations, alternating with relaxation procedures, the lowering of expectations, the restructuring of goal-setting strategies, and the development and application of positive self-statements and evaluations.

Abrahms found that a

... therapeutic program aimed at skill development and cognitive restructuring was significantly more powerful in producing short-term behavioral changes than a less-structured discussion-type group approach. The most significant impact of the program was in the areas targeted for change such as management of stress and anxiety, non-assertiveness, depression and non-productive self-statements. The multi-dimensional approach attempted to teach techniques that could be applied to the patient outside the treatment setting, develop resources and raise expectations regarding the self-management of routine stresses which might be confronted in a non-addicted society, and produce changes designed to promote self-sufficiency and positive self-appraisals without drug-dependency. [1]

Couples Therapy Groups

There is often a natural transition from multiple family therapy (see Chapter 9) to couples therapy groups, since couples who were part of a multiple family therapy group may have resolved problems related to their child and wish to focus on their own problems. When one member of the couple is an addict, the primary focus is on the relationship between the addict and the spouse or potential spouse (5, 6, 7, 9). The couples are generally not permitted to bring in problems related to children. According to Kaufman, three issues are usually primary in couples therapy: money, sex, and intimacy. Money is generally the first problem to be discussed, particularly its use as an instrument of power, since it is the easiest to focus on. Divorced couples who are parents may attend the couples sessions with their new spouses or lovers. The group helps them make a better commitment to their new relationship. Couples work on solving the problems between themselves and defining the generational boundaries between themselves and their children.

A second type of couples therapy with adult addicts and their mates includes couples in residential settings, such as Su Casa in New York and The Awakening Family in Los Angeles. In the former, the couples meet as part of a multiple family therapy group; in the latter, they meet separately. The focus is on building the relationship as the couple prepares to move out into society from the residential setting. Therapists need to be very careful not to get involved in a triangle, with each member vying for the therapist's approval. An important technique is the exploration of hidden agendas and ritual behavior. Substance abuse may be provoked in the addict because of the spouse's need for self-punishment or to keep the addict helpless because the spouse is fearful that he or she may improve and abandon the relationship. A critical point occurs when the addict gives up drug use; the nonusing partner will then have to find an entirely new way of relating, learn to communicate better, and enjoy sex in a nonexploitative way. As in all therapy, trust must be built, and the addict must finally learn to live without drugs as his first love object and overcome his anxiety and depression.

CASE ILLUSTRATION

Dr. Jerry Flanzer of the University of Arkansas School of Social Work believes that treatment in small groups of eight to eighteen members has yielded the most favorable results of all the psychotherapeutic and/or counseling modalities. The following presentation with commentary by Dr. Flanzer utilizes edited excerpts from one long-term couples group, of which some members had been polydrug abusers, although heroin was the common denominator. Flanzer lists the benefits and purposes of group treatment for drug users as: (1) peer resocialization and social reality; (2) behavioral feedback and consensual validation; and (3) treatment in a nondependent relationship with some distance from authority. These are illustrated below.

Peer Resocialization and Social Reality

Second Meeting

Therapist: Everyone seems mighty quiet today. Last week, I couldn't get you to shut up. (Here and now—process comment)

Wife A: We're just tired. Didn't get much sleep. (Avoidance)

Husband A: Yeah—we couldn't get the kids to sleep. (Collusion)

Wife B: Sure was hard putting my two to sleep last night too. Something must be in the air. ("Let's keep it safe.")

Husband B: There sure is something in the air. (Let's play—guessing game. Everyone squirms, ten cigarettes are lit. Husband D begins playing with the tape recorder. Group secret—nonverbal clue to therapist)

Therapist: Something sure is in the air—the air right in the room.

Husband B: Yeah, it sure stinks. (Who would like my anger?)

Husband D: Who stinks? (Stands up. You want to fight?)

Therapist: Sit down, Mr. D. (Guarantees physical safety) It sounds like there is something else we all want to talk about. In the beginning of every group, we wonder, "Who can we trust?"

Wife B: Well, we can't talk with Mr. D. here.

Husband D: What's the matter—afraid you'll cut off your sources?

Therapist: I guess we have a choice—to remember the past or to work in the "here and now."

Wife B: Then we need to make some rules.

Therapist: Right. What rules do we need to make?

During the years of exclusive attention to maintaining their habit, social contact has been increasingly limited to "friends" with similar needs, such as the need for acceptance. The addicts' social reality differs markedly from the outside norm, as collectively their interests remain in immediate gratification. Time is measured between fixes; long-term planning is just a dream. Constantly ripping each other off, yet needing each other to maintain the drug pipeline, drug addicts quickly learn a pleasing style, faking concern and involvement as a defense against the "hurt" and "mistrust" of those they need to retain as friends. Group therapy focuses quickly on this false empathy and trust issue. The group, through the leader and the agency, also begins chipping away at the life-style while inculcating society's values. The successful group begins working in small incremental steps toward goals promoting delayed gratification (5, 6, 7, 9).

It is likely that members of the drug addict group may have "ripped off" each other on the streets. This magnifies the difficulty of the therapist's task. The lack of trust permeating such a group often prevents the members from focusing on the primary agenda. The leader must exhibit appropriate empathy, warmth, and genuineness, particularly at these beginning times, while keeping the focus on the "here and now" and away from the "there and then." In this way, the emphasis remains on the client's inability to form interpersonal relations and on the addictive behavioral life-style itself. "War stories" and other non-relevant games are thus thwarted, forcing the client to remain responsible for his/her drug-taking behavior. An important rule of thumb for many skilled therapists in the field is that at least ten minutes of every hour must be spent on the precipitating reason or problem for their being in the group in the first place. If not, the group will fail.

Behavioral Feedback and Consensual Validation
Eighth Meeting

> Wife A: My husband and I have a problem we want to bring up.
> Husband A: That's right. We want your help.
> Therapist: Is this what you called me about yesterday evening?
> Couple A: Yes.
> Therapist: Don't you think the whole group can help you? (Keeping process within the group)
> Wife A: Well, maybe . . . but we really want to know what you think about it.
> Therapist: Go ahead.
> Husband A: Well, as we told you yesterday . . .
> Wife A: (Interrupts) I'm supposed to talk. (Brief squabble—continuing:) Our friend Harry called yesterday. He asked if he could come for dinner. Well, he's with us no more than five minutes and he's trying to push stuff on us, and you know what? He gives our daughter some free to sniff. Well, if we don't take any we lose one of our oldest and best friends; if we do, we don't know where it will lead us. That's when we called you. You told us to tell him we wanted his friendship without his merchandise. We couldn't do it.
> Therapist: Tell everyone what happened.
> Wife A: Well, I pretended that we just heard that my father-in-law was sick.
> Husband A: Yeah, and we left Harry standing there in the kitchen as the three of us ran out of the house. (The group applauds)
> Therapist: Well, it looks like you found your own way out of the dilemma. That was really quick thinking. That was a brilliant move. Has this happened to anyone else in the group? (Feedback) . . .
> Therapist: Well, you see, you aren't the only ones struggling with

this. Let's role-play the situation. Mr. A., you be Harry, and I'll play you . . .

The group offers the drug addict a place to try out new behaviors. Since behavior is learned, generally through role-modeling, the group leader as the prime role model offers a behavioral set to mimic. Conscious mimicry, as Yalom has noted (17), "is an especially unpopular concept as a creative mode since it suggests a relinquishing of individuality—a basic fear of many group patients." The drug addict therefore quickly rejects attempts at prescribing behavior. Yet it is precisely a structured behavior set that is needed. The therapist, then, must help the addict approach an acceptable behavioral response strategy, leaving its ultimate form to the client. Addicts, not unlike other clients, are much more likely to follow through on behavior when the decision or choice remains in their control and when they retain responsibility. In that way the addict-clients use their own feedback to alter their input into the group and thus have a share of the input (process) and ultimate output (behavior change). Successful outcome and channeled control increase the consensual validation of self-worth and integrity, decreasing the chance of sliding back to the addictive depreciating life style (5).

Treatment in a Nondependent Relationship and Distance from Authority
Fourteenth Meeting

Therapist (to women): Do you see what it really means if your husband starts working? (Reflection)

Wife A: Everything will be fine; plenty of money. (Denial)

Wife B: We'll have less money, we made more money on the streets. (Reality—groping with the moral issue)

Therapist: You all married inadequate guys. There must be a reason why you married your husbands.

Wife A: I loved him.

Wife B: We had a habit in common.

Husband A: What else could we talk about?

Husband B: Well, I'm not bad in bed (laughter). (Attempts at intimacy)

Therapist: When you are working things might be different. (To men:) What are you going to want?

Wife C: Yeah, what's he going to demand this time? (Persecution)

Husband C: You aren't kidding. I'll change things around here. (Macho)

Wife A: When he'll go away to work, I'll miss him. We are so close. (Rescuer)

Husband A: Why don't you go to work? (Persecutor) (Uproar—conversation got too close).

Therapist: This is a delicate subject. Let's help each other look at this. Let's pair off to discuss why we want to avoid this subject and get back together in five minutes. (Distance the relationship)

Groups spread dependency relationships over a number of individuals. First, the dependency is mutual. Mutual dependency leads to mutual trust and interdependence. Addicts are caught in the dependency triangle, featuring the overfunctioning mate (persecutor), the underfunctioning addict (victim), and the rescuing helper. These roles continually change, particularly when all three members, including the therapist, are themselves addicts. The dispersal of the dependency relationships helps to distance the addict from intense encounters with the therapist, who is thus helped to avoid becoming the rescuing part of this devastating triangle (17).

GROUP SELECTION

Perhaps the most important aspect dictating success is the initial membership of the group. The agency itself most often handles only drug-related problems, thus restricting intake to a group that is homogeneous, at least as to drug use. Drug addicts are not welcome in many psychotherapeutic or growth groups. Research supports the importance of having groups within fairly analogous socioeconomic and contemporary age ranges and of keeping the size between eight and eighteen to maximize social interaction. An exception to the age limitation occurs in the case of multifamily group sessions or other groupings focusing upon problems between the generations.

The issue of whether drug addicts should be placed only with other drug addicts or with clients facing dissimilar problems is often debated (10, 11). Placing the drug addict in a homogeneous group increases the likelihood of contacts in the deviant subculture. Placing the addict in a group with non–drug addicts may be ill-advised, for the addict may not be accepted or may be destructive in the group. In reality, there is little purpose in discussing the heterogeneous alternative since time and expense, agency fears, and therapists' lack of training and experience dictate homogeneous groups. Where heterogeneous groups have been used, a number of clinicians have reported that drug addicts make significant contributions in the early phase of the group's development but take on destructive interpersonal roles and eventually flee from the group as it progresses. This rarely occurs in a homogeneous group, but then the homogeneous group has a more difficult time progressing into the working stages of treatment. It jells more quickly than the heterogeneous one, becomes more cohesive, and offers immediate support to the group members. Direct results of this support include better attendance, less conflict, and symptomatic relief.

Phases of Group Development and Worker's Role

Every group proceeds through similar developmental phases, from planning and orientation stages, in which inclusion and group formation are at issue; to the exploring and testing stage, in which control, conflict, and dominance are at issue; to the use of the group as a problem-solving medium, when cohesion, affection, and work are at issue; to the termination stage, in which autonomy and independence are the main issues (6, 9, 10, 11, 17). Leadership behavior that is appropriate at one stage of therapy may be quite inappropriate at another. At the initial stages, the therapist must provide support and structure, helping to provide an atmosphere of trust. Confrontation, not support, may be appropriate at a later stage, but it is certainly inappropriate at the beginning of the group's development.

The therapist must quickly deal with the trust issue. Risk-taking is a strong barrier to overcome. Through active "use of self," the therapist takes risks. The group members learn to imitate this behavior. The therapist knows that soon enough the trust between group members will be violated. Again, utilizing the "here and now," this breakdown of trust is brought to the surface. It becomes grist for the mill: A cardinal rule of the drug culture is never to inform on the others, and this is broken in the group. The confrontation begins, and feelings are brought to the surface. Clients learn it is alright to express feelings again. Since they need to be resocialized, to learn to express feelings and feel pain, the leader becomes a very important model. The group members begin to approach problems by considering what the therapist or other group members would think or do in such a situation. Thus, the imitative behavior takes hold. Successful patients adopt the complex value system of the therapist. Initially, this was done to receive approval; now the clients learn that these imitative behaviors bring favorable feedback; increased acceptance leads to increased self-concept and self-esteem.

The dropout rate for most clients occurs at the point where the "real" work begins—the problem-solving intimacy stage. There are those who believe that drug addicts cannot deal with intimacy issues and must therefore drop out or else retard the group's development. Flanzer believes that the addict can achieve this high level of interaction only a considerable time after cessation of his drug activity. For one reason, the addict may be facing long-lasting or recurring drug-induced distortions of reality and needs time to recuperate. In addition, the drug addict originally turned to drugs out of a need to avoid the pain of intimacy. High levels of social interaction awareness are predicated on having satisfied the more basic needs and having learned or completed the tasks of earlier psychosexual development. The drug addict has not done this. The group serves to "catch members up." It grants them the opportunity to progress toward high-order tasks (5).

Twenty-Third Meeting: Planned Discussion on Parenting with Children Present

Therapist: Who makes the meals?

Children of E: (nine-year-old and seven-year-old) We do. When we eat.

Therapist: Explain!

Children: Well, we eat whatever we find in the refrigerator. Whenever we are hungry.

Therapist: Do you eat leftovers?

7-year-old: Well, we eat what Grandma has left for us. (Child of E)

8-year-old: Our Grandma does the same thing. (Daughter of B)

Therapist: Do you eat together?

9-year-old: I usually get my brother and we eat watching TV. (Daughter of E)

Therapist: When do you eat with your parents?

9-year-old: When we're at Grandma's.

8-year-old: Same here. (B)

Wife E: Well, they are never there when you want to feed them.

Wife B: Yeah, and you can never get them to bed.

8-year-old: I won't go to bed until you do. that way I'm sure you won't run out on us again.

Drug addicts' "need levels" tend to be on a lower plane of Flanzer's model.* The addict cannot discuss the need for better communication with his or her spouse when physical or economic safety is still at stake. The same is true of every member of the family (4, 15). The worker/therapist must "begin where the client group is," helping the group climb up the ladder of human needs. Thus, discussion and role-playing of job interviews, parenting, and meal-planning may be the work of the group and can be in every way as therapeutic as discussion of the transference relationship between group members.

In review, then, drug addicts are described as benefiting from group work and treatment. They are best seen in homogeneous groups, according to Flanzer, until they are comfortable enough to work with highly charged intimacy issues. The group offers support while providing feedback and fostering independence. While not a panacea for all

---

*See pp. 120ff.

drug addicts, therapy groups, whether alone or in conjunction with other approaches, have been shown to have a meaningful impact.

Comment

In this chapter, we described the evolution of group therapy approaches to drug abusers, most always heroin addicts. A brief overview touched on the efforts of early pioneers in such settings as the Riverside Hospital, the two Public Health Service Hospitals at Lexington and Forth Worth, and in probation and parole systems to deal with the acting-out behavior and resistance of such patients. This was followed by the widespread use of encounters in the ex-addict-directed therapeutic communities such as Synanon, Daytop Village, and Phoenix House. This discussion was followed by the author's description of his own experiences at the Lincoln Hospital in the South Bronx, where he conducted groups of cyclazocine and methadone patients and their spouses. The numerous problems and issues involved were detailed.

From here, we moved to present two models for treating groups of drug abusers: the Flanzer-McBroom model, which for the first time breaks down the four different kinds of groups most frequently encountered and the techniques for dealing with them; and the Abrahms model, which is based on cognitive-behavioral thinking. This was followed by a consideration of couples therapy as a natural transition from multiple family therapy. Case examples were cited from an extended couples group conducted by Dr. Flanzer. In the following chapter, we shall discuss family therapy per se—its evolution and rationale; its varied approaches and techniques; and its applications to substance abuse, including alcoholism. Finally, we shall present case illustrations of its use as practiced by Dr. Kaufman and his associates.

References

1. Abrahms, J. L. "A Cognitive-Behavioral Versus a Non-Directive Group Program for Opioid-Addicted Persons: An Adjunct to Methadone Maintenance." *International Journal of the Addictions,* 14, No. 4 (1979): 503–511.
2. Aprill, F. A. "Skills Workshop: Relaxation Training as an Adjunct to Drug Abuse Treatment." Paper delivered at National Drug Abuse Conference, Seattle, Wash., April 3–8, 1978.
3. Brill, L. "Drug Addiction." In *Encyclopedia of Social Work.* 17th Ed. Washington, D.C.: NASW, 1977.
4. Brill, L., and L. Lieberman. *Major Modalities in the Treatment of Drug Abuse.* New York: Behavioral Publications, 1972.

5. Flanzer, J. P. "Family-Focused Management: Treatment of Choice for Deviant and Dependent Families." *International Journal of Family Counseling,* Vol. 6, No. 2. New York: Brunner-Mazel, 1978.
6. Flanzer, J. P. Group treatment of drug addicts. Private communication to author, March 1980. Unpublished.
7. Flanzer, J. P., and F. A. Aprill. "A Diagnostic Treatment Model for Effective Group Treatment of Drug Abusers." *Journal of Psychedelic Drugs,* Vol. 9, No. 2, April–June 1977.
8. Jaffe, J. H., and L. Brill. "Cyclazocine, a Long-Acting Narcotic Antagonist: Its Voluntary Acceptance as a Treatment Modality by Narcotic Abusers. *International Journal of the Addictions,* Vol. 1, No. 1, Jan. 1966, pp. 99–123.
9. Kaufman, E., and P. N. Kaufman. "From Multiple Family Therapy to Group Therapy." In *Family Therapy of Drug and Alcohol Abuse.* E. Kaufman and P. N. Kaufman, eds. New York: Gardner Press, 1979.
10. Laskowitz, D.; M. Wilbur; and A. Zucker. "Problems in the Group Treatment of Drug Addicts in the Community: Observations on the Formation of a Group." *International Journal of the Addictions,* 3, No. 2: 361–379.
11. J. H. Lowinson, and I. Zwerling. "Group Therapy with Narcotic Addicts." In *Groups and Drugs.* H. I. Kaplan and B. J. Sadock, eds. New York: E. P. Dutton, 1973.
12. McBroom, E. *Socialization and Social Casework.* New York: Columbia University Press, 1970.
13. Miller, P. M. "Behavioral Treatment of Drug Addiction: A Review. *International Journal of the Addictions,* 8, No. 3: 511–519.
14. Rasor, W. "The U.S. Public Health Service and Its Institutional Treatment Program for Narcotic Addicts at Lexington, Ky." Chapter 1 of *Major Modalities in the Treatment of Drug Abuse.* New York: Behavioral Publications, 1972.
15. Reiner, B. S., and Kaufman, I. *Character Disorders in Parents of Delinquents.* New York: Family Service Association of America, 1959.
16. Wolpe, J., and A. A. Lazarus. *Behavior Therapy Techniques: A Guide to the Treatment of Neuroses.* New York: Pergamon Press, 1966.
17. Yalom, L. D. *The Theory and Practice of Group Psychotherapy.* New York: Basic Books, 1970.

CHAPTER 10

Family Therapy

THE READER WILL NOTE that some of the distinctions among the different forms of group and family therapy are arbitrary. Thus, couples therapy is frequently considered in conjunction with, and as an outgrowth of family therapy, as the Kaufmans do in their book *Family Therapy of Drug and Alcohol Abusers.* (10). This chapter dwells solely on the family unit, in both multiple-family and single-family substance abuse therapy, in order to separate out and highlight the various approaches being used.

It is fairly well established today that work with the entire family is essential if we are to understand and treat any individual member of that family (1, 2, 3, 4, 7, 9, 11). Our thinking has moved from viewing a problem as solely within the patient to tracing it to the relationship with other family members and understanding that these members are involved in a shared psychopathology with the "identified patient," who serves not only as a scapegoat but as the family agent helping to maintain the family balance and homeostasis. Through a process of "transactional dynamics," the family, apart from being viewed as a pathological entity, has also been seen as containing the potential for encouraging beneficial change and individuation among its various members (2). This is as true for families of drug abusers as for other families. In the 1950s and 1960s, I. Chein and D. L. Gerard thought that families of addicts contributed to the personality defects of their drug-abusing members. Their studies found clear-cut differences between addict families and control groups (6).

In almost all addict families, there was a disturbed relationship ("emotional divorce") between the parents. The mother generally became the most important figure in the child's life, with the father appearing as a shadowy and inadequate or less involved person. The homes

133

were in many ways "far less wholesome" than those of the control group.

Bowen's work in the 1950s at the Clinical Center of the National Institute of Mental Health is also of interest (3). He drew up a paradigm of "schizophrenogenic" families—i.e., families that produce one or more schizophrenic children. The trouble with this model was that it seemed equally valid for families of narcotic addicts, alcoholics, delinquents, gastro-intestinal and colitis cases (as reported by Melitta Sperling), and obesity cases (as described by Hilda Bruch). This raised the difficult issue of "choice of neurosis": why, with seemingly identical family constellations and often social situations, does one person become a narcotic addict, another an alcoholic, and a third a colitis case or a schizophrenic (4)?

Boszormenyi-Nagy, at the Eastern Pennsylvania Psychiatric Institute, felt that involvement of the entire family in treatment gives the therapist the opportunity to study directly the "secret, warded-off feelings which had hitherto either been projected, expressed symbolically or acted out." The families studied were found to have their own internal communications network where "family myths" could be established, shifting alliances formed, and hidden games played out (2). In this context the symptoms of the "scapegoated patient could be comprehended as a logical and coherent expression of the family maladaptation." Pathological behavior was understood as not limited to the patient but observable in all family members. The roles of "sick" and "well" members shifted as the family homeostasis required. The behavior of any one member could be influenced by the "important others" in the family who were in a position to gratify or frustrate. What had started out as a study of the transactional processes in schizophrenic families was soon discovered to be valid for families of addicts, alcoholics, delinquents, and acting-out "character disorders" generally. It was no longer the individual but the family as a biosocial unit that needed to become the primary object of investigation.

The revolutionary concept of treating the entire family has led to a variety of approaches and techniques, which nevertheless share a core understanding and framework. The five basic modes usually delineated are psychodynamic, structural, communications, experiential, and behavioral (11).

Psychodynamic therapy, espoused by Ackerman, Bowen, Boszormenyi-Nagy, and others, uses history to uncover situations inappropriately being applied to the present, creating change through insight (1, 2, 3). It is based on the psychoanalytic belief that we need to "uncover" the past in order to understand its hold on the present and resolve the current problems. There is emphasis, therefore, on eliciting history, uncovering past events, and using this information to deal with current problems.

Structural family therapy, of which Minuchin and Stanton are the founders and prime advocates, focuses on patterns of family interaction and communication and attempts to influence these patterns directly. Past history and insight are deemphasized, with the major emphasis placed on changing current interactions. The therapist also attempts to set boundaries and to restructure the family, often by redefining generational boundaries between parents and offspring. A basic tool used is the "genogram," a pictorial chart of the people involved in a three-generation relationship system, which marks all significant physical, social, and psychological dysfunctions in the family (11).

Communications therapy is the approach advocated by Satir, Bateson, and Haley, who see the patient's symptoms as a communication to the family and as evidence that more appropriate forms of communication are blocked. One of the earliest concepts advanced by these theorists was the "double bind," first demonstrated in families of schizophrenics. Here, two different messages are given simultaneously, often one verbal and the other nonverbal. The receiver of the messages is intimately involved with the sender. The messages are mutually exclusive, and the receiver is not permitted to comment on the double bind. Thus, a mother may repeatedly indicate that she wants her daughter to be assertive and successful but will simultaneously strongly discourage any signs of assertiveness in the girl and foster feelings of helplessness, dependency, and failure. For drug abusers the double message may be more overt and less confusing than for schizophrenics. The goal of communications therapy is to correct discrepancies in communication by having messages clearly stated, clarifying meanings by permitting feedback and other means (11).

Experiential therapy entails dealing with the immediate moment of experience between the therapist and the family. Whitaker explains that the therapist must be involved in a real human encounter with substantial self-disclosure on his part (9).

Behavioral therapy is the approach espoused by Malout, Alexander, and Stuart. They believe that a parent's responses to a child perpetuate his undesirable behavior. The parent must be taught extinction of those responses and how to give reinforcement for desired behavior (10).

Kaufman bases his work with drug families, first on the assumption that drug addiction and alcoholism are behavioral problems (11, 12, 14). This concept leads to the need for treatment methods that will help the patient and family "unlearn" the conditioned behavioral patterns and patterns of social reinforcement. Treatment must be a mutually active process in which the patient takes responsibility for his or her behavior and for changing it. Primary to this behavior is the family. In thinking about the family, we need to extend our perspective beyond the parent-child-sibling constellation and think of intergenerational family structures and multiple family relations as well as the larger social network. Treatment is a complex process that must deal with "family subsystems," such as the spouse subsystem, the sibling subsystem, and individual members of the family (11, 12, 14).

In the family, the drug addict is the symptom carrier of the family's dysfunction and helps maintain the family homeostasis (5). The addict reinforces the parents' need to control and continue parenting, yet finds such parenting inadequate. Parental drug and alcohol abuse are common. Ziegler-Driscoll, at the Eagleville Hospital and Rehabilitation Center in Pennsylvania, finds similarities between the families of alcoholics and of drug dependents with regard to their "myths," their identified roles, their family dynamics, and their prevalence of substance abuse. She describes the initial steps in both relatives groups and conjoint family therapy as follows:

1. Establishing rapport with each family member ("joining")
2. Defining the group's expectations of family sessions
3. Distancing emotionally to replace overreactivity, as in educating families about addiction in order to correct misinformation and distortions
4. Formulating an appropriate course of action for the family, with the consensus of all participants, if the subject returns to drug use
5. Detaching the parent or other participating relative from the subject's addiction problem and placing responsibility for the consequences of the addictive behavior on the substance abuser (16).

Ziegler-Driscoll contends that multiple family therapy is a particularly suitable technique for drug abusers and their families. It can be used in any treatment setting but is most successful in residential settings, where the family is more available and accessible (16).

Flanzer, reviewing the concept of family therapy as applied to drug abuse, reports that research has begun to prove that alcoholic families are not unique populations and that wives of alcoholics have essentially the same range of personality as is found in the population at large (8, 9). He cites studies showing that drug-abuse families are surprisingly similar in their decision-making patterns to other "abnormal" groupings such as families of schizophrenics, delinquents, and other maladjusted persons. Most of our information has been based on clinical descriptions provided by practitioners rather than on research, which might shed light on why these families "choose" drug abuse rather than other disturbed behavior. This is still poorly understood.

According to Flanzer, four categories of explanation for such drug-abusing families have usually been delineated (9).

1. *Inadequate internal family development.* This refers to the family climate or ambience and the fact that one or both of the parents may themselves be drug abusers. The characteristics of such families with a drug-abusing adolescent are:

  a. Poor relationships between the parent and the child of the same sex
  b. Severe marital dysfunction and overinvolvement between the adolescent and one parent
  c. Current or past alcohol or drug abuse by the parents
  d. Dysfunctional family communication and alienation
  e. Problem symptoms in children other than the identified patient

2. *Family systems and role imbalance.* Drug abuse may meet the entire family's needs, so that removal of the addiction may mean only symptom displacement onto another family member. In some families the well-being of other family members depends on the alcoholic's continued drinking; in others, the nondrinking member begins to decompensate as the drinking member gets better. Spouses often seek to sabotage treatment, and drinking relapses are frequently caused by the reentry of the recovered alcoholic into a family that has not changed. Some studies show that alcohol interaction patterns provide a stabilizing rather than a disruptive influence on the couple's relationship and represent attempts to deal with family issues that cannot be approached during sober periods. The drinking may also distract attention from the underlying conflicts. Most families use shifting alliances or shifts that are dysfunctional when they become overly rigid. Wives may adopt a succession of roles, becoming alternately "rescuers," "persecutors," and "dummies" (15).

3. *Selected socialization variances within the family.* This means simply that certain social conditions may be encouraging drug abuse among particular groups and individuals, a subject considered in earlier chapters.

4. *An all-encompassing, psychosocial-interactive approach.* There are many interacting antecedents that can cause drug abuse in families and influence a drug abuser's effect on his/her children. This ties in with the concept of multicausation of any dysfunctional behavior (4, 7, 8, 9).

Regarding treatment, Flanzer notes that families typically react to substance abuse dysfunctioning with denial and avoidance; then by sporadic attempts at resolution, with alternating periods of withdrawal and social isolation; and finally by breaking down into further disorganization and despair. In therapy various modalities may be used, including individual, conjoint, couples groups, and multiple family treatments in a variety of settings. Treating even one or two family members is useful, since a change in any member of the system can affect the entire system. Alcohol-abusing families usually have problems in at least four areas: the provision of a normal growth and development environment; the establishment of clear and consistent behavioral role models; the development of positive communications and relationship models; and mastery of interpersonal relationships, especially in the area of intimacy attainment. Family treatment is the preferred modality, because it exposes existing marital conflicts, provides support for the nonalcoholic spouse, offers opportunities for the partners to work on problems together, makes for greater commitment to treatment because of the partners' common goals, prevents the scapegoating of any partner, and offers opportunities for more objective perception of personal behavior and interactions. Similar goals can be postulated for families with other drug addictions.

Two General Modes of Family Therapy

MULTIPLE FAMILY THERAPY

Like Ziegler-Driscoll, Kaufman prefers the residential therapeutic community as a setting for treating multiple families because the identified patient is drug-free, the general situation is more relaxed, and the families are often required to join the therapy as a precondition for visiting privileges (11). The resulting "group" may include all the families in the therapeutic community or only four or five closely matched families. The group is usually seated in a large circle, with co-therapists seated at equal distances to permit observation of the total group. They begin the session by having the members introduce themselves and state their names and family roles. A group member describes the purposes of the group and the need to communicate and express feelings honestly. The importance of understanding and changing the familial forces that led to the drug abuse is also explained. Once a particular family has begun to discuss its problems, the other families can identify with the conflicts described, express feelings, offer support, and work on their own conflicts. The informal contacts that take place before and after the group meetings are also important. Therapists mingle and interact with the families at these times.

During the early sessions, the families are encouraged to articulate the pain they have experienced at having a drug abuser in the family. They discuss their loneliness and isolation and describe the ways in which they have been manipulated by their children. The families are encouraged not to repeat these patterns. Following the ventilation of anger and resentment, strategies for change are introduced, with the group providing support. As the therapy progresses, the role of the family in producing and perpetuating the abuse of drugs is gradually explored. Patterns of mutual manipulation and coercion are identified. Confrontation and encounter are used in the service of the structural change. The family's need to perpetuate the addict's dependent behavior through scapegoating, distancing, overprotection, or infantilization is discouraged, and new methods of relating are fostered. The parents experience guilt and shame as they focus on their own role and need help in resolving their feelings constructively, without pulling the child out of treatment. This is accomplished, in part, by presenting drug dependency as a family problem in which there can be no scapegoats. Families learn to express love and anger, often for the first time. The identified patient acts as the barometer of the family's functioning: If he or she becomes worse, it is assumed that the entire family is under greater pressure and is moving toward a destructive response. The patient is helped to deal with his or her share of the problem through encounters with his peers in the therapeutic community. Homework tasks are assigned to reinforce the family's structural changes. Beyond this, the therapy focuses on dysfunctional communication. Members of the extended family, including grandparents, friends, and lovers are brought in wherever it is possible and relevant to do so.

CASE EXAMPLE*

The ten families and three therapists were grouped and introduced themselves. In this group, four families were actually worked with intensively, but the remaining families identified strongly with them.

The first family worked with consisted of the identified patient (IP), a twenty-seven-year-old Italian male, his older brother, mother, father, and wife. The mother dominated the family and its communication. The father was crippled and unable to work, so the mother had assumed the financial support of the family. It emerged that the father did not take care of his physical health because of his worry over his addict son. The group then pressured the father to make a dental appointment, and when he was vague about this, they exerted pressure on him to make a commitment, which he did. The son experienced his guilt and began to cry, stating that he still needed his father. His mother cried in response to her son's tears, and the three of them embraced. We learned that the IP, his wife, and his son ate most of their meals at the mother's house prior to treatment. They were continuing this pattern on weekend passes, and the wife and child were eating their meals there during the week. The wife and child were given the task of eating most meals at home during the week,

---

*Adapted with permission of authors and publisher from E. Kaufman and P. N. Kaufman, *Family Therapy of Drug and Alcohol Abusers* (New York: Gardner Press, 1979).

and the nuclear family was asked to eat in its own home three out of four weekends. The mother and father readily agreed to reinforce this individuation. The IP and his wife embraced, bringing tears to the eyes of most group members.

The second family on which we focused consisted of a twenty-three-year-old resident, his mother and father. This family was also Italian, as were two others. We worked with them to consolidate an insight from a previous session. They had devastatingly insulted their son and denied doing so. They had been shown the sequence on videotape to break through their denial. They accepted that they had devastated him, and in getting in touch with their anger at him they were able to refrain from putting him down in this session. The group also pressured them to involve their drug-abusing daughter in therapy.

A third family consisted of the identified patient, a thirty-four-year-old Irish male, a younger sister and brother. The mother had been quite active in MFT (multiple family therapy) but did not attend this session because the family had moved away. The father had never been present but was frequently discussed because of his pattern of severe withdrawal. The father had not left his bedroom in three years and never came out when his son visited. In this session, the son realized how much he had identified with his father's emotional isolation, even to a point of duplicating his posture. He was helped to recognize and experience the rigid control system. His anger towards his father would be a subject for future group work. He also realized how he had attempted to be a father to his younger siblings to the point of neglecting his own needs. The sister reached out to him and partially broke through his isolation with her poignant plea. Another resident who was attending the group with his mother identified heavily and sobbed about not being closer to his own sister. He was asked to talk to the first resident's sister as if she were his own. In doing so, he reached a deep level of yearning and anguish. His mother reached out to him and began to rock him. To diminish his infantilization, the therapist asked the mother not to rock him. Freed from his mother, he was able to sob heavily about missing his sister and his guilt in pushing her away. We returned to the Irish family, but were still unable to break through the IP's emotional isolation. It was pointed out that it was difficult for him to express feelings because of his identification with his father and his need to remain the big brother who had no weaknesses.

Single-Family Therapy

According to Kaufman, the starting point of treatment is the diagnostic family "map" used to help organize the material and set goals (13). Therapeutic tactics usually involve "coupling" or "joining," to enhance the therapist's leverage within the family, and "change production," designed to change dysfunctional sets. There are three types of coupling techniques:

Maintenance entails supporting the family structure and behaving according to the family's rules in order to reduce family stress. This includes supporting areas of family strength, rewarding members, affiliating with a family member, supporting a threatened member, and explaining problems.

Tracking involves adopting the content of a family's communications and using its special language to reinforce the therapist's ideas and objectives. The therapist makes the family's rules work in the direction of his goals for the family.

Mimesis involves adopting the family's style and affect as reflected by the family's actions and ideas. Thus, if the family uses humor, the therapist will use it too, but without the double binds; if they touch, so will he; if they smoke or eat, he will join them.

Unlike the coupling techniques, change production entails a challenge to the family's homeostasis and a restructuring of the family "sets." The starting point is the therapeutic contract, with the therapist and family agreeing on what they consider the workable issues. The therapist may begin with problems which test the family's resilience, resistance to stress, and ability to change. A common example involves disengaging a severely enmeshed mother from the family, excluding members from attending sessions, or having them sit outside the family circle or behind a one-way mirror. Another method is "actualizing family transaction patterns" ("enactment"). Patients are instructed to talk directly to each other instead of talking about each other. They are required to enact and relive transactional patterns rather than describe them. This can be done through role-playing and other devices such as seating arrangements, which reveal much about alliances, coalitions, and antagonisms. The seating may be shifted to create or strengthen boundaries.

Application to Family Therapy with Alcoholics

In a private communication to the author, Dr. Kaufman explains why he shifted to work with alcoholics after twenty years of work with drug abusers (14). Since about half the drug-dependent patients he worked with had at least one parent with problematic drinking, focusing on the family system from the aspect of the alcoholic parent was of value for present or future drug abusers as well as for alcoholics. "The development of family treatment interventions for alcoholism has paralleled the development of the conceptual framework of alcoholism as a family system problem. The first family treatment approaches were developed ten years ago in social work agencies and were primarily based on individual casework methods. This was followed by marital therapy of alcoholic couples. A variant on this theme, recently, has been the joint hospitalization of marital couples, although only one is alcoholic. Later, group therapy for the wives was developed. This was followed by group therapy of alcoholic couples. Currently there is a focus on specific family therapy of whole families, with alcoholism as a problem focus."

In working with alcoholics and their families, the therapist is faced with a unique problem, that of "wet" and "dry" family systems. A "wet" system is one in which the alcoholic continues to drink problematically; while a "dry" system is one where active drinking is not a problem, but the family's problems continue. Some therapists, particularly those who work in A.A.-oriented programs, will only work with dry systems. This should not be a precondition of treatment with family systems in our opinion since many families with a drinking alcoholic who is resistant to treatment desperately need help. A dry system is always preferable; however, it may be an unreasonable expectation for many families at the onset of treatment. In all families, the therapist should suggest measures to effect a dry state, at least temporarily; and in some instances, the therapist should insist on these measures.

"ACHIEVING A DRY SYSTEM"

If the alcoholic is drinking so severely that he or she is unable to attend sessions without being under the influence and/or functioning is severely impaired, then the first principle is to interrupt the pattern of drinking. Thus, the first goal is to persuade the family to pull together to initiate detoxification. This may be done on an outpatient basis, but if the drinking is severe, it may require immediate short-term hospitalization. If the drinking is only moderately severe or intermittent, then the family should be offered alternatives to initiate a temporary alcohol-free state. These should include social detoxification centers, Alcoholics Anonymous, Antabuse, and, very rarely, minor tranquilizers. Antabuse should not be given to a family member for daily distribution, as this tends to reinforce the family's being locked into the alcoholic's drinking or not drinking. Minor tranquilizers are discouraged because they tend to become a part of the problem rather than a solution. Appropriate medication for treatment of that *minority* of alcoholics who drink because of their underlying affective or other psychotic disorders may also help produce a dry system. If the alcoholic refuses to initiate abstinence, then we are limited to working with the wet system.

"WORKING WITH THE WET SYSTEM"

Since the wet system is a reality, the therapist should have techniques available to work with such families. When a member arrives at a session intoxicated, the therapist should not deal directly with this problem. Rather he or she should ask the sober spouse and family members to deal with the intoxicated person. This offers an excellent opportunity to observe how the family interacts during one of the most critical phases of family system function. In subsequent sessions, this behavior can be reexamined. In general, it is easier to ask the hyperfunctioning partner (sober) to change than the underfunctioning (alcoholic) individual. [14]

To illustrate these concepts, Dr. Kaufman and his assistant, Ms. Jane Roschman, prepared the following two cases.

CASE 1: THE K. FAMILY

Mr. K., forty-two, professional man
Mrs. K., forty, housewife
Jennifer, sixteen
Jeff, fourteen
Katie, twelve

This case is an interesting example of therapy focused on an individual family in the context of multiple family treatment. Mr. K. is a recovering alcoholic. The presentation illustrates the various attitudes and roles assumed by his wife and children as well as the role of faulty communication. There is need for better individuation of the children. Auxiliary aid in the form of AA is drawn upon. There is a progressive move from multiple family therapy to couples therapy for the parents.

At the time the K. family entered treatment, Mr. K had been sober for three years. Mr. K. had a history of heavy drinking in the past, which had begun to affect his family life and marriage to the point where Mrs. K. threatened to leave him if he did not stop drinking. Mr. K. complied and quit "cold turkey." He had never attended A.A. or been in therapy prior to attending our outpatient program, and the marriage had continued to deteriorate despite his sobriety. Thus Mr. K. is the typical "dry drunk" who continues his behavior even when sober. Mrs. K. regarded therapy as a "last resort" to save her marriage. Mr. K. agreed to attend for the same reason; however, he was not convinced that he was ever really "alcoholic." Mrs. K. had been attending Al-anon for approximately four years and was sophisticated about alcoholism. Mrs. K. described Mr. K's behavior as "the same as before except he has not been drinking."

The two youngest children had little recollection of ever seeing their dad drink. Mr. K. had taken great pains to hide his drinking from the children. The oldest daughter seemed to be the most affected since she was closest to her mother and more tuned in emotionally to her. The family attended a multifamily group once weekly, and the parents attended a couples group on a second night during the week. They seemed to be locked into a fairly rigid system of communication, which was not working well after three and a half years of "sobriety" for Mr. K. It soon became apparent that the children fitted into roles that are typically seen in alcoholic families. The oldest daughter was closest to the mother and took the role of "emotional caretaker" or parental child in the family. The mother–daughter relationship was enmeshed and helped shelter the two younger children from the full impact of the father's drinking and the dysfunctional marital relationship, as well as reinforcing the mother's distance from her spouse. Jennifer was the most openly hostile to Mr. K. and, as emotional caretaker of her younger siblings, often rescued them from conflicts with either parent. She tried hard to please, and her social behavior was very responsible. Outwardly, Jennifer appeared to be sophisticated and "sexy," but inwardly she was a lonely girl who seldom dated and felt very inadequate in many ways.

The middle child, Jeff, was the achiever. He received recognition for achieving in sports and academics. He pleased his dad in these areas, yet emotionally was distant and angry with him. His anger was more passive and would come out in his refusal to do his chores and other expressions of noncompliance. He covered up his feelings with joking and laughter. He seemed closest to his younger sister.

The youngest child, twelve-year-old Katie, fitted the role of "family mascot." She was cute and playful and seldom taken seriously. The only feelings she seemed to feel safe in showing to the family were positive feelings. She helped distract the family from their common pain. This child was brought into treatment only upon urging by the therapists. The family saw Katie as being "no problem." She was the only one who was "okay." However, the family picture would not have been complete without bringing in this child.

Mrs. K. was still openly hostile and angry at her husband for his drinking. Although he had been sober for more than three years, she still blamed him for their "problems." Their sexual relationship had deteriorated over the past three years and this further complicated their problems. Mrs. K. unconsciously used the sophistication she learned at Al-anon to make her husband look bad. She continued to deny for many months that she answered for Mr. K., though she often "put words into his mouth." Although she was perceptive, sensitive, and rather open with her own feelings, she would unconsciously cut off communication by telling Mr. K. that she knew how he felt rather than listening to his feelings. Mr. K. seemed to be emotionally detached from Mrs. K. and was using the children to try to satisfy some of his emotional needs. He buried himself in his work, and his self-esteem was closely related to his job performance. He felt himself to be a failure as a husband and parent. The guilt he carried over from his drinking days remained unresolved during his first three and a half years of sobriety, and this helped to keep him feeling inadequate even after becoming sober.

After six to nine months of multifamily therapy, the faulty communication patterns were brought to the awareness of all family members and change began. The youngest girl learned to be more assertive and occasionally risked expressing negative feelings. The fourteen-year-old son began to tune in to his dad's feelings more and risked sharing his own feelings. We observed in the group that whenever his mother and father achieved unity in setting limits, he would split them apart by bringing up how much his dad's previous alcoholic behavior was like the kids' acting out. This would provoke an escalating argument between them about "old tapes," and the children would go without needed limits. The oldest daughter was finally able to ask her dad for some time of her own with him. She acquired a part-time job and began planning her own future. She stopped worrying about mom's and dad's relationship. Mr. and Mrs. K. slowly stopped fighting about "picky little things" and began to enjoy each other again. Mr. K. finally believed that he was an alcoholic and began working on his guilt in the couples and alcoholic groups that he attended. Mrs. K. realized that she had been misusing her Al-anon training and began to disown her blaming attitude to the point where it gradually disappeared. The family system became more open and flexible, and everyone was released from their rigid roles.

THE THERAPY

The therapy team consisted of male and female co-therapists. The male therapist is a recovering alcoholic, himself sober for eight years. The inclusion of a recovering co-therapist on the team was an important aspect of the treatment. Mr. K. quickly developed an alliance with the recovering male therapist and was able to work through some of his feelings of inadequacy by identification with another male. The major mode of treatment consisted of meeting with the family in a multifamily setting. The number of families varied from three to five. All three K. children attended regularly.

In the initial stages of treatment, the identified problem was the poor relationship between Mr. K. and his sixteen-year-old daughter. Mrs. K.'s role was to identify family problems. Mr. K. tended to minimize these problems but was willing to work on them when Mrs. K. initiated work on particular problems. Jennifer described one problem as, "He yells at me a lot—I don't know why." Mr. K. would reply somewhat apologetically that Jennifer and his wife were right—he did yell at Jennifer a lot. Our method of working on this type of situation was to attempt to get the family or family members to actualize the problem by giving us a specific situation that had arisen recently. Jennifer would usually be able to think of a specific incident. A typical example follows: The family was sitting down to dinner. Dad seemed to be a little grumpy (no one knew why or asked why before sitting down to eat). Dad began to pick on Jennifer for putting too much food on her plate. (Dad would frequently criticize Jennifer for being overweight—he would do the same to his wife—but neither was more than a few pounds overweight.) Jennifer would react in a childlike way by whining and counterattacking about Dad not being so skinny himself and then threaten to leave the table. When this occurred, Mrs. K. would become involved, side with Jennifer, and rescue her by openly being critical of Mr. K. for picking on Jennifer. Mr. K. would then turn his attention to Mrs. K., and a fight would ensue with Mr. K. accusing Mrs. K. of criticizing him in front of the children and not backing him up when he was only trying to help Jennifer to stay on her diet.

The other children had learned to tune out these fights and often had difficulty even remembering the incident. Jennifer would frequently begin to cry during an actualization, and when Jennifer started to cry, Mrs. K. would cry also. Mr. K. would fold his arms, cross his legs and give a long, deep sigh of frustration. The team would then encourage Mr. K. to describe how he was feeling. Mr. K. would usually feel angry. After further probing, Mr. K. would admit to feeling hurt and hopeless about handling these situations successfully and without everyone ending up in tears. Mr. K. felt totally responsible for everyone's bad feelings. He felt that he was the reason why his family was in therapy. Mrs. K. was so enmeshed with Jennifer that she was unable to separate Jennifer's feelings from her own. Mrs. K. stated many times that Jennifer had felt the impact of her father's drinking more than the other children because she was the oldest and had "seen" more. Jennifer was caught in the middle of a dysfunctional marital relationship, and the spouses' conflicts were triangulated to her.

Our contract with them was (1) to strengthen the marital dyad by encouraging them to spend quality time together, and they were given tasks to accomplish this; (2) to become involved in a couples therapy group in order to focus on their relationship; (3) to encourage Jennifer to individuate by reaching outside of the family—that is, by obtaining a job, spending more time with friends, and reinforcing her mature qualities; (4) to strengthen the parental dyad by having Mr. and Mrs. K. sit down and work out mutual disciplinary techniques and make efforts to consult each other on decision-making that related to the children; (5) to encourage Mr. K.'s participation in A.A. and the development of a broader program for himself in order to enhance his sobriety; and (6) to encourage Mrs. K. to reach out of the home to explore alternatives for herself such as a return to school, volunteer work, or employment.

The K.s have been in therapy for one year. Their relationship is now characterized by egalitarian mutuality. They are role models for other group members both as individuals and as a couple. At this point, they are more directly helpful to other families than to themselves except as helping others reinforces their own strengths. This concept is compatible with the very necessary twelfth step of Alcoholics Anonymous.

CASE # 2—THE C. FAMILY

This case illustrates the treatment of problems in the parental dyad as well as in the father-daughter relationship.

CASE 2: THE C FAMILY

Mr. C., forty-four, blue-collar worker in a supervisory position
Mrs. C., forty-two, bookkeeper
Mary, fourteen, natural daughter of Mr. and Mrs. C.
A 25-year-old daughter of Mrs. C. from a first marriage was very involved with the family, yet lived away from home and never attended the sessions.

Mr. C. had been a practicing alcoholic for most of his marriage to Mrs C. When Mr. C.'s job performance began to be affected by his drinking, he decided to admit himself to a hospital for the treatment of alcoholism. This hospital includes an intensive one-week treatment experience for the entire family, which helps prepare families for outpatient work. After four weeks as an inpatient, Mr. C. and his family entered the outpatient program. They attended multifamily therapy one night a week. Mr. and Mrs. C. attended a couples group periodically.

Mrs. C.'s daughter by a previous marriage, Suzie, was not living at home and never attended any therapy sessions, even though the C.'s were urged to bring her into treatment. Suzie was still very much involved with her family and had a great impact on the family system. She was about five years old when Mr. and Mrs. C. married. They both considered Suzie to be "their failure." Suzie began taking drugs as an adolescent and at age twenty-five was still involved with drugs to some degree. They felt she was a bad influence on Mary.

Mary felt close to her half-sister and resented her parents' attitude toward Suzie. She felt her mother was always trying to sabotage their relationship. Mary frequently found herself in the middle of conflicts between Suzie and Mrs. C. Mr. C. took the role of observer and would "analyze" what transactions occurred. He seldom became actively involved in this triangle. He communicated to both daughters through Mrs. C., thus giving Mrs. C. a switchboard role and the power to act as controller of the family. In reality he was controlling in a passive manner. Mrs. C. felt overly responsible for raising both daughters and took out her resentment by overeating. Since Suzie lived away from home, Mary carried the burden of receiving Mrs. C.'s projected feelings of failure for Suzie.

It became apparent that Mrs. C. was a "co-alcoholic" (a facilitator of alcoholism and alcoholic behavior) to Mr. C. and a co-drug-abuser to her oldest daughter. She had been protecting Suzie from many of the consequences of her behavior just as she protected her husband from parental responsibilities and relationship responsibilities.

Mary was a quiet, withdrawn girl who was academically slow. She and Mrs. C. had a mutually enmeshed relationship. One could not feel without the other's having the same intense feeling. Mary was emotionally immature and looked to her mother for approval almost every time she spoke in the group. Mary and Mrs. C. were both overweight. Mr. C. deferred to Mrs. C. in most family matters. He displayed the passive-dependent personality pattern seen in the stereotyped alcoholic.

Mrs. C. quickly became an involved group member. She began to "own" her need to control. She and Mary worked together exploring their emotional dependency. Mary began to be able to assert herself with her mother and to feel safe doing this at home as well as in the group. Mrs. C. was able to get in touch with the many unmet needs she had been feeling in her marital relationship. She had been unable to express hurt and anger at her husband when he had been drinking and had misdirected much of these feelings toward Mary. Slowly Mr. and Mrs. C. began to rebuild their own relationship. A marriage encounter weekend was very helpful in building their dyadic spouse relationship.

Mary and Mr. C. also began communicating more openly. Mr. C. began to recognize that he really did have feelings and experimented with expressing them in the group. Mr. C. still carried around much unresolved guilt and became depressed periodically, which could have been relieved if he had attended the couples and alcoholic groups. As the family communication patterns became more open, Mr. C. was gradually able to receive more emotional gratification from his family. He was urged to begin participation in an alcoholic group. At last report Mrs. C. revealed that Suzie was receiving treatment for her drug abuse.

THERAPY

It soon became apparent that Mr. C. had encouraged his wife and fourteen-year-old daughter to become involved in family therapy because he thought they had many problems to work on. Mr. C. would frequently initiate or identify a problem and then sit back and try to remain uninvolved even to the extent of actually falling asleep on occasion. Upon inquiry, Mrs. C. shared that Mr. C. seldom became involved in "their" fights and separated himself from them. He wanted us to "fix" his family but did not see how he fitted into "their" problem. While he was actively drinking, he would drink after dinner until he fell asleep and seldom was aware of what was going on between Mrs. C. and Mary. Mrs. C. saw her relationship with Mary as the main "problem" in the family. She saw herself as a failure as a mother. She referred to her older daughter as being her biggest "mistake" because Suzie had begun using drugs as a teenager and at age twenty-five was still "fucked up." It seems that Mrs. C. took the majority of the responsibility for the older daughter's problems, because she was not Mr. C.'s natural child and Mrs. C. had encouraged a "hands off" policy concerning discipline of this older daughter. Mr. C. had followed suit with Mary and had established a very peripheral role in her parenting. Mrs. C. resented this greatly but was reluctant to "upset" Mr. C. by bringing this subject up, so she continued to fight with Mary and feel like a failure until she began therapy.

A typical example of a "fight" would go as follows: Mary would ask Mom to take her and a friend somewhere on a Saturday afternoon. Mrs. C.'s first reaction was to gripe and say no and then reluctantly agree. Later on in the day, when Mary would return home, Mrs. C. would still carry the resentment and begin to pick on her. Mary would be confused and not know why Mom was mad and yell back and eventually go to her room and cry. Mr. C. would observe passively. At times he would attempt to lecture either Mrs. C. or Mary on her behavior and try to analyze it. When Mr. C. began to lecture and analyze, our therapy team encouraged him to describe his feelings—as we did for Mrs. C. and Mary. Mrs. C. was usually the first to identify her feelings. In this particular situation she was able to identify her resentment toward Mr. C. for lecturing and analyzing. As the team probed further, we found that Mrs. C. wanted Mr. C. to become more actively involved in the parenting of Mary, yet was reluctant to lose her control over the girl. Mrs. C. was displaying behavior that is quite typical of a co-alcoholic: She wanted to keep control and feared any change in the status quo other than taking away the alcohol. Mr. C.'s behavior until the fifth or sixth month of recovery had remained constant, except that he was no longer drinking.

Treatment goals were: (1) to enlist Mr. C. into a role of actively parenting Mary by teaching him parenting skills through tasks and encouraging Mrs. C. to ask for and reinforce Mr. C.'s active parenting; (2) to strengthen the father–daughter dyad by having father plan occasional outings for them (This was done also to give Mrs. C. some time to herself); (3) to strengthen the marital dyad by planning for Mr. and Mrs. C. to spend more time alone; (4) to reinforce Mrs. C.'s positive qualities and to give her opportunity to express fears and learn to risk showing her vulnerability; and (5) to help Mr. C. to see himself as a feeling person and an important member of the family.

The C. family terminated therapy after one year. Mr. C. remained sober and had begun to show some spontaneous expression of feelings in the group. The marital relationship was greatly enhanced, and Mr. C. was "getting to know" his daughter Mary. The therapy ended with a going away party and included a cake commemorating one year of sobriety and their successful treatment.

References

1. Ackerman, N. W. *Psychodynamics of Family Life.* New York: Basic Books, 1958.
2. Boszormenyi-Nagi, I., and J. L. Framo, eds. *Intensive Family Therapy.* New York: Hoeber Medical Division, Harper & Row, 1965.
3. Bowen, M. "A Family Concept of Schizophrenia." In *Etiology of Schizophrenia.* D. O. Jackson, ed. New York: Basic Books, 1960.
4. Brill, L. "Drug Addiction." In *Encyclopedia of Social Work.* 17th ed. Wash, D.C.: NASW, 1977, 1: 24–38.
5. Cannon, W. B. *The Wisdom of the Body.* New York: Norton, 1932.
6. Chein, I.; D. L. Gerard; R. S. Lee; et al. *The Road to H.* New York: Basic Books, 1964.
7. Flanzer, J. P. "Family-Focused Management: Treatment of Choice for Deviant and Dependent Families." *International Journal of Family Counseling.* Vol. 6, No. 2. New York: Brunner-Mazel, Inc., 1978.
8. Flanzer, J. P. Group treatment of drug abusers. Private communication to author, 1980.
9. Flanzer, J. P. "Treating Drug-abusing Families." Paper presented at the First International Conference on Substance Abuse, Phoenix, Ariz., November 1977.
10. Kaufman, E., and P. N. Kaufman. "From Multiple Family Therapy to Couples Therapy." Chapter 7 in *Family Therapy of Drug and Alcohol Abusers.* E. Kaufman, and P. N. Kaufman, eds. New York: Gardner Press, 1979.
11. Kaufman, E., and P. N. Kaufman. *Family Therapy of Drug and Alcohol Abusers.* New York: Gardner Press, 1979.
12. Kaufman, E., and P. N. Kaufman. "The Application of the Basic Principles of Family Therapy to the Treatment of Drug and Alcohol Abusers." In Kaufman and Kaufman, eds., *Family Therapy of Drug and Alcohol Abusers.*
13. Kaufman, E., and P. N. Kaufman. "Multiple Family Therapy with Drug Abusers." In Kaufman and Kaufman, *Family Therapy of Drug and Alcohol Abusers.*

14. Kaufman, E., and J. Roschman. Family therapy approaches with alcoholics. Private communication to author. March 1980.
15. Steiner, C. *Games Alcoholics Play*. New York: Grove Press, 1971.
16. Ziegler-Driscoll, G. "The Similarities in Families of Drug Dependents and Alcoholics." In Kaufman and Kaufman, eds., *Family Therapy of Drug and Alcoholic Abusers*.

PART III

THE ADJUNCTS OF TREATMENT

CHAPTER 11

Interdisciplinary Collaboration

THE "FIELD" OF DRUG ABUSE did not develop in an orderly, planned fashion but was rather the amorphous result of a variety of pushes and pulls, contingencies and happenstances (1, 2, 6, 7, 8). Much usually depended on the particular interests of individuals and groups: on whether there was community interest in, or resistance to, a particular modality such as chemotherapy or therapeutic communities; on the extent of public alarm about the drug problem; on the interest of governmental agencies in funding programs; and, frequently, on the political climate and public presures.

By the 1960s large numbers of storefront centers serving primarily as information and referral centers had proliferated in areas such as the South Bronx, often without suitable follow-up resources to which a client could be referred for help. Duplicative programs mushroomed, competing with each other for clients and making extravagant claims of success while serious gaps in service remained unfilled. There was limited planning until the city, state, and federal governments intervened to ensure that the "three C's" prevailed: comprehensiveness, continuity, and coordination of services. New York was among the first to set up a statewide coordinating and overseeing agency, known initially as the Narcotic Addiction Control Commission (NACC) in 1967. In 1973 the federal government established the Special Action Office for Drug Abuse Prevention (SAODAP) to serve as the federal coordinating agency for the new "Single State Agencies" (SSAs) to be set up in every state (7). The most recent trend has been to decentralize and regionalize the state so that a full range of integrated services can be provided in each area of the state, tying in closely with mental health and other health services as well

The administrative and other personnel recruited to staff these facilities reflected the same lack of planning and forethought that had characterized the early agencies. Many of the individuals were "professionals" from nonrelevant fields who lacked prior experience in the rehabilitation and treatment of drug abusers. Centers such as the therapeutic communities made use of ex-addicts to serve as role models, counselors, and administrators as part of their "concept" for the new residences. Various professionals were needed for such chemotherapy modalities as methadone maintenance and the narcotics antagonists, along with ex-addicts who had graduated from a prototype facility (3, 4, 6). But problems were raised by the use of doctors, nurses, pharmacists, dentists, and other staff who had had no prior experience with the treatment of drug abuse and had little understanding of the elements of personality organization and behavioral dynamics. Funding agencies were concerned about the staff's lack of administrative know-how and experience and their poor understanding of research and evaluation parameters.

The need for effective interdisciplinary collaboration and for a clearcut definition of roles and responsibilities within each program posed additional problems. There was frequent friction between professionals and paraprofessionals, which interfered with their teaming up in behalf of the client. Paraprofessionals were often ambivalent about working with professionals, on the one hand looking up to them for help because of their advanced training and credentials, yet on the other hand resenting and mistrusting them because of their superior position in the hierarchy of power and control. The professionals found working with these "untrained" members of the team a new experience. Some looked down on them, not recognizing that they had a great deal to offer clients on the basis of having shared experiences on the streets and similar backgrounds so that they could now serve as role models and bridges to treatment for them. Other professionals went to the other extreme, agreeing with the ex-addicts that professionals had nothing to offer clients since they had not themselves experienced the drug scene and drug life. For a long time the needs for staff training, for a better definition of roles and responsibilities, and for administrators who knew how to structure a program and define goals and objectives remained unfulfilled (3, 4, 6, 8).

As public funding became harder to obtain by the 1970s, there was increased emphasis on the need for better administration and evaluation of programs and on "cost effectiveness." Specialized personnel were called for, some with expertise in the new area of "grantsmanship" and in federal–state–city liaison. Programs now needed to justify carefully residential or inpatient treatment (as opposed to ambulatory treatment) if they were to continue receiving their funding as before. A sudden drop in clients could be disastrous to a program, because a certain number of "slots" or client openings was assigned, which had to be kept filled at a certain level to maintain federal funding. Within each program, a core of problem clients emerged who needed more intensive psychological services. More highly trained staff such as psychiatrists, psychologists, and social workers were required to deal with these more troublesome and disturbed cases. More professionals began to appear in the therapeutic communities, and more intensive psychological services were added to many methadone maintenance programs once it was found that at least 25 percent of the patient population became seriously involved with problems of alcoholism and other drugs while stabilized on methadone. Others needed to be treated for serious emotional, including psychotic, problems (4, 6).

Social workers gradually began to serve in a variety of roles in keeping with their training and experience: as community organizers, as supervisors and trainers of other staff, and as community liaisons, intermediaries, and coordinators. Because of their training in counseling, guidance, and personality dynamics they proved especially useful in training indigenous and paraprofessional staff. They could, further, be used in individual and group therapy. Still other areas for social workers were vocational rehabilitation and referral. When funds became scarcer in the 1970s and program administrators needed to curtail staff, difficult decisions had to be made: whether to trim the more expensive professional staff or the paraprofessional workers. Paraprofessionals served as the primary counselors or workers in the early 1960s. For example, they were the main counselors in the Beth Israel–Morris Bernstein Institute Methadone Maintenance Program, with only a few social workers on hand. This was changed as the need for more intensive treatment of the more disturbed patients was recognized and more professionals were added to provide these services. In the therapeutic communities, their "concept" called for the use of ex-addicts who had "graduated" from a residential community to serve as the main administrative and treatment staffs though the facility might be directed overall by a psychiatrist, psychologist, or social worker. More professional personnel were used later to supplement the ex-addict staff. The use of professional and paraprofessional personnel to carry out the treatment responsibilities often led to confusion and friction.

In practice, for effective interdisciplinary collaboration to occur, all staff must have a rational understanding of drug abuse, including behavioral dynamics. The team must have a common perception of how to structure a program; of what the cutoff point must be for limiting a patient's acting-out behavior; of the roles and functions to be assigned to different staff members; what the program's goals are; and what techniques are to be used to achieve them. There should be further consensus on what is success and how it is to be evaluated; how the team should work together in the patient's behalf; who supervises whom; what resources should be available for supervision and training; what the intake process entails; the criteria for acceptance and rejection; where the decision-making responsibility resides; and how differences of opinion are resolved. Previous studies of hospitals and therapeutic communities have demonstrated the importance of the staff's working together harmoniously if the client is to be helped. Subterranean power struggles and differences of approach that are not confronted and resolved inevitably undermine the treatment process.

Different agencies have adopted different approaches to interdisciplinary collaboration as a means of implementing treatment. What follows is a description of how an agency can deal with this issue.

At the Lower Eastside Service Center the social worker is used to

> ... weave together traditional psychoanalytic psychodynamic theory, crisis intervention theory, the provision of concrete social services, and sociocultural factors into an eclectic social work and psychotherapy program, developing treatment plans based on a differential diagnosis. The social worker must be prepared to provide long-term services, feel satisfied with slow progress, work with clients while they are still engaged in drug abuse and antisocial behavior, maintain a caring yet firm attitude with the clients, accept their frequent recidivism before they can progress, cope with the underlying anxiety and depression of the clients and with their acting-out and hostile behavior, do aggressive follow-up, balance on the tightrope between being a surrogate caring and professional worker, and maintain respect and tolerance for the clients even while he is being tested, challenged, or manipulated. The staff as a whole must be close-knit, constantly sharing feelings of frustration and inadequacy through regular staff meetings and in-service training and understanding how to utilize feelings of countertransference and transmute them into therapeutic tools. [2]

These points, offered by Herbert Barish, emphasize the frustrations ordinarily voiced by workers dealing with confirmed drug abusers.

At the Albert Einstein College of Medicine Drug Abuse Program the staff was initially composed of ex-addict counselors who were themselves successful graduates of methadone programs. They had had at least a year of employment experience outside the field of methadone or drug abuse treatment. A high school diploma was required, but some had postsecondary education. The idea behind the hiring of ex-addicts was that they would serve as role models for patients and as interpreters of the addict subculture to the professional staff—especially the doctors, nurses, and social workers. Other community-based paraprofessionals were subsequently hired with some experience in a medical-social agency and an inside knowledge of the South Bronx community (5).

As services in the clinics expanded, degreed counselors with expertise in the areas of education and vocational rehabilitation were hired. Their focus on specific rehabilitative needs was in keeping with the changing profile of the patient population, which grew progressively younger, less motivated, and more deficient in behavior skills. Social workers were then hired to provide more clinically oriented services and to train and supervise counseling staff in recording, psychosocial diagnosis, therapeutic processes, and effective utilization of bureaucratic institutions on behalf of the patients.

The introduction of the newly recruited social workers led to friction and insecurity among the long-term paraprofessional staff. It proved to be threatening because of the greater prestige, training, and therefore authority of the social workers; but also because of the new program requirements, which made it appear that there would be less emphasis on the use of paraprofessionals. This ultimately proved to be the case since, in subsequent layoffs of some of the paraprofessional counselors with greater seniority, the social workers were retained because of the new clinical requirements. [5]

On the other hand, programs in other regions cut corners by recruiting paraprofessional staff rather than professionals because of the scarcity of funds allocated.

Case Illustration of Interdisciplinary Collaboration in a Long-Term Situation

Like the long-term case presented in Chapter 8, this case is offered in considerable detail, at the risk of taxing the reader, because it accurately illustrates the routine "bread-and-butter" cases one finds in most drug-abuse agencies, which call for endless patience on the part of workers and limited expectations of success. The case describes the effective use of a variety of staff to deal with different aspects of the client's problems. Staff apparently collaborated very well in sharing their information and findings in the client's behalf. Treatment included individual and group therapy, the day program and workshop, psychiatric and medical care, and other modes. The staff also effectively supplemented their own resources by calling upon outside agencies wherever indicated: welfare, hospitals, and so on. The bracketed statements are by Herbert Barish, reflecting on the course of treatment (2).

Mr. F., a thirty-two-year-old Italian male, was referred to the Center by the Welfare Department for treatment of alcohol abuse. Mr. F. completed the application and was asked to return the next day to the Orientation Group, whose goal is screening and enhancing motivation. After he attended two O.G. sessions, the group leaders decided to schedule an intake appointment for him. In the Center, each social worker or paraprofessional is assigned responsibility for intake on a rotating basis, including also suitability for a particular patient. The screening interviewer need not be the same person as the intake worker. Both the screening interviewer and the O.G. leaders felt that Mr. F. had very little motivation. He said he had stopped drinking ten days earlier, after spending eight days in a hospital detoxification center. He had recently lost a friend from the effects of excessive drinking. He showed no understanding of what therapy is or can do.

Mr. F. had an eighteen-year history of drug abuse. In that time he had been detoxified four times on an outpatient basis and had never entered any treatment program. Between the ages of eleven and sixteen he had experimented with many substances and continued to use multiple drugs, although heroin and alcohol were his main substances of abuse. He became addicted to heroin at sixteen. At the age of twenty-two he was arrested and convicted for attempted robbery and received a four-year sentence. He served three years and was paroled for the remaining year. Mr. F. said he was wrongly charged. While on parole, he was arrested for purchasing two bags of heroin and was sent to a municipal prison for sixty days and then to a state prison for the remainder of the one-year period of parole. [It is not clear why Mr. F. received such a severe sentence, since he had no other arrests. His own poor attitude may have been a factor. He said later that he had no trouble adjusting to institutional life, and one wonders whether he sought imprisonment as a means of finding structure and safety in his life or possibly of punishing himself.]

Mr. F. was an only child and had grown up in East Harlem. His parents were separated and both were in new common-law relationships. His father was now in California. His grandmother told him that the father had beaten the mother regularly. Mr. F. had completed three years of high school at a technical school. His work record was rather sparse: like his father, he was a drummer and had had a number of "gigs" (jobs) as a young man. He had been involved in a common-law relationship for four years and had one son, who was living with the mother. He hadn't seen the son or wife for several years. [This intake information will need to be reexamined repeatedly in light of later information during the course of treatment. It was later reported by Mr. F. that his grandmother claimed his father had actually beaten his mother to death.]

The intake worker presented the initial information to the Intake Review Committee, noting that Mr. F. was "a drug habituate and not currently a drug addict"; that he used drugs more to handle anxiety, and that he had an "inadequate personality."

PSYCHIATRIC EVALUATION

A psychiatric evaluation was then arranged. Following are excerpts from the initial psychiatric evaluation:

Mr. F. was recently hospitalized for serious medical complications related to alcoholism. Since then he has not drunk for six weeks. He was on the verge of death
then and had a friend who had died recently from alcohol. His fear of surgery and
death have helped him stay drug-free. He used heroin for nine years but claims he
has no "tracks" because they "dried up." The only thing he wants to do vocationally
is play the drums. He feels no need for Antabuse or AA now, because he's stopped on
his own. He is motivated to stop his drinking. His father earlier suggested he move to
California to be with him. This relationship should be explored as well as his feelings
about his mother's and father's separation. Best diagnosis is alcoholism in remission.
His personality is more compatible with that of an alcoholic than an "inadequate
personality."

TREATMENT PLAN

Following the psychiatric evaluation, Mr. F.'s case was again reviewed and a treatment plan outlined. It was felt that his prognosis was poor, anxiety level high, and
insight capability low, but he was currently motivated by the death of a friend from
alcohol abuse. The Intake Team felt they had to provide an alternate life-style opportunity through an intensive multiservice program plan. Mr. F. was therefore assigned
first to individual counseling and also to a group that met four times weekly. He was
to enter the therapeutic day workshop program at a later date and receive psychiatric
evaluation and medication whenever necessary.

TREATMENT: FIRST THREE MONTHS

Mr. F. accepted the treatment plan. During the first months of treatment, he attended
almost all his individual and group sessions. He expressed feelings of helplessness,
anxiety, depression, and hostility. When he saw the psychiatrist, he was placed on
tranquilizers. He made serious efforts to remain "dry." Though he expressed negative feelings about his therapy, he nevertheless followed directions and attended
sessions. He viewed the counselor as "tough" but seemed to want such firmness. By
the end of this three-month period, Mr. F. was being prepared to enter the therapeutic
workshop. One objective here would be to help him start and finish projects. Mr. F.
was also encouraged to move from the welfare hotel room where he was living, since
it was felt that it was exercising a negative influence on him.

SECOND THREE MONTHS OF TREATMENT

During this interval, Mr. F. continued to report regularly for his individual and group
therapy and maintained contact with the psychiatrist. Ventilation became his main
support during this period, with the counselor continuing to be the "tough worker on
the case." Medication continued to be a major support since he had little ability to

understand the therapeutic process and goals. Mr. F. needed many concrete services such as help with his welfare checks, housing, and clothing. The workshop was attempting to help him plan for some future vocational orientation. He remained abstinent from alcohol all this time.

He became upset when a group member left the workshop to enroll in school. Mr. F. felt that he was being left behind and that this had happened to him all his life. A joint session was therefore arranged for the patient with the group leader and his individual counselor. The therapists could begin to make connections between his feelings and his actions. He was told that he must focus on the past relationships and understand how they still influenced him. Mr. F. cried during this session, asked for advice, and agreed to follow it. [This session was useful as confirmation of the therapists' concern as well as in involving Mr. F. more actively in planning his treatment.]

GROUP THERAPY REPORT

At the beginning, Mr. F. was quiet and withdrawn. Shortly afterward, he began interacting. He didn't respond to group material, but to his own agenda. He soon became supportive of the other group members and responsive when this was pointed out to him. The group leader focused on Mr. F.'s family background, and Mr. F. was able to express anger toward his father for beating his mother. He also showed some identification with the father. Mr. F. complained frequently, and the group leader focused on the fact that the complaints were a defense against feeling people's concern for him, which threatened to break down his facade and expose him to feeling. This defense also allowed him to accept direction without taking responsibility. Mr. F. has been better able to talk when tense and anxious, which has strengthened his ability to abstain from alcohol use. He felt other group members were smarter than he and had fears of being tested vocationally. The group experience has been successful thus far and is to be continued.

INDIVIDUAL COUNSELING

The counselor continued to meet with Mr. F. and to focus more on his past. This proved to be very difficult for Mr. F., and the counselor needed to slow his pace. The counselor continued to help him with his concrete problems.

THERAPEUTIC WORKSHOP PROGRESS REPORT

For the second three-month period, Mr. F.'s attendance, time concept, and appearance were good. He was viewed as highly emotional and sensitive. He related well to the staff and other patients and was interested in learning particularly printing, but was slow. He needed a great deal of structure and direction. It was here that he first brought out the details of his mother's having been killed by the father—according to the grandmother. Mr. F. didn't remember school, teachers, peers, or daily activities of the past. His grandmother moved in with him when the mother died. He remembers that the father used heroin with his friends and had constant arguments with the grandmother. He had some fond memories of trips with the father and described his sexual experiences starting at the age of twelve. He now reported that he had a child by a common-law relationship but showed no remorse over not having seen the family for the past six years.

SECOND SIX MONTHS OF TREATMENT

Mr. F. continued to attend his sessions regularly and to cooperate with the treatment program. He was aware that this was helping him avoid self-destructiveness and loneliness. The individual counselor continued to do much intervening and confronting of Mr. F.'s immature reactions and served as a control for Mr. F.'s acting-out by fighting and so forth. Mr. F. permitted himself to be dependent on the counselor and to use this dependency as a control for his own impulsive behavior. [The intense dependency that develops with many patients and the counselor's need to function as a surrogate parent plus the continuous demands are a most severe drain and burden on the counselor and often lead to the counselor's becoming "burned out." The worker must be aware of this pull and guard against artificially creating distance between himself and the patient, unless this is therapeutically indicated.] During the remainder of the first year Mr. F.'s complaints continued as before. On occasion, he acted out by getting into fights or abusing cocaine, which usually occurred when the counselor was on vacation.

GROUP THERAPY: SECOND SIX MONTHS

During this period the group leader noticed that Mr. F. was withdrawing from the group. This resulted from the group's confronting Mr. F. with his need to monopolize attention with his stories of street activities. The group confronted him with his constant expressions of ineptness in his workshop as well as in his relationships with women, usually street "hookers." The group felt this betrayed Mr. F.'s low self-esteem. Mr. F. needed to reorient his approach to the group. During the summer he acted out by using cocaine when his counselor was on vacation and he felt depressed. During this time Mr. F. was requested to have an educational evaluation. He was nervous about this but went through with it. The tests showed that he could read on a sixth-grade level but was not motivated to improve. It was recommended that no attempt be made at this time to institute educational tutoring toward a high school equivalency diploma.

WORKSHOP PROGRESS REPORT: SECOND SIX MONTHS

Mr. F. continued to attend regularly but expressed fears of not being able to do as well as the other patients. Still very nervous and sensitive, he complained about his individual counselor's "being too hard" on him. He got upset less easily and began to develop attachments to other patients. He rarely speaks positively about himself, appears depressed and angry in an attempt to get attention. He manipulates others into making decisions for him and gains approval by getting others to ask him to join in or make decisions. He is very fearful of work and of dealing with the frustrations of a job. He likes the staff member in charge of the print shop and is dependent on his approval. [The vocational counselor in this clinic also functions as a therapy counselor, group leader, and observer of behavior. Here she has focused on the passive-aggressive aspects of Mr. F.'s behavior, seeing much of this behavior as manipulative as opposed to inadequate. It would be important for the staff to challenge Mr. F. continually to make his own decisions and confront his manipulative behavior since his dependency only reinforced his low self-esteem.]

At the end of the year, the final comment of the workshop leader was that Mr. F. was still a "cry baby," demanding a lot of attention and continually saying he wanted to get back into shape with his drums though never attempting to do so. He was still a loner, though he had made some friends. [These latter statements reflect something that occurs frequently in treatment: the staff begin to feel drained because of the patient's excessive demands and dependency and obsessive complaints.]

PSYCHIATRIC EVALUATION: END OF FIRST YEAR

The psychiatrist had originally felt the prognosis was poor and was surprised at the progress Mr. F. had made. The mellaril had been very effective, and Mr. F. had abstained from alcohol despite much pressure from friends. Effective use of leisure time, boredom, and loneliness were still major problems.

SECOND YEAR OF TREATMENT

In the thirteenth month of treatment, the individual counselor was preparing to terminate his employment at the Center, and this was a great disappointment for Mr. F. For the following eight weeks he reacted intensely. His case was therefore reviewed by the interdisciplinary team, and another psychiatric interview was scheduled. Mr. F. had become hostile, negativistic, and withdrawn as well as disruptive in the workshop and was also acting-out by using cocaine. The review team, led by the chief psychiatrist, decided to remove Mr. F. from the workshop temporarily, resume the mellaril, which had been discontinued earlier, and transfer Mr. F. temporarily to the group leader for individual counseling. Mr. F. showed little awareness of the reasons for his anger and acting-out but was able to express his rage in the group. His relationship to the group remained good. He began to explore how he had adopted his father's behavior patterns, which kept him from assuming responsibility for himself. [The staff never took these thoughts farther in helping Mr. F. understand his identification with the father and thereby helping him to individuate himself.] In the eighteenth month of treatment, Mr. F. was returned to the workshop, because his behavior was now more controlled and less hostile. The group leader felt that Mr. F. was more related interpersonally, had less tendency to interrupt, and was able to generate some warmth toward the other patients. He showed no major acting-out or flight from treatment. This was viewed as a sign of developing ego strength. [The acceptance of even small steps of growth is crucial to being able to continue working with this population and still remain optimistic and energetic in treatment. Long-term treatment is indicated for many of the patients.]

Mr. F. was able to explore his feelings about separation from the past counselor and similar feelings about his father. The mother was rarely mentioned. Throughout the entire treatment, Mr. F. needed help with concrete services, particularly in relation to welfare, housing, and management. He needed to learn how to manage and account for his money rather than just spend it. He reduced his borrowing from other patients and friends. For the first time, he expressed an interest in contacting his father in California.

WORKSHOP REPORT AT TWENTY-ONE MONTHS

It was noted that Mr. F. had made friends with an elderly male onto whom he displaced feelings from his father. He showed a somewhat better ability to assume responsibility and follow through on concrete tasks. He was also able to articulate his anger and negative feelings better, with resulting decrease of anxiety. The worker felt that his anger was generally used as a defense againse closeness and positive feelings. Mr. F. then began to hang out with another patient who was having a negative effect on him.

TEAM MEETING: TWENTY-SECOND MONTH OF TREATMENT

Mr. F. was again having feelings of having been abandoned by males, whom he saw as failing him and not giving to him. A team meeting was therefore called to help Mr. F. understand and deal with these feelings. It was important to show him that he was making progress and that his expressions of anger were beneficial. This would help counteract his current acting-out of his anger and efforts to punish and disappoint the staff. Soon after the discussion with Mr. F., he had a fight with the friend who was having a negative effect on him and broke off the relationship. Mr. F. was also transferred to a new counselor. [The staff made no connection between this and the fact that Mr. F. was being prepared for transfer to the new counselor, which may have triggered his acting-out behavior. He would have a chance to work out his feelings toward the father in this new relationship, since the counselor came from the same background as he.] Mr. F. tried to engage the new counselor in a "negative contract" by telling him he was using coke and had spent all his welfare money to do so. The counselor pointed out that Mr. F. was attempting to test him. This confrontation immediately checked Mr. F. and started the relationship off on a more positive basis. [It would have been easy to fall into a recriminating approach with Mr. F. or to enter into extensive discussions of drug use. By focusing on the underlying motives of Mr. F.'s behavior, the counselor was able to check the acting out and establish the relationship on a firm basis.]

THIRD YEAR OF TREATMENT

At the twenty-sixth month of Mr. F.'s treatment, the group leader needed to be hospitalized for minor surgery, and Mr. F. acted out by using drugs and taking up again with his former friend who had had a negative effect on him. He also expressed to the print shop supervisor a desire to leave the workshop program and get a job. He was not considered ready for this and was encouraged to explore vocational training opportunities instead. Mr. F. again experienced stomach pains and needed to see the psychiatrist for evaluation and medication. By means of a urinalysis test, a psychiatric interview, and individual counseling, it was ascertained that Mr. F. had been main-lining heroin for weeks on a daily basis. He was advised to enter a hospital for detoxification, which he did. After returning from the hospital, he used the group sessions for months to ventilate feelings of anger but appeared to be influenced by peer feedback. He expressed anger toward his parents. Joint sessions were arranged with the patient friend and the social workers of both Mr. F. and the friend as a means of breaking through their negative contract, using drugs together, hanging out in bad neighborhoods, and so on. [Such joint sessions have been found useful in helping patients understand how they are using each other and acting out their fears of succeeding in treatment.] The two joint sessions proved successful in separating out the two patients and helping them become aware of what they were doing. Mr. F. asked the other patient to move out of his apartment, which he did. [In fact, the new counselor was having difficulty advancing the therapeutic relationship.] Mr. F.'s desire to leave the clinic and workshop were really an expression of his desire to change his counselor. He verbalized this, and his request was approved. Mr. F., in the thirty-second month of treatment, was transferred to a new counselor, a woman. Mr. F. attempted to involve his new worker in defending his decision to change counselors, but she refused to take any position, except for making it clear that it was all right for him to want to change and that separations could often have beneficial effects. This relieved Mr. F.'s anger and guilt. He then made a swift, positive transference to the new worker. He talked about women and about his mother. Mr. F. had thoughts about terminating from the workshop and group and attempted to force the counselor to make the decision for him. The worker refused to do this and put the responsibility on him.

Mr. F. continued to see his counselor regularly. Because she was a woman, he didn't have to act competitively or "macho," as he did with a man, and he could open up better with her. She avoided giving direction but joined him in his problem-solving efforts. He left the workshop for a while and was surprised that no one fought him. He took up an opportunity to play in a band with other musicians, then returned to the workshop and moved into the most productive stage of treatment thus far. He had a good relationship with the print shop supervisor and was pleased that he had not forgotten his printing experience.

FOURTH YEAR OF TREATMENT

Regrettably, Mr. F.'s new worker was planning to leave the clinic in the thirty-eighth month of his treatment. [This turnover was unfortunate. It was good that Mr. F. was receiving multiple services and was relating to a variety of staff so that he had a connection somewhere when a particular counselor left. Patients like Mr. F. develop intense and sensitive transference relationships. He was able to maintain a strong attachment to the program and different staff at different times, which helped him remain in treatment.] Mr. F. was able to talk about his feelings when prior counselors had left and then made connections with his mother and also with his own abandonment of his common-law wife and children. The psychiatrist was also leaving at this time, but Mr. F. was able to take this too in stride.

ASSESSMENT OF NEW COUNSELOR

The arrival of a new counselor and the assessments made by the new counselor represented an important opportunity to take a fresh look at a long-term case and to obtain a new perspective on what had been happening and what further needed to be done. The new counselor made the following appraisal of Mr. F.:

Mr. F. appears considerably younger than his stated age because of his preference for 1950s-type clothing and his highly affected "hip" manner. He relates in a friendly and cooperative manner, though he is very anxious and tense and frequently becomes angry, withdrawing at the slightest frustration. His difficulties in obtaining and maintaining employment appear to be related to difficulties with interpersonal relationships rather than problems as a musician. In treatment, he relates in the pseudo-communicative style cited—that is, he will talk about superficial matters unless confronted. He then resorts to a variety of generalized obscure expressions which serve to cover up his real feelings. He is very sensitive to the social worker's reactions and gets "confused" if he senses anything negative. His progress in treatment to date has been hampered by his periodically resorting to acting out in times of stress and crisis. He appears to be heavily invested in maintaining his angry passive-aggressive and dependent stance to the world. He has never been able to deal effectively with his rage toward the father. He blames the father for the loss of the mother. His relationships with women are extremely narcissistic, based on unmet dependency needs. Treatment will continue to involve long-term supportive ego-building therapy toward the goal of enabling him to feel strong enough to confront some of his self-defeating patterns. It will be important to build sufficient trust so that he can relinquish his defensive anger and deal with the underlying hurt."

By the 43rd month, Mr. F. was building a firmer relationship with the social worker and also with a girlfriend. Treatment focused on his maintaining distance in all his relationships, lacking trust, and fearing closeness and loving. A psychiatric diagnosis made at this time was "Borderline Personality Disorder with Drug Addiction". [The borderline personality is not easy to describe briefly. Essentially, the ego structure has been split and compartmentalized. The patient internalizes his early object relationships and splits off the opposing feelings. A rigid structure is organized which protects the contradictory ego states, thus allowing opposite reactions to coexist. Such patients will often feel impotent rage when a therapist becomes important, are quick to feel attacked, and are very sensitive. Such patients can be explosive and display a lack of impulse control and weak reality testing. They often reveal a chaotic nature in therapeutic situations.] In treatment Mr. F. continued to overreact and create crises in his life.

FIFTH YEAR OF TREATMENT

Mr. F's attendance record had declined over the past four months and was viewed as symptomatic of increased resistance. He continued to maintain his position as a helpless victim, and treatment was slow and difficult. His drug use had ceased with the relationship with the new girlfriend.

JOINT SESSION WITH GIRLFRIEND

In his fifty-fifth month, the social worker asked Mr. F. to bring his girlfriend in for joint sessions. Additional crises had occurred, and the worker felt the time was ripe to confront Mr. F. about his crisis orientation to life. The joint sessions were conducted weekly. Mr. F. began to recognize some of his dependency needs. At the same time he had new outbreaks of rage toward his girlfriend. He had relapsed to drinking but stopped and began to feel better. He found a better place to live with his girlfriend. His ulcer acted up, but he refused to get medical care for it. A special meeting was therefore arranged with the social worker, the supervisor of the Mental Hygiene Clinic, and the psychiatrist to underline the seriousness of his condition and the need for medical care. Mr. F. agreed to go to the hospital and get treatment but was fearful of surgery.

SIXTH YEAR OF TREATMENT

By the sixty-fourth month the social worker reported that Mr. F. was manifesting the highest level of motivation since he started treatment. The confrontation two months before had had a major impact. He showed greater motivation to maintain the relationship with his girlfriend, which had survived a great deal of acting-out on his part. He accepted the fact that people cared about him and could accept this better than before. His judgment had improved along with his self-control, and he had been able to walk away from several street fights. [Treatment has finally made a significant impact. Mr. F. was able to internalize caring and thus begin to care more about himself. Though more years of treatment apparently remain, and crises will still occur, a major inroad has been made.]

As we have seen, this case was chronic and long-drawn-out, requiring the combined efforts of a variety of staff members working together consistently and harmoniously to provide the extensive supports this patient needed because of his frequent crises, periods of acting-out, regressions, relapses, and stubborn lack of movement and awareness. The work was indeed slow-moving, painstaking, frustrating, and tedious. The staff needed to invest very large efforts with the expectation of only small gains over many long months of treatment. The case is typical of many such chronic situations, opposed only by the other extreme of clients or patients who come in only sporadically and on a crisis basis until they can be involved on a more sustained basis in regular, ongoing treatment.

References

1. Aprill, F. A. Some notes on the intake process. Private communication to author, March 1980.
2. Barish, H. Some notes on the Lower Eastside Service Center. Private communication, October 1979.
3. Brill, L. "Drug Addiction." In *Encyclopedia of Social Work.* New York: NASW, 1971, pp. 24–38.
4. Brill, L. "Drug Addiction." In *Encyclopedia of Social Work,* Washington, D.C.: NASW, 1977, pp. 30–42.
5. Curet, E., and J. Page. The role of the supervisor in a methadone maintenance program. Private communication, February 1980.
6. "Programs for Drug Abuse Treatment." Chapter 4 in *Community Crime Prevention.* Washington, D.C.: National Advisory Commission on Criminal Justice Standards and Goals, January 23, 1973.
7. SAODAP. *Community Action for Drug Abuse Prevention.* Washington, D.C., 1972.
8. Social Work Symposium, National Drug Abuse Conference, Seattle, Wash., April 3–8, 1978. "The Professional and His/Her Role in the Interdisciplinary Team in Substance Abuse Treatment." Floyd A. Aprill, Leon Brill, and Jerry Flanzer.

CHAPTER 12

Training

It SHOULD GO WITHOUT SAYING that staff training is an indispensable ingredient of any drug treatment program: only to the extent that staff members understand the program's goals and their own roles and responsibilities will the program be effective (3, 8). Staff must be trained to understand the complexity of the problems encountered and the diversity of techniques needed to deal with them. They must understand the chronic-relapsing nature of drug addiction and the crisis orientation of clients and realize that treatment is often a long-drawn-out process which must use all the reinforcements at hand; that they will need to settle for limited goals in spite of their huge efforts to treat and rehabilitate; and that they will be challenged and tested frequently in the course of treatment and will need to be aware of their own feelings and reactions to the client's acting-out and dependency in order to maintain their objectivity. They will, finally, need to be eclectic, choosing from among a range of modalities those that can best be applied to a particular client and to have a thorough understanding of behavioral dynamics and personality organization as well as the meaning of relationships as the central factor in treatment (3, 8). Training staff members in these matters must be emphasized especially, because there is still so much we do not understand about drug abuse and its treatment.

Since personnel in the drug field come from such diverse backgrounds, the need for training assumes still further urgency if we are to develop teamwork and effective interdisciplinary collaboration among them. Training can be pursued along various lines, such as the indoctrination of new workers by supervisors and administrators, provision for ongoing training, individual and group supervision supplemented by in-service training, and special seminars and workshops, as well as outside academic courses and education. The following sections will discuss the content and substance of training and examine methods used in different agencies to train professional as well as paraprofessional personnel.

The Content of Training

J. P. Flanzer has suggested several necessary directions for counseling, administration, and planning in relation to training generally. His comments are relevant for drug abuse training as well (7).

1. _Counseling_. Counseling training must clearly educate workers in the basics of a case-management approach and a counseling "follow-through." Case management must be learned at two levels: (1) the professional management of client cases from intake to termination, from environmental manipulation and agency linkage to resources development and the coordination of intra- and interagency efforts; (2) the process of helping clients meet their basic human needs so that their energy is freed for counseling efforts. Counseling must be learned in its various manifestations: individual, family, and group; from short-term to long-term; from remedial to rehabilitative; and from analytic to behavioral (1, 7). These emphases are discussed in various contexts at different points in this book.

2. _Administration_. The administrator must be able to run an agency efficiently, operate and evaluate programs, maintain staff harmony, generate funding, maintain physical integrity, and protect the staff from external forces: that is, allow them to work without interference. Specific training of administrators must include staff and organizational development; management information and activity systems; and grant-writing and budgeting.

3. _Planning_. Planners must have knowledge of changing populations and consumer needs, political-legal awareness and know-how, and professional and institutional interests.

4. _Drug Content_. There must be some understanding and knowledge of drugs, their nature, abuse, misuse, and usefulness on a cognitive, affective, and behavioral level. Courses must be developed that present this information on a dynamic basis, not on a moralistic or punitive basis as in the past, and can be used to supplement our understanding of what is involved (6).

5. _Sequentiality_. Training must be continuous and sequential, leading progressively to specific goal attainments. By having courses sequenced, increased levels of expertise and focused knowledge can be brought to bear. Learning can be measured, and professional experience and competence levels differentiated (1, 7).

Training Professionals

Careful preliminary screening is needed if we are to recruit staff with the requisite personality characteristics: a large fund of empathy, flexibility, and patience, and freedom from bias, rigidity, and moralistic and punitive attitudes in relation to drug-dependent individuals. For a number of years, as indicated, it was widely believed that only ex-addicts had the attributes for dealing with drug abusers, whether in treatment or in prevention. It is now better understood that not all ex-addicts have the personal qualities and qualifications to play such a role. Nor can we say, after years of experience, that any one discipline, profession, or background is exclusively or best equipped to work with users. Rather, a variety of skills, attributes, and disciplines is called for, with added training and orientation required. The specific modality will also help dictate the kinds of staff and disciplines needed (3, 9).

In training professionals, the mental health professions have usually relied on "practicums" where the social worker, psychiatrist, or psychologist treats clients under supervision as a supplement to their previous educational and internship experiences. In the Milwaukee Mental Health Center Drug Abuse Program, staff members needed to combat many of their own stereotypes in relation to addicts, such as the belief that drug abusers are not responsive to treatment, that very little can be achieved in treatment, and that any addiction is irreversible. The Milwaukee Social Work School was also concerned about the dangers of exposing untried students to very complicated situations and to "unrewarding case experiences" that could not justify the efforts expended (2). Staff members were further apprehensive initially about the students' ability to relate to clients and show flexibility in working in a nontraditional setting. Clients were all written off by the staff as "sociopathic personalities" or "character disorders." They tended to view addicts as "losers" and as untreatable. It was implied that no efforts would work until the client had "burnt out" (reached bottom). A high probability of failure even then was assumed.

These stereotypes were examined and found to be not justified by experience. Student cases were selected both for their educational value and for the benefit of the individual client. Because of their reduced caseloads, students were able to work intensively with each client and family. A criterion of the majority of the cases selected was the client's willingness to acknowledge and work on a psychosocial problem. It was found that drug abusers are a very heterogeneous group of individuals and represent a broad range of personalities with various degrees of motivation, ego strength, and psychosocial functioning. Goals had little meaning unless they were also accepted by the client. In this experience, clients assigned were found to be able to relate to their counselors, set

realistic goals and "treatment contracts," and demonstrate progress toward these goals. The students' traditionally narrow view of
psychotherapy needed to be abandoned in favor of a much broader and
more flexible definition of "social psychotherapy," including individual,
family, and marital counseling; vocational counseling; job development;
welfare intermediation; legal advocacy; and other roles as required. Students needed to learn the value of flexibility. It was felt that many of the
difficulties in establishing a relationship could be avoided by returning
to the social work basics of "beginning where the client is," utilizing
feedback to understand the client's position, and so forth. Insight and
intensive therapy may have a place in a drug abuse program but must be
flexibly and nonrigidly provided, with innovation and professional imag-
ination. It was concluded that the training of mental health professionals in drug abuse settings need not be radically different from training in other mental health specialities (2). These conclusions of Aprill
and his colleagues closely approximated those of the New York Demonstration Center staff in New York City in 1963 (1, 2, 4, 9).

The Training of Paraprofessionals or Mental Health Aides

The training of paraprofessionals and indigenous personnel has a
long history, at least reaching back to the early 1930s. F. Riessman and
A. Pearl in 1965 described what was then a new approach to the "War on
Poverty" (8). It was hoped that as many as 6 million "new careers," not
just jobs, could be developed for the poor in the helping professions:
social work, teaching, recreation, and the health services. Among the
purposes outlined were reducing the manpower shortage in education
and social work; providing more, better, and "closer" services for the
poor and reaching the unreached; rehabilitating many of the poor themselves through meaningful employment; and freeing the professionals
for more "creative" and supervisory duties. It was hoped to foster upward mobility in our society by establishing a continuum of careers,
ranging from nonskilled entry positions; extending through inter-
mediate, subprofessional functions; and terminating in full professional
status. The poor would no longer be eliminated from these areas by
requiring five to eight years of prior college experience. The use of indigenous personnel and nonprofessional aides would help bridge the gap
between the professional agency and the lower socio-economic segments of the community and make services less remote and impersonal.
Guided by the professional team, a mental health aide could assume
certain psychological and psychotherapeutic roles within his capability,
such as role model or a listener to provide catharsis; in a supportive role

to express concern; as an intervention person with the hospital or clinic and outside agencies; and as an auxiliary "healer" in group treatment (8).

What attributes are required for the nonprofessional? Riessman and Pearl single out flexibility as highly significant, since it is the "trainability" of the aide that will probably be decisive: he or she must be not too moralistic, judgmental, and punitive and must be able to accept supervision and criticism and to function in a group. Interestingly, the authors also stress the "helper principle" or the principle of differential association. This means that aides who are engaged in training others will, in the process, be learning a great deal themselves.

It was found that a major difficulty in supervising, training, and administering an indigenous staff was the task of molding workers in the professional image. On the one hand, this could cause them to lose their ability to help clients by virtue of their natural "style," experience, and abilities. On the other hand, the trainees needed to be instructed in specific skills and to be taught how to relate positively to other members of the staff and to clients in their care. They had to develop a feeling of belonging and to understand the need for training if they were to function meaningfully and competently in the program. Training should provide an opportunity to screen candidates, assess their work performance, and eliminate those who do not measure up. Training should be job-related rather than general and should provide the trainee with a portfolio of specific skills geared to a specific job. After initial job assignment, the role of ongoing supervision becomes crucial (8).

Among the problems to be considered in the training of nonprofessionals, Riessman and Pearl stress the need for confidentiality, the acceptance and proper use of supervision, and an understanding of the role of authority and its proper use in treatment; the dangers of over-identification with the institution and underidentification with the community or client population, and of over-optimism and defeatism in helping and treating; the relationship of the nonprofessional to professionals both inside and outside the program; and the hazard of becoming overwhelmed by individual case situations. The training methodology should be oriented to learning through doing (job simulation, role-playing, on-the-job learning), on the assumption that this approach is the basic style of low-income people. More reading and writing assignments can be introduced as the training proceeds. There should be continuous on-the-job training and almost immediate initiation to work; an activity rather than a lecture approach; an intensive team approach aimed at building strong group solidarity among the nonprofessional workers; informal individual supervision on request, supplemented by group discussion and group supervision; a down-to-earth teaching style emphasizing concrete tasks presented clearly and in detail; utilization of the "helper principle"; and freedom for the nonprofessional to develop his or her personal style (8).

Many of the training concepts advocated by Riessman and Pearl were subsequently carried out at the Lincoln Hospital Mental Health Service Clinic. Indigenous personnel were most useful in helping the clinic assess the needs of the South Bronx community and organize services accordingly. They also helped to staff the neighborhood service centers established in the area. In training, it was found useful to employ a problem-oriented approach rather than attempt sensitivity training methods, which generated anxiety among the workers.

In the 1970s there was increased focus on the importance of credentialing nonprofessional staff. Workers have received credit for life experience in establishing job levels and credentials, including advance credits toward academic degrees. There has been emphasis on both horizontal and vertical mobility, that is, vertical escalation, and expanding a worker's skills beyond the drug field to include other areas of mental health and other fields. A number of states have established standards and criteria for the credentialing of staff and licensure of programs. Since "paper credentials" may be misleading and may not accurately reflect a worker's real level of ability, there would appear to be a need for additional competence checks through actual observation of on-the-job performance, as the New York State Department of Education does in certifying teachers.

PARAPROFESSIONAL TRAINING: ALBERT EINSTEIN COLLEGE OF MEDICINE METHADONE MAINTENANCE PROGRAM

The AECOM training program is concerned with two issues: (1) the management of individual caseloads by paraprofessional workers; and (2) the supervisory relationship between the counselor and the social worker. Supervision consists mainly in ensuring that there is proper treatment planning and intervention as well as follow-up of treatment. In addition, there must be proper recording to comply with state and federal mandates related to methadone maintenance treatment (5).

E. Curet assisted by R. Page, in a private communication to the author, indicate that supervision is also needed to relate to different kinds of paraprofessional counselors: the non-degree-holding counselors, some of them ex-addicts, and the degreed counselors, with special skills and experience in an area such as education or vocational counseling. Some of the problems encountered by the authors are outlined in the following case illustrations (5).

1. *Dealing with crisis situations and setting limits.* Because addicts are so frequently involved in crisis situations, counselors must learn to deal

with these crises and help patients begin to avoid precipitating the crises. This is illustrated in the case of Mr. W.

Mr. W. is a forty-four-year-old alcoholic who has been in and out of treatment for nine years. He was maintained on a low methadone dosage and was required to pick up his medication at the clinic six days a week. This patient repeatedly disregarded welfare appointments and had his case closed on numerous occasions as a result of his negligence. Because Mr. W. usually comes to the clinic intoxicated and is often unmanageable, his counselor usually handles most of the red tape involved in getting his welfare case reopened. The dependency thus fostered caused Mr. W. to become increasingly demanding, asking for carfare, use of the telephone, release of bottles of medication, and so on. When the counselor discussed the situation with the social worker, the social worker guided the counselor in setting limits to the patient's behavior. Mr. W.'s response was that of a spoiled child whose demands were suddenly thwarted. The counselor needed to learn some hard lessons as to how the client's dependency would be increased and even mushroom out of control if limits were not set from the beginning. The meaning of the patient's behavior and the reasons for the counselor's inability to set limits were also explored.

2. *How to intervene appropriately*. The methods of intervening appropriately and then monitoring the effects of the intervention are basic elements of supervision among paraprofessionals as well as other counselors engaged in treatment. In one case situation, a patient's laboratory urine reports showed evidence of previously undetected secondary drug use, and the patient appeared to be coming into the clinic sedated. It became imperative that the counselor not intervene punitively, as he had been doing, thus threatening to drive the patient from treatment. It was more important to help the counselor explore the underlying problems and factors contributing to the patient's relapse.

The patient, Mrs. R., is a twenty-five-year-old Puerto Rican mother of two children who has been a patient in the clinic for five years. In her first four years of treatment she had achieved a stable family life, had discontinued illicit drug use, and was generally cooperative and responsible. However, during the fifth year of treatment sporadic dirty urines (indicating heroin use) began to appear and became steadily more frequent. Because she had been so stable in treatment and had merited a three-day pickup schedule of medication rather than the usual six days' pickup per week, she was not disposed to approach her counselor to discuss her problems for fear she would be required to come to the clinic more frequently. The counselor, for his part, had not intervened at the first signs of abuse because of the patient's good record of adjustment. As a result of his delayed intervention, however, he now acknowledged that the patient needed to be restricted and compelled her to come in more frequently to give urine samples. The consequence was the development of hostility between patient and counselor and avoidance by the patient of further therapeutic contacts with the counselor.

This situation came to the attention of the social work supervisor, who felt it necessary to intervene in order to reinvolve the patient in therapy. A meeting was held with the counselor and the patient jointly. The patient was vehement in not wanting to continue with the counselor, and it was necessary to transfer her to another worker. The new counselor was able to discover that there was a crisis in the life of Mrs. R. Her husband, who had had a prior drug abuse history but was not currently in treatment, had gone back to heroin use. Because her husband and family had been a major source of Mrs. R.'s motivation to do well in treatment, she followed the same route as her husband. In addition to intensive counseling, it became necessary to raise the patient's methadone dose. The supervisor was able to use this situation to emphasize the fact that lab reports should not be used to punish the patient but rather as an occasion for learning what had made the patient regress and use drugs. It also demonstrated the need for family involvement (5).

Another area frequently requiring intervention relates to the question of child custody. The counselor must be careful not to get caught in a conflict between members of the family and forced to side with one member or another rather than preserve a more objective stance. Child custody issues further involve the question of whether the counselor is the advocate for the patient and family or for a governmental agency. The mother usually expects the counselor to serve as advocate for her efforts to retain or regain custody. Overidentification with the patient may be detrimental if this clearly does not serve the best interests of the child.

Mrs. D. is a thirty-one-year-old patient who has been in treatment for three years. She has a consistent pattern of sedative-hypnotic drug abuse (Valium and Elavil) and had previously been subjected to disciplinary action (increased pickup schedule to six days weekly) when she acted out and became pregnant, which violated the program's rules. Her decision to carry the pregnancy to term as well as the immediate cessation of secondary drug abuse were viewed by her counselor as signs of her intent to become a responsible partner in her treatment. Consequently, her pickup schedule was reduced as the pregnancy advanced, resulting in less frequent contact with the counselor. In the patient's eighth month of pregnancy the counselor was transferred to another clinic. At this point, Mrs. D's two-day pickup schedule made the establishment of a trusting relationship with the new counselor difficult. It was not until Mrs. D. gave birth that the new counselor learned that she had discontinued prenatal care months earlier and was without housing, staying at the home of her alcoholic husband's parents. At the request of the hospital social worker, the Bureau of Child Welfare was asked to make a recommendation for the infant's custody. The counselor, basing her intervention on the positive effect of Mrs. D.'s pregnancy and on her rehabilitative efforts in treatment, was concerned that the denial of custody would lead to regression. The counselor was unable to see the total picture objectively or to understand Mrs. D.'s inability to plan adequately for her infant's care. Once the social worker's advice was sought, the patient, her counselor, and the social worker met jointly. The session served as a learning experience for the counselor in terms of making an objective assessment of the patient's motives regarding custody of her child. It also helped the patient to verbalize her ambivalence about the pregnancy and to deal with her feelings in this area. Under the social worker's direction, a conference was arranged at the hospital where the child was delivered. The Bureau of Child Welfare worker, Welfare Department caseworker, hospital social worker, and counselor planned together in behalf of the patient. In keeping with the patient's request, a coordinated plan of follow-up, including preventive care visits by the BCW, medical follow-up, and psychiatric evaluation, was developed and implemented. Mrs. D. could thus be granted custody of her child and provided with the necessary support to ensure adequate child care (5).

3. *Recognizing more serious emotional problems.* The ability to recognize more serious emotional problems, including psychotic symptomatology, is an important dimension in a counselor's learning, as indicated in the following case example.

Mr. H. is a twenty-eight-year-old Italian male who had been in the program four years and was transferred to our clinic because of his involvement in a physical fight at another clinic. He maintained a distance in spite of the social worker's repeated efforts to engage him in psychotherapy. He seemed to be more interested in talking to one of the counselors in the clinic, discussing the "oppression of the poor" and the "coming end of the world." When the social worker indicated to the counselor her feeling that the patient had more severe psychopathology and a thought disorder, the counselor responded accusingly that the social worker lacked sensitivity and an understanding of the problems of the poor.

About a week later the patient came into the social worker's office presenting the picture of a beginning psychotic episode. Mr. H. had been obsessed with suicidal and paranoid thoughts for a few weeks prior to this contact. He was aware that he was undergoing a psychotic episode and was reaching out for assistance. The social worker was supportive and accompanied the patient to the nearest psychiatic hospital, remaining there with him until he could be admitted. Follow-up was done until the patient was discharged and returned to the clinic.

The case was used as an example for the next staff development session. It was important to provide didactic training and to make certain that the counselors responded appropriately when they encountered such situations and were being provoked by the patient. The counselor in Mr. H.'s case recognized his need to learn more about psychotic symptomatology and not to collude with the patient's illness. Such collusion seemed more likely to emerge if the counselor collaborated with the patient in locating the causes of the patient's problems in the larger social situation, thereby helping him project his problems and tensions. This proved to be especially dangerous for the indigenous counselors who shared these attitudes and needed to learn to distinguish between occasions when anger about the social situation was based in reality and when it was a projection of the patient's problems. Only in this way could the counselor learn to intervene appropriately and head off more serious problems. It was important for the counselor to realize when the patient was crying out for help under the guise of his social concerns and also to understand the need for help from the social worker if the patient's problems were beyond the counselor's capacity.

4. *Overidentification with the patient.* The problem of overidentification is implicit in some of the case illustrations presented earlier. The counselor, especially if he is an ex-addict or indigenous worker from the same area as the patient, may be inclined to identify with the patient against the clinic and outside agencies as well as against other members of the patient's family. Other problems may derive from the frustration of ex-addict counselors when the patient isn't doing well. They may become punitive and rejecting out of a feeling that "if I could make it, so can you." There will be little recognition of individual differences among the patients.

Mr. J. is a thirty-year-old Vietnam veteran whose drug addiction began after he was wounded and permanently disabled in the war. He is very personable, intelligent, and artistically inclined. Before the injury and subsequent addiction, he had been highly motivated to enter fashion design. His history in methadone treatment showed a continued pattern of heroin and cocaine abuse. He still talked abour pursuing a career and, indeed, made what turned out to be several false starts. His counselor instead of recognizing his need for intensive psychotherapy, continued to support his unrealistic and self-defeating attempts to pick up where he had left off before. When this came to the attention of the social worker, a supervisory session was held with the counselor to discuss the unrealistic treatment course and the counselor's problem with overidentification. A new treatment plan was then designed to accord better with the patient's psychological needs of the moment (5).

Overidentification may also be the result of the split loyalty the ex-addict counselor may have because he feels torn between the "straight" world and the drug world. Counselors may waver between extremes of lenience and punitiveness, and it is important for the supervisor to help them maintain a balance, especially when the patient fails to meet their expectations. Counselors may also feel disloyal to the patient when they are siding with the straight world.

5. *Countertransference feelings.* A crucial element in supervision is helping the counselor understand and deal with his or her own feelings in relation to the patient. The counselor may be unable to express anger and other feelings and may unwittingly get caught up in venting these

feelings in hidden ways, thus undermining the relationship with the patient and the progress of treatment. The counselor may be so involved in attempting to please the patient that he or she is unable to set limits or discourage acting-out behavior. The supervisor needs to help counselors become more aware of their true feelings in relation to different patients and the unconscious need to encourage acting-out of forbidden impulses or excessive dependency needs.

6. *Developing confidence.* Because of his or her previous life, the ex-addict or indigenous counselor may have many areas of insecurity and need to receive all the support possible from the supervisor in dealing with the very difficult and trying patients. The need to accept the higher ranking of the professional personnel and to be dependent on them is often discouraging. It is important to recognize the special skills and experience indigenous counselors bring to treatment and the fact that professionals can learn a great deal from them. The program should establish an open, nonthreatening, and noncompetitive environment in which the counselors feel free to raise questions and seek help. At the same time, professionals need to examine their own stereotypes about indigenous personnel and ex-addicts if they are to work effectively with them (5).

References

1. Aprill, F. A.; J. P. Flanzer; and L. Brill. Social Work Symposium on "Social Work and Drug Abuse Treatment" National Drug Abuse Conference, Seattle, Wash., April 3–11, 1978.
2. Aprill, F. A.; T. R. Johnston; and T. E. Grazer. "Training of Mental Health Professionals in a Multi-modality Drug Abuse Setting." Unpublished paper. Milwaukee County Mental Health Center Drug Abuse Program, Milwaukee.
3. Brill, L. "Drug Addiction." In *Encyclopedia of Social Work.* 17th Ed. Washington, D.C.: NASW, 1977.
4. Brill, L., et al. *Rehabilitation in Drug Addiction: A Report on a Five-Year Demonstration Center.* Mental Health Monograph # 3. Washington, D.C.: PHS NIMHM, 1963.
5. Curet, E., and R. Page. The supervisory role of the social worker in a methadone clinic. Private communication with author, February 1980.
6. Delone, H. R. "The Ups and Downs of Drug Abuse Education." *Saturday Review of Education,* November 11, 1972.
7. Flanzer, J. P., et al. Symposium on "The Role of the Social Worker in Drug Abuse Treatment." At the National Drug Abuse Conference, Seattle, Wash., April 3–11, 1978.
8. Pearl, A., and F. Riessman. *New Careers for the Poor.* New York: Free Press, 1965.
9. "Program for Drug Abuse Treatment and Prevention." Chapter 4 in *Community Crime Prevention.* Washington, D.C.: National Advisory Commission on Criminal Justice Standards and Goals, February 1973.

Summary and Retrospect

THE WORD "SUMMARY" WAS CHOSEN in preference to "conclusion," because there can obviously be no conclusion to what is a constantly evolving and unfolding subject, treatment. Looking back to the intentions outlined in the Preface, we recall that our goal was to fill the gap in the existing literature and to outline specific modes and techniques of treatment for workers in the helping field and others involved more peripherally with the substance abuse problem. Though the book had originally been planned for social workers only, it was soon apparent that many other disciplines were involved, including paraprofessionals and indigenous persons, and that drug abuse could no longer separate itself from alcoholism. Our discussion has therefore included all helping persons and the shared dynamics and treatment of both drug abuse and alcoholism.

Basic to our discussion has been the effort to formulate a more rational approach to drug abuse treatment and management than has hitherto prevailed, and to focus on the *person* rather than the substance if we are to understand what is involved. Liberal use was made of case illustrations of the different modes being used today: individual, individual supplemented by other forms such as relaxation and sexual therapy, marital counseling, and others, as well as couples therapy, family therapy, and multiple family therapy. To accomplish this, contributions were solicited from five different treatment centers in the country. Their willingness to share their thinking and experiences was acknowledged with gratitude in various sections of this book. As indicated, also, several of the contributors added their thoughts to other sections, such as intake, training, group techniques, and standards.

The representatives of these centers reflect a variety of approaches and options in treatment, ranging from the traditional psychoanalytic approach to more eclectic and pragmatic techniques. As mentioned, this undoubtedly had to do with the fact that the five centers deal with different regions and client populations as well as their employment of different kinds of staff, with varying perceptions and expectations of treatment and varying levels of expertise, training, and experience. One of the central problems in treatment derives from the fact that too few staff have the requisite experience and training to diagnose accurately and select out from a range of options the one or ones best suited to help a particular patient. In presenting this material, the author sought not to espouse any individual approach, but rather to reflect the range and scope of what is available and what is needed to cope with the great diversity of clients and patients encountered. What emerged as surprising was the remarkable uniformity of approach and thinking evidenced on the whole. Also noteworthy was the skill with which the general treatment modalities had been adapted to the needs of substance abusers.

The central portion of the book, Part II on treatment, was supported by two auxiliary sections. The four chapters of Part I offered a historical overview of the management of substance abuse in the United States since passage of the Harrison Narcotics Act in 1914; a review of current treatment modalities and the rationales for them; a consideration of general and specific issues related to the treatment of substance abuse; and a discussion of drug classifications terminology, and detoxification. A chapter on prevention was included in Part I in order to emphasize its importance and the need for greater activity in this area.

Part III dealt with the "adjuncts" of treatment; that is, those crucial components of programming without which no program can operate effectively: interdisciplinary collaboration, training, and supervision. The Appendixes list the major informational resources available through the federal government and also outline the federal guidelines and standards developed over recent years for the assessment and treatment of substance abusers. These guidelines must be a reference point for all helping persons and should serve as their base for treatment.

It will be recalled from the Preface that the author hardly aspired to lay down absolute principles of treatment or to be "definitive" in any sense. It was emphasized, rather, that the field of substance abuse is in a constant state of flux and that there are still too many unknowns about substance abuse and treatment to permit any final formulations. It was emphasized that our techniques must be multifaceted if they are to begin to address the needs of such a diverse population of users. Workers further needed to develop imaginative and innovative methods, which yet fitted in comfortably with their own treatment and life experiences, inclinations, personal styles, and perceptions of the needs of each client. They needed, above all, to avoid the previous stereotyping by recognizing the complexity of substance abuse and by individualizing each patient and client rather than being overwhelmed and misled by the label of "drug abuser."

APPENDIXES

APPENDIX I

Selected Sources of Drug Abuse Information

THE FOLLOWING INFORMATION HAS been extrapolated from various brochures issued by the National Clearinghouse for Drug Abuse Information (NCDAI), the main resource for drug abuse information of the Federal Government, by the National Institute on Alcohol Abuse and Alcoholism (NIAAA) and ADAMHA, the acronym for the overall agency for the three combined federal institutes on drug abuse, alcoholism, and mental health.

The National Clearinghouse for Drug Abuse Information (NCADI) was established in the 1960s. It collects, classifies, stores, and disseminates scientific and general information on drug abuse and misuse; develops information resource materials such as bibliographies, fact sheets, and directories; responds to mail and telephone inquiries; maintains a multimedia Resource Center, which provides library and bibliographic services to the public; and supports a nationwide Drug Abuse Communications Network (DRACON) of satellite information centers affiliated with federal, state, and local government agencies, universities, and training centers.

a. *NCDAI User Services.* The NCDAI maintains an inventory of more than three hundred publications, which are disseminated free to the public in response to inquiries. These include publications targeted to parents, educators, students, community program workers, trainers, prevention/treatment program personnel, legislators, criminal justice system personnel, health professionals, racial/ethnic minorities, and scientists. Single copies of items in the inventory as well as publications listings, which are updated monthly, can be obtained free by writing the NCDAI at P.O. Box 416, Kensington, Maryland, 20795.

b. *Audiovisual and Publication Loan Service.* A free audiovisual loan service is operated through the NCDAI Resource Center. The center's library consists of more than three hundred films and filmstrips, recordings, games, tapes, video cassettes, and so forth. One item at a time can be borrowed for a two-week period. The request can be submitted by mail. It is recommended that the borrower contact the center first to reserve the item and learn about the specific procedure for borrowing it. The phone number is (301) 443-6614.

The Resource Center also maintains a book collection of more than eight thousand titles; subscribes to more than four hundred scientific/technical journals and newsletters; and maintains a collection of journal articles on microfiche. The Resource Center has a brochure entitled *NIDA Resource Center Journal Holdings,* which lists the large number of journal titles available for literature searches, microfiche, loans, and so on. Information concerning these collections and the loan policies for each can be obtained by writing the NIDA Resource Center at: Room 10 A54, Parklawn Building, 5600 Fishers Lane, Rockland, Maryland, 20857.

c. *Mailing Lists.* The NCDAI has six mailing lists by subject areas: epidemiology, laws/policy, documents, prevention/education, research papers and reports, training, and treatment. This includes new publications. To be placed on one of these mailing lists, write to: NCDAI, Department ML, Room 10 A53, Parklawn Building, 5600 Fishers Lane, Rockville, Md. 20857.

d. *Research Issue Series.* This series, available free upon request, includes abstracts of research studies, a bibliography, and two essays on current issues of interest. The active listing (with others added since publication of this volume) follows:

Drugs and Employment. Issue 1
Drugs and Sex. Issue 2
Drugs and Attitude Change. Issue 3
Drugs and Family/Peer Influence. Issue 4
Drugs and Pregnancy. Issue 5
Drugs and Death. Issue 6
Drugs and Addict Life-Styles. Issue 7
A Cocaine Bibliography. Issue 8
Predicting Adolescent Drug Abuse: A Review of Issues, Methods, and Correlates. Issue 11
Drug Abuse Instrument Handbook. Issue 12
Data Analysis Strategies and Designs for Substance Abuse Research. Issue 13
Drugs and Personality. Issue 14
Cocaine: Summaries of Psychological Research. Issue 15
Drugs and Crime. Issue 17
Drug Users and the Criminal Justice System. Issue 18
Drugs and Psychopathology. Issue 19
Drug Users and Driving Behaviors. Issue 20
Drugs and Minorities. Issue 21
Research Issues Update, 1978. Issue 22
International Drug Use. Issue 23
Perspective on the History of Psychoactive Substance Use. Issue 24

e. *Films.* The films in NIDA's Drug Abuse Film Collection deal with the following categories:

Drugs and Their Effects
Opinions and Overviews of Society and Drug Use

Prevention and Alternatives for Drug Use
Community Planning and Action
Treatment, Rehabilitation, and Issues Related to Them

A brochure describing the various films is available including the procedure for borrowing a film. For information on how to reserve a film and other details, call the Resource Center at (301) 443-6614.

There is also a listing of films suitable for doctors, nurses, therapists, and counselors. To borrow a film, call Dick Sackett, Visual Information Specialist, Communications and Public Affairs, NIDA, (301) 443-6500.

f. *National Directory of Drug Abuse and Alcoholism Treatment Programs.* This directory is a compilation of approximately 9,100 federal, state, local, and privately funded agencies responsible for the administration or provision of alcoholism or drug abuse services throughout the United States and its territories. It includes state authorities and VA medical centers. The directory is available from the NCDAI and the National Institute on Alcohol Abuse and Alcoholism (NIAA), at 5600 Fischers Lake, Rockville, Md. 20857. Directories of treatment programs and publications in Spanish are also available.

g. *Handbook on Drug Abuse.* This handbook, edited by Robert I. Dupont, Avram Goldstein, and John O'Donnell and issued by NIDA in January 1979, is an outstanding collection of articles covering all important aspects of drug abuse, prepared by the foremost authorities. The handbook is organized into nine sections: "Overview of Drug Treatment"; "Treatment Modalities for Narcotic Addicts"; "Treatment Methods for Specific Needs" including alcoholism; "Drugs of Recent Public Concern"; "Drug Problems in Specific Populations"; "Psychosocial Studies of Drug Users"; "Epidemiological Studies"; "Special Issues" (program management, prevention, and training); and "Drug Treatment in the Future." The handbook is available without cost from the NCDAI.

i. The following two bibliographies related to women are available from the National Institute of Mental Health:

Changing Directions in the Treatment of Women: A Mental Health Bibliography
Women and Health: A Bibliography

j. *The ADAMHA News.* This Newsletter, issued monthly by the Alcohol, Drug Abuse, and Mental Health Administration, offers an excellent summary of events related to all three institutes and also provides special articles or interviews on issues of current importance. The January 1980 issue, for example, has reports on teen marijuana use; the endorphins, the powerful substances manufactured by the brain that serve as pain-killers; phencyclidine (PCP) abuse; the assessment of treatment effectiveness; the future role of ADAMHA; and other subjects. There is also information about new publications and releases by the Institute. A regular mailing can be obtained free by writing ADAMHA at 5600 Fishers Lane, Rockville, Md. 20857.

k. *The National Library of Medicine.* Computerized abstracts covering such fields as alcohol, marijuana, and so on are available through the National Library of Medicine through their MEDLAR, TOXLINE, and TOXBACK systems, as are *Psychological Abstracts, Biological Abstracts, Chemical Abstracts,* and others.

1. *Summary Reports. Alcohol and Health and Marijuana and Health*, reports to the U.S. Congress from the Secretary of the Health, Education and Welfare, are issued periodically and can be obtained without charge from the National Clearinghouse (NCDAI). They provide excellent summaries of the state of our knowledge in this area.

APPENDIX II

Federal Standards and Criteria

Preface

THE FOLLOWING DOCUMENTS, Appendix II, A–F, are included to illustrate the federal government's continuing efforts to define effective criteria and standards of treatment. Because of limitations of space, not all the pertinent documents could be included, and portions of those listed here have been deleted in some cases. Thus, in IIA, "Federal Funding Criteria" for drug treatment services, the introduction by the then Director of the Special Action Office for Drug Abuse Services, Dr. Robert L. DuPont, which contains his "General Statement," was omitted. Portions of the Standards by the Joint Commission for the Accreditation of Hospitals, a unit of the Accreditation Council for Psychiatric Facilities, sponsored by the National Institute of Mental Health (II C), were also left out for the same reason. Only a few areas from the National Institute on Drug Abuse Model Records Manual (II E) are included here as examples. Following is a listing of the actual documents appended:

A. *Federal Funding Criteria for Drug Treatment Services* were developed by NIDA for all programs receiving full or partial federal funding.

B. *Federal Funding Criteria Audit Form* was newly developed and supersedes the older Audit Form.

C. *JCAH Standards for Drug Abuse Treatment Programs* were developed as a basis for accrediting programs and were used in this way until they were superseded by the JCAH Consolidated Standards. They are included here to indicate how these standards were first defined and how they evolved.

D. *JCAH Consolidated Standards* are the current JCAH Standards, which all programs will have to meet for their new accreditation. They do not include a special section on social service, as did the now outdated standards. The National Association of Social Workers has been working with the JCAH to remedy this oversight. This revision was to be available by September 1980.

E. *National Institute on Drug Abuse Model Records Manual*, a model record-keeping system developed by NIDA, supposedly meets all federal funding criteria and the JCAH criteria. As indicated, because of its length, only a few areas were included here.

F. *Psychohistory History Form* was developed by NIDA as part of its model records package. There has been some question about the usefulness of the checkoff format, which may have been intended as a firm guide, in agencies where there was no professional staff, since the clinical subtleties may be lost between the interstices of the questions. Many agencies use a narrative social history, with guidelines to ensure that the necessary areas are covered by the workers.

A. Federal Funding Criteria:* Special Action Office for Drug Abuse Prevention

Part 1402 is added as set forth below:
Sec.
1402.01 Applicability.
1402.02 Definitions.
1402.03 General requirements.
1402.04 Minimum standards for physical and laboratory examinations.
1402.05 Pre-admission interview.
1402.06 Medical services.
1402.07 Mental health consultation.
1402.08 Counseling.
1402.09 Provision for supportive services.
1402.10 Procedures for urine surveillance.
1402.11 Vocational rehabilitation and employment programs.
1402.12 Patient record system.
1402.13 Program hours for services.
1402.14 Provision for meals.
1402.15 Compliance with all Federal and State regulations.
1402.16 Exceptions to requirements.

AUTHORITY: Secs. 210, 231, 222, the Drug Abuse Office and Treatment Act of 1972, Pub. L. 92–255. (21 U.S.C. 1120, 1131, and 1132).

§ 1402.01 Applicability

This part sets forth the criteria which all Federal departments and agencies shall apply with respect to standards of treatment to be maintained in programs or projects (other than research or demonstration) funded by them, by means of grants or contracts awarded or renewed after the effective date of this part, for drug abuse treatment services, including but not limited to outpatient methadone, residential methadone, residential drug free, out patient drug free and day care drug free, whether such services are performed directly by the recipient of any such grant or contract or indirectly through subcontracts, grants, or means in implementation of the recipient's contract or grant with the Federal agency or department supplying the funds. In the case of a program funded by several sources, only one of which source is Federal, the standards of treatment set forth in this part shall apply to all segments of such program which provide the type of services to which this part applies. This part, however, does not apply to programs conducted within or by departments and agencies of the Federal Government.

§ 1402.02 Definitions.

(a) *Patient*. The term "patient" means any person who has applied for or been given diagnosis or treatment for drug abuse at a treatment program or Central Intake Unit which administers services to which this part applies.

(b) *Program*. The term "program" means any drug abuse project or activity which administers services to which this part applies.

(c) *Program director*. The term "program director" means the person having the ultimate responsibility for managing and supervising a drug abuse program which administers services to which this part applies.

(d) *Medical director*. The term "medical

Federal Register, vol. 40, no. 102 (1975).

director" means a duly licensed physician who has been appointed to assume responsibility for all medical affairs conducted by a program which administers services to which this part applies.

(e) *Treatment and treatment plan.* For the purposes of this part, the term "treatment" includes interviewing, counseling, and any other services or activities carried on for the purpose of, or as incident to, diagnosis, treatment, or rehabilitation with respect to drug abuse, whether or not conducted by a member of the medical profession; and the term "treatment plan" means the mode of treatment that is determined appropriate to meet the objective needs of the patient.

(f) *Qualified mental health professional.* The term "qualified mental health professional" means a person who, by virtue of education, training, or experience, is capable of assessing the psychological and sociological background of drug abusers to determine the treatment plan most appropriate for patients in programs administering services to which this part applies.

§ 1402.03 General requirements

The grantee or contractor shall provide the necessary facilities, materials, services and personnel for the operation of a drug abuse program to which this part applies. The contractor or grantee shall establish and operate, or shall engage a subcontractor to establish and operate, such facilities, and shall provide such material, services, and personnel as are deemed necessary to provide patients with services in accordance with the provisions of this part. The grantee or contractor shall:

(a) *Appropriate facilities.* Provide services through such drug abuse treatment facilities as may be appropriate at such site or sites as shall be approved by the contracting or awarding authority.

(b) *Maintain in sanitary condition.* Maintain all facilities in a clean, safe, and sanitary condition in accordance with applicable standards established under Federal, State and local laws.

(c) *Admission criteria.* Develop criteria which meet the requirements of this part for the admission of patients and the termination of services to them. The admission criteria are applicable only to those individuals with a primary drug abuse problem other than alcohol. Services to a patient must be terminated whenever there is evidence that the level of services does not

meet the requirements of this part or where legitimate, person or person, services are not provided at least once per month on a regular scheduled basis.

(d) *Equipment and furnishings.* Install and maintain appropriate equipment and furnishings which are suitable for the type of treatment services being conducted.

(e) *Personal, medical and drug history.* Establish procedures under which a complete personal, medical, and drug history for each patient will be secured upon the patient's entry into the program and shall be maintained and kept up to date throughout the patient's treatment. This is essential for the purpose of identifying symptoms of flashbacks, psychotic manifestations, and severe physical illness requiring immediate psychiatric or medical care and also for the development of the patient's treatment plan. The intake process must proceed expeditiously to avoid discouragement and shall be completed within the earliest practicable time. A treatment program need not secure personal, medical, or drug information which already had been obtained by a Central Intake Unit on a patient who was referred to the program by such unit unless the information is deemed incomplete or appears questionable. The documentation and results of these CIU examinations must be transferred to the treatment program as such results became available.

(f) *Notice and review of termination of treatment.* In any case in which a decision is made that a patient's treatment to which this part applies be terminated or substantially changed by the program director, the patient shall be given written notice of this fact and the right to have such decision reviewed in accordance with procedures established for that purpose.

§ 1402.04 Minimum standards for physical and laboratory examinations.

(a) *Performance requirements.* A physical and laboratory examination shall be administered by qualified personnel as soon as practicable but not later than 21 days after admission of the patient. The results of the physical and laboratory examination and their implications for the patient's treatment shall be detailed in his treatment plan. Residential drug-free programs are required to perform physical examinations at the earliests practicable time because of the possibility of the existence of infectious diseases which might affect other patients. In the event that the residential program requires a period of induction, the physical examination should be administered during that period. A treatment program need not repeat any part of a physical or laboratory examination which had been completed by a Central Intake Unit from which a patient was referred unless the results of the examination are incomplete or questionable. The documentation and results of these examinations should be contained in the patient's intake record upon transfer to the treatment program. When special circumstances warrant an exception to the required physical and laboratory examination, a request for such exception may be made in accordance with § 1402.16 of this part. Such request must be submitted by the Medical Director and must contain a full explanation of the need for the exception to the requirements. However, the granting of an exception under this part shall not be considered as an exception to any applicable regulation of the Food and Drug Administration.

(b) *Physical and laboratory examination.* The physical and laboratory examination of each patient shall include:

(1) Investigation of the possibility of infectious disease, pulmonary, liver, cardiac abnormalities, dermatologic sequelae of addiction and possible concurrent surgical problems;

(2) Complete blood count and differential;

(3) Serological test for syphillis;

(4) Routine and microscopic urinalysis;

(5) Urine screening for drug (toxicology);

(6) Multiphasic chemistry profile;

(7) Chest x-ray;

(8) Australian antigen [HbAg testing (HAA testing)] as appropriate, and

(9) EKG and biological tests for pregnancy, as appropriate.

§ 1402.05 Pre-admission interview.

(a) *Information to be obtained.* Each patient seeking admission or re-admission for the purpose of obtaining treatment services shall be interviewed by a qualified mental health professional having qualifications as described in paragraph (f) of § 1402.02, or by a qualified intake counselor under the supervision of such a professional. Under the supervision and guidance of such professional, the staff shall obtain a complete

personal history including information relating to the patient's social, economic, and family background, his education and vocational achievements, any history of past drug abuse and treatment, any record of past criminal conduct, and any other information which is relevant to his application and which may be helpful in determining an appropriate treatment program.

(b) *Development of appropriate treatment plan.* A primary objective of the admission interview is to determine the most appropriate mode of treatment for the patient and to assure that he understands the nature of the program and what may be expected of him. Any program of treatment recommended must be designed to meet the needs of the patient consistent with the projected program expectations. If a Central Intake Unit provides intake screening, it is the responsibility of the program to which the patient has been referred by such Unit to develop an individually tailored treatment plan based on the interview and his case history.

(c) *Reexamination and reports.* For persons receiving outpatient treatment, individual treatment plans shall be reexamined by the treatment team at least once in each ninety day period and altered where necessary to satisfy any needed changes. For all other modalities, the individual treatment plan shall be reexamined at least once in each 30 day period. A complete report of each review shall be recorded in the patient's record.

(d) *Information to be documented.* Each treatment plan must include documented information relating to (1) short and long term goals for treatment generated by both staff and patient, (2) the assignment of a primary counselor, (3) a description of the type of counseling services to be provided, and the frequency thereof, and (4) a description of the supportive services determined to be needed by the individual patient.

§ 1402.06 Medical services.

(a) *Designation of medical director.* Each grantee or contractor shall designate a medical director who must assume responsibility for the administration of all medical services performed by the program. He must be licensed to practice medicine in the jurisdiction in which he administers medical services. It will also be his responsibility to assure that the initial evaluation is properly performed, the medical needs of each patient are periodically evaluated, and that any emergency medical services, when needed, are adequately provided. The medical director shall also be responsible for determining what emergency medical equipment and supplies are needed to deal with possible overdoses and other medical emergencies that might arise and to make certain that such equipment and supplies are provided.

(b) *Services to patients (other than methadone) receiving prescription medication.* Each grantee or contractor shall, for those patients receiving prescription medication through the program, establish procedures under which consultation with the medical director or other program physician will be provided, at a minimum, once in every four week period or more frequent depending upon the needs of the patient.

(c) *Provision for emergency medical services.* (1) Each program is required to formalize a written agreement with a licensed hospital or hospitals in the community for the purpose of providing emergency, inpatient and ambulatory medical services, when needed.

(2) Medical services which are not directly related to the provision of drug abuse treatment services are not reimbursable under Federal contracts or grants. To the extent practicable, however, each program should arrange for the provision of such services.

§ 1402.07 Mental health consultation.

Each program shall provide, through a qualified mental health professional, a minimum of five hours per week of mental health consultation for each 100 patients. The objective of this consultation should be to review selected cases and to provide assistance to the staff in the management of patient services or for the purpose of referral for psychiatric services.

§ 1402.08 Counseling.

All counseling services are required to be performed by trained personnel under the supervision of a qualified professional, utilizing the individual, family, or group counseling technique which best meets the needs of the patients. In the case of group counseling, the size of the group should be left to the discretion of the professional under whose supervision the group counseling services are administered. For outpatient methadone and outpatient drug-free programs, a minimum of three hours of formalized counseling per week shall be made available for each patient either by the program or by an outside qualified consultant under a contract. For residential drug-free, residential methadone, and day care drug-free programs, a minimum of 10 hours of formalized counseling per week shall be made available for each patient either by the program or by an outside qualified consultant. The hours of counseling actually provided should vary according to the needs of the patient.

§ 1402.09 Provision for supportive services.

The following supportive services shall be provided:

(a) Educational:

(b) Vocational counseling and training:

(c) Job development and placement; and

(d) Legal services through local licensed lawyers to the extent such services are related to the patient's treatment.

To the maximum extent possible, programs shall utilize community resources to provide these services. Copies of any agreements for the provision of such services shall be furnished to the contracting or awarding authority. If any program is unable to obtain any of the requisite supportive services, a formal request to provide such services directly must be made to the project officer for the contract or grant award.

§ 1402.10 Procedures for urine surveillance.

The following standards shall be applied for urine surveillance:

(a) *Procedures.* Urine specimens from each patient must be collected in a manner that minimizes falsification and on a randomly scheduled basis. In programs dispensing methadone, urine specimens for all patients must be analyzed weekly for opiates and monthly for methadone, amphetamines, barbiturates, as well as other drugs as indicated. For all other programs it is recommended that urine specimens from all patients be analyzed at least monthly for opiates, methadone, amphetamines, barbiturates, as well as other drugs as indi-

194   **APPENDIX II**

cated. More frequent testing should occur when clinically indicated.

(b) *Compliance with other standards.* Laboratories used for urine testing shall comply with all applicable Federal proficiency testing and licensing standards and all state standards in conformity therewith. Laboratories covered by this requirement include any independent, clinical, government or program facility that offers to perform presumptive analysis for screening purposes as well as definitive qualitative analysis for confirmed identifications.

(c) *Use of urine testing results.* Urine testing results shall be used as one clinical tool for the purposes of diagnosis, and in the determination of patient treatment plans. Patient records must reflect the manner in which test results are utilized, and shall distinguish presumptive qualitative laboratory results from those which are definitive.

(d) *Use of laboratory analysis.* Program and medical directors electing to rely on the results of presumptive urinalysis for patient management must demonstrate reasonable access to definitive qualitative laboratory analysis for use when necessary, e.g., criminal justice system records, intake urine testing on all prospective methadone clients, any loss of patient privileges based on urinalysis results, and any frequency of use of other drugs not detectable by a screening method.

§ 1402.11 Vocational rehabilitation and employment programs.

All patients enrolled in outpatient treatment should be encouraged to participate in an educational or job training program or to obtain gainful employment as soon as appropriate but not later than 120 days from the date of enrollment. In the case of patients enrolled in residential programs, such patients should be encouraged to participate in one of such programs or to obtain gainful employment within sixty days from the date of admission. All efforts toward either of these objectives and the results derived therefrom must be noted in the patient's treatment plan and the notes of his progress. If, for any reason, a patient is not encouraged to pursue one of these alternatives, the reasons therefore also shall be recorded in the patient's records.

§ 1402.12 Patient record system.

Each program shall establish a patient record system to document and monitor patient care. This system shall comply with all Federal and State reporting requirements. All records shall be kept confidential in accordance with the applicable regulations (currently 21 CFR, Part 1401; proposed to be incorporated in 42 CFR, Part 2; see 40 FR 20522, May 9, 1975).

§ 1402.13 Program hours for services.

(a) *General requirements.* A reasonable effort must be made to adjust the hours of program operation to meet patient needs. For outpatient treatment programs, consideration should be given to the employment hours of patients, and, to the extent practicable, clinic operating hours should be scheduled at such times as will accommodate the working hours of such patients. Patients who are not employed or who are not attending school or training programs are expected to arrange their schedules in such manner as to receive services at suitable times. Where necessary to accommodate the needs of patients, the program must recognize that the usual 9 a.m. to 5 p.m. workday shall not be rigidly adopted for outpatient treatment. In many clinics with large patient admissions, a 12 hour day of operations is frequently necessary.

(b) *Minimum hours of operation.* The following minimum hours of operation shall be maintained:

(1) *Outpatient methadone.* Each outpatient methadone program shall provide services seven days each week. Services provided on at least five of these seven days shall be on the basis of an eight hour day provided that services for a minimum of two hours of such eight hour day must be scheduled at a time other than the regular 9 a.m. to 5 p.m. day. Services administered during the remaining two days must be scheduled for a period of at least four hours each day at a time most convenient to the patients.

(2) *Residential methadone and residential drug-free.* Each residential methadone and residential drug-free program shall provide services seven days per week, twenty-four hours per day.

(3) *Outpatient drug-free.* Each outpatient drug-free program shall provide services at least six days per week. Services provided on at least five of these six days shall be on the basis of an eight hour day provided that a minimum of two hours of such eight hour day must be scheduled at a time other than the regular 9 a.m. to 5 p.m. day. Services administered during the re-

maining (sixth) day must be scheduled for a period of at least five hours.

(4) *Day-care drug-free.* Each day-care drug-free program must provide services at least five days per week, teh hours per day. Services provided for the remaining two days may be so scheduled as to accommodate the needs of the patients.

(5) *Central intake unit.* Each central intake unit must provide services at least five days per week, eight hours per day.

§ 1402.14 Provision for meals.

Residential methadone and residential drug-free programs shall provide each patient a minimum of three meals per day. While meals are not required for day-care drug-free programs, such programs are encouraged to provide each patient one meal daily, if practicable.

§ 1402.15 Compliance with all Federal and State regulations.

All programs which use methadone for detoxification and maintenance treatment must comply with all applicable regulations of the Food and Drug Administration, as well as other applicable Federal and State regulations and directives.

§ 1402.16 Exceptions to requirements.

Exceptions to the requirements set forth in this Part 1402 may be requested by submitting a request to the Director, Division of Community Assistance, National Institute on Drug Abuse. 11400 Rockville Pike, Rockville, Maryland 20852. The request must fully explain and justify the necessity for the exception.

Part 1403 is added as set forth below:
Sec.
1403.01 Applicability.
1403.02 Definitions.
1403.03 General requirements.
1403.04 Operation of facilities and examination of patients.
1403.05 Medical services.
1403.06 Agreement for emergency medical services.
1403.07 Pre-admission interview.
1403.08 Patient file.
1403.09 Referral for treatment.
1403.10 Adoption of procedures to avoid duplication.
1403.11 Procedure for urine surveillance.
1403.12 Patient recordkeeping.
1403.13 Agreements between CIU and community programs.
1403.14 Requirements to be adopted in CIU procedures.
1403.15 Compliance with all Federal and State regulations.
1403.16 Exceptions to requirements.
AUTHORITY: Secs. 210, 221, 222. Drug Abuse Office and Treatment Act of 1972 Pub. L. 92-255. (21 U.S.C. 1120, 1131, and 1132.)

§ 1403.01 Applicability.

This part sets forth the criteria to be applied by all Federal departments and agencies with respect to standards to be maintained for drug abuse programs or projects (other than research or demonstration) funded by them by means of grants or contracts awarded or renewed after the effective date of this part, for the conduct of central intake services, whether such services are performed directly by the recipient of any such grant or contract or indirectly through subcontracts, grants, or other means in implementation of the recipient's contract or grant with the Federal agency or department supplying the funds. In case of a program funded by several sources, only one of which source is Federal, the standards of treatment set forth in this part shall apply to all segments of such program which provide the type of services to which this part applies. This part, however, does not apply to programs conducted within or by departments and agencies of the Federal Government.

§ 1403.02 Definitions.

(a) *Patient.* The term "patient" means any person who has applied for or been given diagnosis or treatment for drug abuse at a treatment program or central intake unit which administers services to which this part applies.

(b) *Program.* The term "program" means any drug abuse project or activity which administers services to which this part applies.

(c) *Central intake unit.* The term "Central Intake Unit" (CIU) means a centralized facility which is responsible for the initial screening, evaluation, diagnosis and orientation of a patient for purposes of referral to an appropriate modality for drug abuse treatment.

(d) *Qualified mental health professional.* The term "qualified mental health professional" means a person who by virtue of education, training, or experience is capable of assessing the psychological and sociological background of drug abusers to determine the treatment plan most appropriate for patients in programs to which this part applies.

(e) *Treatment and treatment plan.* For the purposes of this part, the term "treatment" includes interviewing, counseling, and any other services or activities carried on for the purpose of, or as incident to, diagnosis, treatment, or rehabilitation with respect to drug abuse whether or not conducted by a member of the medical profession; and the term "treatment plan" means the mode of treatment that is determined appropriate to meet the objective needs of the patient.

(f) *Program and medical director.* The term "program director" and "medical director" shall have the meaning set forth in §§ 1402.02(c) and 1402.02(d), respectively, of Part 1402 of this chapter.

§ 1403.03 General requirements.

The grantee or contractor shall provide adequate facilities, material, services, and personnel for the operation of a central intake facility. The contractor or grantee shall establish and operate, or shall engage a subcontractor to establish and operate, such facilities and provide such material, services, and personnel as are necessary to render such services to drug dependent persons in accordance with the provisions of this part. The Central Intake Unit shall be established at such site or sites as shall be approved by the awarding authority. The unit shall operate under procedures which provide (a) criteria for the admission of patients and for the termination of services rendered to them and (b) informal, standardized, initial patient orientation, multiphasic health screening, and referral to an appropriate treatment modality for new or readmitted patients.

§ 1403.04 Operation of facilities and examination of patients.

(a) *Hours of operation.* Each CIU facility shall remain open at least eight hours each day, five days per week. The intake process must proceed expeditiously to avoid discouragement and should not exceed a period of two days. The facility shall be appropriately furnished to provide the required services and shall be maintained in a condition consistent with applicable regulations of Federal, State and local authorities.

(b) *Examination.* At the time of intake, an initial personal, medical, and drug history shall be obtained and a physical and laboratory examination administered by qualified personnel. Such examination shall check the possibility of infectious diseases, pulmonary, liver, cardiac abnormalities, dermatologic sequelae of addiction and possible concurrent surgical problems. The laboratory examination shall include:

(a) Complete blood count and differential;

(2) Serological test for syphillis;

(3) Routine and microscopic urinalysis;

(4) Urine screening for drugs (toxicology);

(5) Multiphasic chemistry profile;

(6) Chest x-ray;

(7) Australian antigen [HbAg testing (HAA testing)] as appropriate;

(8) EKG and biological tests for pregnancy, as appropriate; and

(9) Pap smear and gonorrhea culture, as appropriate.

§ 1403.05 Medical services.

(a) *Designation of medical director.* Each grantee or contractor shall designate a medical director who shall assume responsibility for the administration of all medical services performed by the CIU. Such director must be licensed to practice medicine in the jurisdiction in which the program is located.

(b) *Initial evaluation.* It will be the responsibility of the medical director to assure that the initial evaluation is properly performed and that the appropriate needs of each patient are evaluated and the type of treatment, if any, prescribed. The evaluation shall include an initial diagnostic work up, an identification of medical and surgical problems for referral to other treatment facilities, and a periodic review of the patient's records. If the patient has a previous medical record and it is available, the medical director should obtain it if possible and include it with the records sent to the treatment center to which the patient has been or is being transferred.

§ 1403.06 Agreement for emergency medical services.

(a) Each program is required to formalize a written agreement with a licensed hospital or hospitals in the community for the purpose of providing emergency, inpatient and ambulatory medical services, when needed.

(b) Medical services which are not directly related to the provision of drug abuse treatment services are not reimbursable under Federal contracts or grants. To the extent practicable, however, each program should arrange for the provision of such services.

§ 1403.07 Pre-admission interview.

Programs shall conduct an interview by a mental health professional, or by a qualified intake counselor under the supervision of such a professional, of each patient or former patient re-admitted. In the course of the interview, the staff shall obtain a complete personal history, including information relating to the patient's social, economic, and family background, his education and vocational achievements, any history of past drug abuse and treatment, any record of past criminal conduct and any other information which is relevant to his application and which may be helpful in determining an appropriate treatment program. The staff should then discuss with the patient the various treatment modalities available to him. After discussing the availability of these modalities in the light of the patient's particular needs (including the results of physician's evaluation), a treatment plan should be selected by mutual agreement and an appropriate referral made.

§ 1403.08 Patient file.

The program should maintain a file for each drug dependent patient. This file should be kept up to date by the particular agencies and all transfers to other programs and terminations noted. All records shall be held confidential in accordance with the Confidentiality Regulations set forth in Part 1401 of this chapter.

§ 1403.09 Referral for treatment.

Upon reaching an agreement as to the modality to be applied, the patient should be referred to treatment within 48 hours and his intake records transferred to the center administering such treatment.

§ 1403.10 Adoption of procedures to avoid duplication.

Each program shall adopt such intake procedures as will avoid the duplication of services by programs receiving patients through the central intake process.

§ 1403.11 Procedure for urine surveillance.

Urine specimen shall be obtained by CIU from each patient under appropriate supervision. The specimens must be analyzed for morphine, methadone, cocaine, codeine, amphetamines, barbiturates, as well as other drugs if indicated. Laboratories which are used for urine testing must comply with applicable Federal proficiency testing and licensing standards and all State standards in conformity therewith.

§ 1403.12 Patient recordkeeping.

Each CIU program shall establish a record system for patients processed which must be adequate to meet all Federal and State reporting requirements and all patient records shall be maintained in accordance with the Confidentiality Regulations (currently set forth as Part 1401 of this chapter; proposed to be incorporated in 42 CFR Part 2; see 40 FR 20522, May 9, 1975).

§ 1403.13 Agreements between CIU and community programs.

Each CIU program shall establish and provide the contracting or awarding agency with documentary evidence of formal agreements with community based drug abuse treatment programs. Such documentary evidence shall include the treatment program's agreement to utilize the CIU for patient intake functions. The agreement should also provide for the acceptance of only those patients who have been processed through the CIU.

§ 1403.14 Requirements to be adopted in CIU procedures.

Each CIU program shall adopt procedures relating to the following:

(a) Orientation of patients with particular instructions on the available treatment options and the specific treatment program recommended to meet the needs of the patient;

(b) Consideration and determination of the most appropriate method to be followed for referral to treatment;

(c) The negotiation of an agreement with the patient covering the terms and conditions of referral to treatment; and

(d) Subject to approval by Federal and State project representatives, establishment of standards for meeting the needs of patients referred to CIU for rescreening and for referral to a modality or program determined to be more suitable for their needs.

§ 1403.15 Compliance with all Federal and State regulations.

All programs using methadone for detoxification and maintenance treatment must comply with all regulations of the Food and Drug Administration as well as all other relevant Federal and State regulations and directives.

§ 1403.16 Exceptions to requirements.

Requests for exceptions to the criteria and requirements set forth in this Part 1403 shall be submitted to the Director, Division of Community Assistance, National Institute on Drug Abuse, 11400 Rockville Pike, Rockville, Maryland 20852, for his consideration and action. Each request shall fully explain and justify the necessity for the requested exception.

[FR Doc.75-13602 Filed 5-23-75;8:45 am]

B. Federal Funding Questionnaire

NAME OF PROGRAM: Milwaukee County Mental Health Center
Drug Abuse Program

MODALITY: Outpatient

NUMBER OF STATIC SLOTS (Both
National Institute on Drug Abuse
[NIDA] and Non-NIDA Funded):

230	NIDA
137	Non-NIDA
367	TOTAL

FEDERAL FUNDING CRITERIA QUESTIONNAIRE

Please answer all questions below (yes, no, or not applicable). For all questions that you have answered with a "no" please state on the back of the sheet either a) what steps you will be taking to bring your program into compliance or b) the reasons why you feel it would be appropriate to request an exemption from this requirement. Please bear in mind that Federal Funding Criteria apply to *all* treatment slots in your program and not just to those slots that are NIDA funded.

	RESPONSE		
FEDERAL FUNDING CRITERIA	Yes	No	N/A

General Requirements (1402.03)

1. The facilities used for drug treatment are clean, safe, and in a sanitary condition.   X
2. There are written criteria for admission to the program. (Please attach these standards to this questionnaire.)   X
   See Appendix A.
3. There are written criteria for termination (both voluntary and involuntary) from the program. (Please attach this criteria to this questionnaire.)   X

	RESPONSE		
FEDERAL FUNDING CRITERIA	Yes	No	N/A

See Appendix B.

4. All clients admitted to the program have a primary drug abuse problem other than alcohol or marijuana.   X

5. All clients are seen in face to face contact by a program staff member at least once every 30 days on a regularly scheduled basis.   X
   (Please indicate how these contacts are documented.)
   Progress notes are entered in the client's clinical record.

6. Adequate equipment and furnishings are available for the type of treatment services being conducted.   X

7. A complete personal, medical, and drug history is written up and placed in the record for each client as he/she enters the program.   X
   (If you use forms for obtaining this information, please attach them to this questionnaire.)

See Appendix C.

8. These histories are updated throughout the client's treatment.   X

9. The intake process proceeds expeditiously to avoid discouragement and is completed within the earliest practicable time (how long is your intake process from first contact with client to actual admission to treatment?).   X
   Admission services are completed in 1 day.

10. Written notice is given to all clients when their treatment is to be terminated or substantially altered.   X

11. A written appeal procedure is given to the client in the event that he wishes to protest this termination or change in treatment.   X
    (Please attach this statement to this questionnaire.)
    See Appendix D.

Physical and Laboratory Examinations (1402.04)

1. A physical and laboratory examination is administered by or under the supervision of a licensed physician not later than 21 days after admission to the program.   X

2. The results of the physical and laboratory examination and their implication for the client's treatment are detailed in his treatment plan.   X

3. The physical and laboratory examination on each client includes the following:
   a. Investigation of the possibility of infectious disease, pulmonary, liver or cardiac abnormalities,   X

	RESPONSE		
FEDERAL FUNDING CRITERIA	Yes	No	N/A

dermatologic consequences of addiction or possible concurrent surgical problems.

b. Complete blood count and differential.   X

c. Serological test for syphilis.   X

d. Routine and microscopic urinalysis.   X

e. Urine screening for drugs (toxicology).   X

f. Multiphasic chemistry profile.   X

g. Chest x-ray.   X

h. Referral of female clients for complete OB/GYN   X
examination.

4. The client's medical history is reviewed by a program   X
physician or medical director.

Pre-admission Interview (1402.05)

1. Each client seeking admission or readmission to the   X
program is interviewed by a mental health professional
or by an intake interviewer who is supervised by a
mental health professional.

2. The personal history obtained during the pre-admission interview includes information relating to the
client's:

a. social, occupational and family background;   X

b. educational and vocational achievements;   X

c. history of drug abuse and treatment;   X

d. record of past criminal conduct.   X

3. A treatment plan is developed and written down for
each client and includes:

                          See Appendix E

a. short and long term goals for treatment generated   X
by both staff and client;

b. the assignment of a primary counselor;   X

c. a description of the type of counseling services to   X
be provided and the frequency thereof;

d. a description of the supportive services determined to be needed by the individual client.   X

(If you use a form for recording treatment plans, please
attach it to this questionnaire.)

         See sample cases in Policy and Procedure book.

4. The treatment plan is reviewed, revised, and recorded
in client's record according to the following schedule:

a. outpatient treatment: at least every 90 days;   X

b. all other modalities: at least every 30 days.   X

Medical Services (1402.06)

1. There is a designated medical director who assumes   X

	RESPONSE		
FEDERAL FUNDING CRITERIA	Yes	No	N/A

    responsibility for the administration of all medical ser-
vices performed by the program.

    (Please attach a copy of the written agreement with the physician for provision of medical services to the program.)

    Two full-time physicians staff the Drug Abuse Program.

2. The medical director sees that the initial medical evalu-   X
ation is properly performed, that the medical needs of each client are periodically evaluated and that any emergency medical services, when needed, are adequately provided.

3. The medical director sees that supplies and equipment   X
for medical emergencies are readily available.

4. Consultation with a program physician is provided at   X
least once a month for all clients who are receiving prescription medication (other than methadone) through the program.

5. There is a formal, written agreement between the pro-   X
gram and a licensed hospital in the community for the purpose of providing emergency (inpatient and ambulatory) medical services when needed.

    (Please attach a copy of this agreement.)

    As part of the Medical Complex, medical services are available on an as-needed basis from other Medical Complex components.

Mental Health Consultation (1402.07)

1. Consultation by a qualified mental health professional   X
is provided to the staff for a minimum of five (5) hours per week per each 100 clients (if there is a qualified mental health professional on the staff, this requirement can be met by arranging for that person to formally consult with the rest of the counseling staff members for the required amount of time. Please indicate how many hours of mental health consultation are scheduled for the staff.

    Three full time PSWs staff the Drug Abuse Program. The Psychiatric Social Service Supv. or PSW provide scheduled consultation to the Addiction Specialist. Psychiatric and psychological consultation is available from the appropriate depts. of the Mental Health Ctr.

Counseling (1402.08)

1. All counseling staff are supervised by a qualified pro-   X
fessional.

	RESPONSE		
FEDERAL FUNDING CRITERIA	Yes	No	N/A

2. The required number of hours or formalized counseling time is made available by the program to each client according to the following schedule:

   a. outpatient programs (methadone and drug free): three (3) hours per week;   X

   b. residential and day care programs (methadone and drug free): ten (10) hours per week.   X

(What is the average amount of time each client actually spends in some form of formalized counseling per week?)

                        Approximately 1 hour per week.

Provision of Supportive Services (1402.09)

1. The following supportive services are provided either at the program or through cooperative agreements with the community agencies:

   a. educational;   X

   b. vocational counseling and training;   X

   c. job development and placement;   X

   d. legal services.

                        See Appendix G.

(Please attach copies of the appropriate cooperative agreements.)

Procedures for Urine Surveillance (1402.10)

1. Methadone programs: urine specimens are analyzed at least weekly on all clients for opiates and monthly for methadone, amphetamines, barbiturates and other drugs as indicated.   X

2. Non-methadone programs: urine specimens are analyzed at least monthly for opiates, methadone, amphetamines, barbiturates and other drugs as indicated (optional).   X

3. Urine specimens are collected in a manner that minimizes falsification and on a randomly scheduled basis.   X

4. Laboratories used for urine testing comply with all applicable Federal proficiency testing and licensing standards.   X

5. Urine testing results are used as a clinical tool for the purposes of diagnosis and in the determination of client treatment plans.   X

6. Results of all urine tests and the manner in which these test results were utilized with the client are recorded in all client's records.   X

	RESPONSE		
FEDERAL FUNDING CRITERIA	Yes	No	N/A

7. If the program relies on any of the immunoassay urine testing methods (e.g., FRAT, EMIT, RIA, or HI) it also has access to more definitive qualitative laboratory analysis (e.g., TLC, GC, or SPG) for use when identification of the specific drug is required.   X

        TLC is the primary method of testing.

Vocational Rehabilitation and Employment Programs (1402.11)

1. Outpatient programs: all clients are encouraged to participate in an educational or job training program or to obtain gainful employment not later than 120 days from the date of enrollment.   X

2. Residential programs: all clients are encouraged to participate in an educational or job training program or to obtain gainful employment no later than sixty (60) days from the anticipated date of discharge.   [N/A: X]
(What percentage of your clients are working or in training within this time frame?)

3. All efforts toward the objectives described above and the results derived therefrom are noted in the client's treatment plan and in the progress notes in his record.   X

4. If, for good cause, a client is not encouraged to pursue one of these alternatives, the reasons are recorded in client's record.   X

Client Record System (1402.12)

1. A record is set up for each client in treatment to document and monitor his progress.   X

2. This record includes the following records:
   a. complete intake history;   X
   b. record of physical and laboratory examinations;   X
   c. treatment plan plus periodic revisions;   X
   d. progress notes;   X
   e. notes by program medical director or physician regarding medical contacts and/or medications prescribed.   X
   f. signed consent forms for release of information (when necessary);   X
   g. urine test results;   X
   h. attendance record (for counseling, medication, and other program activities);   X
   i. discharge summary.   X

	RESPONSE		
FEDERAL FUNDING CRITERIA	Yes	No	N/A

Program Hours for Service (1402.13)

1. An effort is made to adjust the hours of program operation to meet client needs with special attention to the working hours of employed clients. — X
2. The following *minimum* hours of operation are maintained: — X
   a. Outpatient methadone programs:
      (1) Service is provided seven (7) days a week. — X
      (2) On at least five (5) of those seven (7) days, the clinic is open for eight (8) hours, with a minimum of two (2) of those hours scheduled at a time other than the regular 9:00 a.m. to 5:00 p.m. day. — X
      (3) Services administered on the remaining two (2) days are scheduled for a period of at least four (4) hours each day at a time most convenient to the clients. — X
   b. Residential methadone and drug free programs: services are provided seven (7) days per week, twenty-four (24) hours per day. — — — X
   c. Outpatient drug free programs:
      (1) Services are provided at least six (6) days per week. — — — X
      (2) Services on at least five (5) of those six (6) days are provided for eight (8) hours a day, with a minimum of two (2) of those hours scheduled at a time other than the regular 9:00 a.m. to 5:00 p.m. day. — — — X
      (3) Services administered during the sixth day are scheduled for a period of at least five (5) hours. — — — X
   d. Day care programs:
      (1) Services are provided at least five (5) days per week, ten (10) hours per day. — — — X
      (2) Services provided for the remaining two (2) days are scheduled to accommodate the needs of the clients (optional). — — — X

Provision for Meals (1402.14)

1. Residential programs: clients are provided with a minimum of three (3) meals per day. — — — X
2. Day care programs: clients are provided with one meal per day (optional). — — — X

	RESPONSE		
FEDERAL FUNDING CRITERIA	Yes	No	N/A

SIGNATURE: _____

Program Director   Richard L. Wiesen, M.D.

DATE: _____

Further documentation of the requirements listed in this survey are available in "Survey Report—Document Book Standards—Alcohol and Other Drug Abuse for Outpatient Treatment Programs PW-MH 61.03, Milwaukee County Mental Health Center, Drug Abuse Program" which is available upon request for your inspection.

C. Standards for Drug Abuse Treatment and Rehabilitation Programs

Accreditation Council for Psychiatric Facilities

Joint Commission on Accreditation of Hospitals

20. Social Services

0.1
D A For each applicant/client, a social assessment shall be undertaken and should include information relating to:
- Environment and home;
- Religion;
- Present family situation;
- Childhood history;
- Military service history;
- Financial status;
- Drug and alcohol usage among other members of the individual's family or household; and,
- Reasons for seeking treatment.

0.2
CD The coordinator of the social services shall provide consultation in interviewing, intake, case management, referral, and client advocacy procedures.

0.3
D The program should establish at least informal working relationships with outside resources, such as:
- Other drug abuse treatment and rehabilitation programs in the community;
- Community social service agencies;

- Public assistance and welfare agencies;
- Hotels, rooming houses, realtors, apartment managers or landlords who are willing to provide living quarters to clients;
- Child care agencies; and,
- Homemaker services.

20.4
CD
At least semiannually, the coordinator of the social services component shall prepare and make available a social services progress report that shall contain for the reporting period information describing the functions and accomplishments of the social services component. This report shall also contain information on the number of referrals made to outside social service resources, and the types of resources to which referrals were made.

22. Intake

22.1
A
The types of intake and assessment services and manner in which they are provided shall be determined by the needs of the programs the assessment and referral program serves. There shall be documentation verifying that intake and assessment procedures are undertaken in a manner consistent with procedures approved by the coordinators of the client service components of the programs with which the assessment and referral program has formal agreements.

22.2
CD A
There shall be clearly stated written criteria for determining the elibigility of individuals for admission.

22.3
CD A
The program shall have written policies and procedures governing the intake process that define:
- The types of information to be gathered on all applicants prior to admission;
- Procedures to be followed when accepting referrals from outside agencies or organizations;
- The types of records to be kept on all applicants;
- The statistical data related to the intake process that is to be compiled on a regular basis, as well as the frequency with which statistical reports are to be made available to the staff; and,
- Procedures to be followed, including those for referrals, when an applicant is found ineligible for admission.

22.4
CD A
The following information shall be collected and recorded for all applicants prior to or at the time of admission:
- Name;
- Address;
- Telephone number, when applicable;

- Date of birth;
- Sex;
- Race of ethnic origin;
- Presenting drug problem, recorded using a classification system common throughout the program;
- Date the information was gathered;
- Signature of the staff member gathering the information; and,
- Name of the referring agency, when appropriate.

5 The applicant shall retain the right to withhold any information that is not
) A demonstrably necessary to the treatment process or to essential program operations.

22.5.1. Where a program finds it necessary to require certain information as a condition of admission, there should be a written policy delineating such information.

22.5.2. When an applicant refuses to divulge information, the refusal shall be noted in the client case record.

6 Information gathered in the course of the intake and assessment process shall be
) A recorded on standardized forms. The completed forms shall become part of the applicant's case record.

.7 When an applicant is found to be ineligible for admission, the reason shall be
) A recorded in the client case record, and a referral to an appropriate agency or organization should be attempted.

.8 A written log shall be maintained of all referrals made by outside agencies or
) A individuals to the program that will indicate the nature and disposition of the referrals received.

.9 During the intake process, every effort shall be made to assure that applicants
) understand the:
- General nature and goals of the program;
- Rules governing client conduct and infractions that can lead to disciplinary action or discharge from the program;
- In a nonresidential program, the hours during which services are available; and,
- Treatment costs to be borne by the client, if any.

.10 *Sufficient information shall be collected during the intake process so that a tentative*
) A *treatment plan can be developed.* The information shall be gathered in a manner

consistent with procedures developed by the coordinators of the client service components, and shall be recorded on standardized forms. The completed forms shall become part of the applicant's case record.

23. Treatment Plans

23.1 An assessment and referral program shall prepare a limited treatment plan defi-
A ning the types of actions required to meet an applicant's immediate needs. This plan shall be used only until a more extensive treatment plan can be developed by the program to which the applicant is referred.

23.2 Based upon the assessments made of a client's needs, a written treatment plan
CD shall be developed and recorded in the client's case record. A treatment plan shall be developed as soon after the client's admission as feasible, but before the client is engaged in extensive therapeutic activities.

23.2.1. A treatment plan shall integrate the specific plans developed for the client by each of the client service components.

23.3 Treatment plans should be developed in partnership with the client, reviewed
C regularly with the client, and revised as often as necessary.

23.4 The treatment plan shall contain clear and concise statements of at least the
CD short-term goals the client will be attempting to achieve, along with a realistic time schedule for their achievement.

23.5 Treatment goals should be set by the client with the participation and guidance
C of appropriate staff members.

23.6 Treatment goals should be written in terms of measurable criteria of expected
C performance or behavior.

23.7 The treatment plan shall define the services to be provided the client, the
CD therapeutic activities in which the client is expected to participate, and the sequence in which services will be provided. It shall also designate those staff members to be involved in the client's treatment.

23.9 Reviews of and changes in the treatment plan shall be recorded in the client's
CD case record. The date of the review or change, as well as the individuals involved in the review, shall also be recorded.

23.9
C
The use of abstract terms, technical jargon, or slang should be avoided in the treatment plan, and the plan should be written in a manner readily understandable to the average client.

11. Activities

11.1
CD A
For each applicant or client there shall be an activities assessment, which should include information relating to the individual's current skills, talents, aptitudes, and interests.

11.2
C
In a comprehensive rehabilitation program, the activities assessment shall include information relating to:
• Physical abilities and limitations;
• Ability to financially afford various forms of activities;
• The amount of leisure time available;
• Expectations as to the benefits to be derived from activities;
• Potential for improving current skills and talents or for developing new ones; and,
• Motivations for engaging in various forms of activity.

11.3
C
At least semiannually, the coordinator of the activities component shall prepare and make available an activities progress report that should contain for the reporting period the following information:
• The number of clients who have participated in each form of organized activity provided by the program;
• The number, nature, and source of complaints about existing activities;
• The number, nature, and source of requests for additional activities;
• Updated inventory of equipment and supplies;
• The number and types of contacts made with outside activity resources; and,
• The number of volunteers used and the types of services the volunteers provided.

11.4
C
The coordinator of the activities component shall take steps to ensure that a regularly revised list of activity resources is made available to clients and is conspicuously posted in appropriate areas of the program. This list may be limited to those resources that clients may utilize without a program referral.

11.5
CD
In comprehensive rehabilitation programs and in residential short-term detoxification programs, there should be a variety of activities available to clients, as appropriate to the needs and level of maturation of the clients served.

11.6
C
In comprehensive rehabilitation programs, the size and geographic location of the program shall also be taken into account in determining the types of activities to be made available to clients.

11.7 The activities that the program makes available should be those that can eventu-
C ally become integrated into the clients' lives.

16. Legal Assistance

16.1 No part of these standards dealing with legal assistance is intended to con-
CDEA travene any laws or rules of court now established or any principle of ethics
related to the practice of law. Where a conflict between these standards and laws
or rules of court or ethical principles exists, said laws, rules, or principles shall
prevail.

16.2 The information gathered on each applicant/client relating to legal assessment
CDA shall include as a minimum:
  • Legal history; and,
    • A preliminary discussion to determine the extent to which the individual's
    legal situation will influence progress in treatment and the urgency of the
    legal situation.

16.3 The coordinator of the legal assistance component shall provide advice and
CD counsel to the program in its attempt to deal with the legal problems of clients,
and should provide counsel and assistance to the governing body, executive
director, and staff members in their capacity as agents of the program.

16.3.1. The program may choose to appoint an attorney to provide legal assistance to clients and another attorney to provide counsel to the governing body,
executive director, and staff members.

16.4 The coordinator shall provide counsel in at least the following areas:
CD • Confidentiality provisions of federal, state, and local laws, and statutes on
    privileged communications;
  • Public or private contracts into which the program may enter;
  • Zoning matters in which the ability or right of the program to locate within a
    community is questioned;
  • Issues relating to liability for acts performed by staff members in carrying out
    their duties for the program;
  • Interpretation of federal, state, and local laws regulating the prescribing, dis-
    pensing, and administering of controlled substances; and,
    • The legal limitations and requirements that apply when a program is engaged
    in research that makes use of controlled substances or potentially hazardous
    procedures.

16.5 The coordinator of the legal assistance component shall conduct regular and
CD timely reviews of any changes in the laws or regulations significantly affecting

the program, and shall distribute to the staff written interpretations of how the changes will affect program operations and what procedures should be followed in order to comply.

16.6
CD
The program should establish at least informal relationships with the following:
• Public defenders;
• Legal aid clinics;
• Legal organizations having special knowledge, interest, or experience in drug abuse treatment;
• Federal, state, and local law enforcement agencies;
• Federal and state probation and parole authorities;
• District or states' attorneys and their assistants; and,
• Bar associations.

16.7
CD
Within the context of existing laws and rules of court, and in compliance with established ethical principles of conduct related to the practice of law, the coordinator shall develop written policies and procedures dealing with but not limited to the following:
• The legal services to be made available to clients directly by the program;
• Legal assistance costs that are to be borne by the client, if any;
• Regular review of clients' legal status to ensure that clients' legal difficulties are being addressed; and,
• The maintenance in clients' case records of a legal history that includes the client's legal status, both civil and criminal, at the time of admission and that reflects changes during the course of treatment.

16.8
CD
The program shall take all reasonable steps to ensure that a client has access to legal assistance when, in the judgment of the coordinator, the program's involvement in procuring legal assistance is warranted. The program may refuse to aid the client in procuring legal assistance whenever in the judgment of the executive director the provision of legal assistance would have an adverse effect on program operations.

16.8.1.   When the coordinator of the legal assistance component or the executive director makes a judgment that the program will not attempt to procure legal assistance for a client who has requested such assistance or whose case record reflects a legal need, the reason for not providing such assistance shall be entered in the client's case record.

16.9
C
Where a client's legal problem is evident, and with the client's consent, a legal assistance plan shall be entered in the client's case record within one month of the completion of the legal review or sooner if delay would be legally detrimental.

16.10 Where a client's legal problem is evident, and with the client's consent, a legal
D   assistance plan should be entered in the client's case record immediately upon
completion of the legal review.

16.11 When the program offers to assist a client and the client refuses such assistance,
CD   the client's signed acknowledgement that legal assistance was offered and refused should be entered in the client's case record.

16.12 When it is found to be appropriate to refer a client to a private attorney, the client
CD   shall be given the names of at least three private attorneys unless, due to the
circumstances of the client's legal situation, a particular attorney has agreed to
handle the matter at no cost or minimal cost to the client.

16.13 With the exception of a program under the direct administrative control of a law
CD E enforcement agency, correctional institution, or court, a program shall avoid
entering into any agreement or taking on any responsibility that places it in the
position of an agent of a law enforcement agency, correctional institution, or
court. A program may enter into agreements with law enforcement agencies,
correctional institutions, or courts, but only where there is clear evidence that
such agreements will in no way compromise the program's right to conduct
treatment and rehabilitation in a manner it finds appropriate, or compromise the
program's responsibilities for ensuring the confidentiality of client information.

16.14 A program may agree to accept as clients individuals who are on probation or
CD   parole, who are referred in lieu of prosecution or imprisonment, or who are
referred under civil commitment statutes when all of the following conditions
are met:
  • The referred individual or his or her guardian agrees in writing that he or she
    wishes to enter the program;
  • The individual or guardian is informed in writing, prior to admission, of the
    nature of the agreement between the program and the referring law enforce-
    ment agency, correctional institution, or court;
  • The individual or guardian is told in writing what the legal repercussions will
    be if he or she refuses to enter or remain in the program;
  • The referring law-enforcement-related agency clearly states in writing, prior to
    the individual's admission to the program, what information it requires and
    the frequency with which it requires the information;
  • The applicant is informed in writing, prior to admission, of the types of infor-
    mation to be released and the frequency with which it is to be released; and,
  • The applicant is informed, prior to admission, of the legal implications of
    refusing to allow the release of information.

16.15 At least semiannually, the coordinator shall prepare and make available a legal
CD   assistance progress report that should contain for the reporting period the following information:

- The number of clients who required legal assistance;
- The number of clients rendered legal assistance;
- The number of clients referred to legal aid agencies or private attorneys;
- The total number and types of charges pending against clients and the total number of clients against whom these charges are pending;
- The total number of cases disposed of under the provisions of criminal diversion statutes, if applicable;
- The number of individuals referred to the program under civil commitment statutes;
- The number of criminal cases in which a court discharged a client as a result of successful participation in the program; and,
- The number and types of opinions rendered to the governing body, executive director, or staff members by program attorneys.

18. Mental Health

.1 There shall be an assessment procedure for the early detection of mental health
D A problems that are either life-threatening, indicative of severe personality disorganization or deterioration, or that may seriously affect the treatment or rehabilitation process.

.2 For each applicant/client, a psychological history shall be entered in the client
D A case record. This history shall cover but not necessarily be limited to:
- History of psychological problem areas;
- Family history; and,
- Previous psychiatric treatment received.

.3 In a short-term detoxification program, where the ability to take a psychological history may be limited by the patient's condition, the program should attempt to do so prior to discharge.

.4 When indicated by an individual's psychological history or behavior, a mental
D A status examination shall be undertaken.

.5 The coordinator of the mental health component shall have responsibility for
D developing policies and procedures related to the assessment, prevention, and treatment of psychopathology, such as neuroses, personality disorders, psychophysiological disorders, transient situational disturbances, psychoses, mental retardation, organic brain disorders, and behavior disorders of childhood and adolescence.

18.5.1.   The coordinator shall develop or adopt a classification system for categorizing the types of mental health services provided to clients.

18.6
C D   At least semiannually, the coordinator of the mental health component shall prepare and make available a mental health progress report that should contain for the reporting period the following:
- The incidence of various mental health problems among applicants and clients;
- Using the classification system adopted by the program, the number of applicants and clients receiving various types of mental health services;
- The number of clients receiving medication prescribed by staff psychiatrists and physicians for the treatment of psychiatric problems, reported by class of drugs; and,
- The number of referrals made to outside mental health resources, reported by type of resource.

18.8
C D   The program should have available, at least on a consulting, as needed basis, both a qualified psychiatrist and a qualified psychologist.

18.7.1.   The coordinator may serve in one of the above mentioned positions if he or she is duly qualified.

18.9
C D   The program psychiatrist(s) shall take part in the development, review, and updating of the program formulary (see 17.3).

In situations where medication is prescribed for the treatment of a psychiatric problem, the standards dealing with the prescribing, dispensing, and administering of drugs (17.1 through 17.16) shall be followed.

18.9.1.   At least every thirty days a physician, preferably a psychiatrist, shall review the client case record of any client receiving medication for the treatment of psychiatric problems, and revise the prescription if necessary.

18.10
C D   At least informal relationships with the following outside resources shall be established:
- Acute and long-term inpatient, outpatient, and residential psychiatric facilities;
- Community mental health centers;
- Psychiatrists, neurologists, clinical psychologists, and other mental health specialists, as necessary; and,
- Individuals or agencies qualified to do psychological assessments.

21. Vocational Rehabilitation

21.1
C A   For each applicant/client there shall be an assessment of his or her vocational status, which should include:

- Vocational history;
- Educational history, including academic and vocational training; and,
- A preliminary discussion between the individual and the staff member doing the assessment concerning the individual's past experiences and attitudes toward work, present motivations or areas of interest, and possibilities for future education, training, and/or employment.

1.2   It is recommended that a vocational assessment be undertaken by a short-term **)**   detoxification program as defined in 21.1.

1.3   A program may delegate vocational rehabilitation responsibilities to an outside **C**   vocational rehabilitation agency. However, the agency must assign, with the approval of the program, a specific individual to serve as the program's coordinator of the vocational rehabilitation component, and the agency must agree to follow the provisions of the standards presented herein.

1.4   The program should attempt to establish at least informal working relationships **C**   with the following outside resources:
- The state vocational rehabilitation agency;
- The state employment service;
- Private employment agencies;
- Employers;
- Trade schools and other vocational training resources;
- General or remedial education resources;
- Colleges and universities;
- Individuals or agencies qualified to do vocational testing;
- Industrial organizations and private sector manpower groups; and,
- Trade unions.

1.5   Vocational services shall be provided in a manner consistent with an indi- **C**   vidualized written vocational rehabilitation plan. The vocational rehabilitation plan shall be developed in partnership with the client and shall reflect his or her strengths and weaknesses in the following areas:
- Current work skills and potential for improving these skills or developing new ones;
- Educational background;
- Amenability to vocational counseling
- Aptitudes, interests, and motivations for engaging in various job-related activities;
- Physical abilities;
- Skills and experiences in seeking jobs;
- Work habits as related to tardiness, absenteeism, dependability, honesty, and relations with co-workers and supervisors;
- Personal grooming and appearance; and,

- Expectations regarding the personal financial and social benefits to be derived from working.

21.6
C

As part of the vocational rehabilitation plan, a client shall receive counseling specifically oriented to his or her vocational needs. These counseling sessions should be used to increase clients' understanding of the demands of their present and future jobs, their vocational strengths and weaknesses, and their responsibilities in holding a job, and should attempt to assist clients in facing and overcoming problems related to vocational training, placement, and employment.

21.7
C

The counseling sessions should be used to review with the client the mutually agreed upon vocational rehabilitation plan to ensure that both the program and the client understand the reasons for and the objectives of the plan and to decide upon the appropriate use of relevant resources.

21.8
C

The program, either on its own or by joining with other interested agencies, shall become involved in an active program of job development, which shall include:

- Identification of those occupations in which there is a labor shortage and those with a labor surplus, as well as specific employers and industries that are characterized by labor shortages;
- Orientation programs for demonstrating to employers the employability of clients, while realistically conveying to them an understanding of the special vocational problems affecting clients;
- Identification of affirmative action employers and those who offer on-the-job training; and,
- Efforts to convince employers, unions, governmental agencies, schools, and training centers to alter discriminatory policies against individuals with drug abuse histories who are in the process of rehabilitation.

21.8.1.   Every attempt shall be made to develop jobs that range from unskilled to highly skilled, commensurate with the abilities and interests of clients.

21.8.2.   A record shall be kept of these activities, which shall include the date as well as a description of the activity, participants, and results.

21.9
C

The criteria for determining a client's job-readiness shall be stated in the client's individualized vocational rehabilitation plan. The program should not attempt to place a client until he or she is ready.

21.10
C

Prior to the scheduling of a job interview, the client shall be informed of the nature of the relationship between the program and the employer and what attempts the program will make regarding follow-up. The client should be given a description of the job duties, salary, and benefits. Clients shall not be referred to an employer until the client has given the program written authorization to do so. This authorization shall be included in the client's case record.

1 The program's obligation to meet the client's vocational needs does not end with job placement; it should also include job upgrading, career development, and the enhancement of job satisfaction. There should be regular follow-up and review of the client's vocational status. If the program wishes to discuss a client's progress with an employer, the client's written permission shall be obtained prior to contacting the employer.

12 Changes in vocational or employment status shall be entered in the client's case record and should include but not necessarily be limited to:
   • Dates of the commencement of employment or training, employer's name, brief job description, job title, and starting salary;
   • A record of all major promotions and demotions, including reasons and dates; and,
   • Dates and results of follow-up.

13 The program shall be able to demonstrate that it has procedures for keeping clients aware of vocational opportunities, using, for example, newsletters, bulletin boards, or meetings.

14 At least semiannually, the coordinator shall prepare and make available a vocational rehabilitation progress report that should contain for the reporting period the following information:
   • Employment rate for new clients entering the program;
   • Summary of major vocational problems demonstrated by clients;
   • The number of job placements attempted;
   • The number and percentage of placement attempts that led to actual placement;
   • The number and types of referrals made to outside vocational resources; and,
   • The number and types of employers and other resources contracted for the purposes of job development.

D. Consolidated Standards for Child, Adolescent and Adult Psychiatric, Alcoholism, and Drug Abuse Programs, 1979 Edition: Joint Commission of Accreditation of Hospitals

PATIENT MANAGEMENT

13 INTAKE

13.1 The acceptance of a patient for treatment shall be based on an intake procedure and assessment of the patient.

   13.1.1 Acceptance of a patient for treatment shall be based on an intake procedure that determines the following:

   a. a patient requires treatment which is appropriate to the intensity and restrictions of care provided by the program or program component; and/or

   b. the treatment required can be appropriately provided by the program or program component; and

   c. alternatives for less intensive and restrictive treatment are not available.

   13.1.2 Criteria for determining the eligibility of individuals for admission shall be clearly stated in writing.

   13.1.3 Assessment shall be done by members of the clinical staff and be clearly explained to the patient.

      13.1.3.1 The assessment shall be explained to the patient's family, when appropriate.

13.2 When a patient is found to be ineligible for admission, the reason shall be recorded in the patient intake record, and a referral to an appropriate agency or organization should be attempted.

   13.2.1 The results of that referral attempt shall be documented.

13.3 A written confidential log shall be maintained and shall indicate the nature and disposition of all referrals received by the program.

13.4 Methods of intake shall be determined by the nature of the program and the needs of the patients it is designed to serve.

   13.4.1 The program shall have written policies and procedures governing the intake process, including the following:

   a. the types of information to be obtained on all applicants prior to admission;

   b. the procedures to be followed when accepting referrals from outside agencies or organizations;

   c. the types of records to be kept on all applicants;

   d. statistical data to be kept regarding the intake process; and

   e. the procedures to be followed, including those for referrals, when an applicant is found ineligible for admission.

   13.4.2 During the intake process, every effort shall be made to assure that applicants understand the following:

   a. the general nature and goals of the program:

     b. the rules governing patient conduct and the types of infractions that can result in disciplinary action or discharge from the program;   _____

     c. the hours during which services are available in a non-residential program;   _____

     d. the treatment costs to be borne by the patient, if any; and   _____

     e. the patients' rights.   _____

13.4.3 When a patient is admitted on court order, the rights and responsibilities of the patient and family shall be explained.   _____

    13.4.3.1 This explanation shall be fully documented in the patient's record.   _____

13.4.4 Sufficient information shall be collected during the intake process so that a tentative treatment plan can be developed.   _____

13.5 The following information shall be recorded on standardized forms and shall become a part of the accepted patient's record:

     a. name;   _____

     b. home address;   _____

     c. home telephone number;   _____

     d. date of birth;   _____

     e. sex;   _____

     f. race or ethnic origin;   _____

     g. next of kin;   _____

     h. education (current school and grade if applicable);   _____

     i. marital status;   _____

     j. type and place of employment;   _____

     k. date of initial contact or admission to the program;   _____

     l. legal status, when appropriate, including relevant legal documents;   _____

    m. other identifying data as indicated;   _____

     n. date the information was gathered; and   _____

     o. signature of the staff member gathering the information.   _____

13.6 All programs which house patients overnight shall document the following items for each patient:

     a. a responsibility for financial support;   _____

     b. responsibility for medical and dental care, including consents for medical or surgical care and treatment;   _____

     c. arrangements for appropriate family participation in the treatment program;   _____

     d. arrangements for appropriate phone calls and visits when indicated;   _____

     e. arrangements for clothing, allowances, and gifts; and   _____

     f. arrangements regarding the patient's departure from the program with or without clinical consent.   _____

13.7 Staff members who will be working with the patient, but who did not participate in the initial assessment, shall be informed about the patient prior to meeting him or her.   _____

                                    Overall compliance: intake   _____

Comments and recommendations

Provide specific documentation for each 2 or 3 rating.

14. ASSESSMENT

14.1 The program shall be responsible for a complete patient assessment that includes clinical consideration of each of the fundamental needs.

    14.1.1 This shall include, but is not limited to, an assessment of the physical, psychological, chronological age, developmental, family educational, social cultural, environmental, recreational, and vocational needs of the patient.

    14.1.2 Clinical consideration of each area of the fundamental needs of the patient shall include the determination of the type and extent of special clinical examinations, tests, and evaluations necessary for a complete assessment.

14.2 The assessment of the patient's physical health shall be the responsibility of a qualified physician.

    14.2.1 The physical health assessment shall include a complete medical and drug history.

    14.2.2 In inpatient programs, the physical health assessment shall include a complete physical examination and, when indicated, a neurological assessment.

        14.2.2.1 A complete physical examination must be completed within 24 hours after admission to any adult psychiatric or child/adolescent inpatient program.

        14.2.2.2 In inpatient alcoholism and drug abuse programs, a physical examination must be completed before commencing detoxification or before administering prescription drugs.

    14.2.3 In residential and outpatient programs, documentation shall verify that a determination of the necessity of a physical examination was made prior to the development and implementation of the patient's treatment plan.

        14.2.3.1 There shall be a written procedure for determining the necessity of a physical examination.

            14.2.3.1.1 Documentation shall verify that this procedure was developed in consultation with a physician.

        14.2.3.2 The steps employed in determining the need for a physical examination shall include, but are not limited to, the following:

            a. routine inquiry of every patient of when last treated by a physician and when last complete physical examination was done;

  b. awareness of the presence of any medical problem; and
  c. what, if any, medication is being taken.

14.2.3.3 If a physical examination is determined to be necessary, the process and results of this examination
shall be documented in the patient's record.

14.2.3.4 Documentation shall verify that the physical examination is obtained during the patient's present course
of treatment.

14.2.4 Residential and/or outpatient programs shall have a written
plan for the provision of physical examinations, if such services are not directly provided by the program.

14.2.5 The physical health assessment shall include an appropriate
laboratory workup.

14.2.6 If, just prior to admission to the program, a complete physical
history has been recorded and a complete physical examination has been performed by the patient's physician, the signed
report of this examination and history may be made part of the
patient's record.

14.2.7 In addition to the requirements outlined in Sections 14.2
through 14.2.6, the physical health assessments in child and
adolescent programs shall include evaluations of the following:
  a. motor development and functioning;
  b. sensorimotor functionings;
  c. speech, hearing, and language functioning;
  d. visual functioning; and
  e. immunization status.

14.2.7.1 If a patient's immunization is not complete according
to the USPHS Advisory Committee on Control of Infectious Diseases of the American Academy of Pedi-
atrics, then the program shall complete it.

14.2.7.2 Child and adolescent programs shall have available
all necessary diagnostic tools for physical health assessments, including EEG equipment, a qualified
technician training in dealing with children and adolescents, and a properly qualified physician to inter-
pret the electroencephalographic tracing of children
and adolescents.

14.2.7.2.1 Programs without EEG equipment and
such staff must have written arrangements with another facility to provide
such services.

14.3 There shall be an assessment procedure for the early detection of mental
health problems that are life threatening or indicative of severe personality disorganization or deterioration, or that may seriously affect the
treatment or rehabilitation process.

14.3.1 For each patient, a psychological assessment shall be completed
and entered in the patient's record. The psychological assess-

ment shall include, but is not limited to, the following items:
a. history of psychological problem areas;
b. family history;
c. previous psychiatric treatment;
d. direct psychological observation and behavioral appraisal;
e. a psychodynamic appraisal;
f. when indicated, intellectual, projective, and personality testing; and
g. when indicated, evaluations of language, cognition, self-help, and social-affective and visual-motor functioning.

14.3.2 In child and adolescent programs, the psychological assessment shall also include an assessment of the developmental/chronological age of the patient, including, but not necessarily limited to, the following items:
a. a developmental history from the prenatal period to the present;
b. the rate of progress;
c. developmental milestones;
d. developmental problems;
e. an evaluation of the patient's strengths as well as problems; and
f. an assessment of the patient's current age-appropriate developmental needs, which shall include a detailed appraisal of peer and group relationships and activities.

14.4 For each patient, a social assessment shall be undertaken and shall include information relating to the following areas:
a. environment and home;
b. religion;
c. childhood history;
d. military service history;
e. financial status;
f. drug and alcohol usage among other members of the family or household;
g. evaluation of the characteristics of the social, peer-group, and environmental settings from which the patient comes;
h. evaluation of the patient's family circumstances, including the constellation of the family group, the current living situation, and all social, religious, ethnic, cultural, financial, emotional, and health factors; and
i. evaluation of the expectations of the family regarding the patient's treatment, the degree to which they expect to be involved, and their expectations regarding the length of time and type of treatment required.

14.5 For each patient, a vocational status assessment shall be undertaken which shall include the following areas:
a. vocational history;
b. educational history, including academic and vocational training; and

c. a preliminary discussion between the individual and the staff member doing the assessment concerning the individual's past experiences with and attitudes toward work, present motivations or areas of interest, and possibilities for future education, training, and/or employment. _____

14.6 A nutritional assessment shall be included in the patient's record for those patients who, for medical reasons, require a special diet regimen. _____

14.7 For each patient, an activities assessment shall be undertaken which shall include information relating to the individual's current skills, talents, aptitudes, and interests, and include assessments of the following:

a. physical abilities and limitations: _____
b. ability to financially afford various forms of activities; _____
c. amount of leisure time available; and _____
d. motivations for engaging in various activities. _____

14.8 In drug abuse programs, a legal assessment of each patient shall be undertaken which shall include the following areas as a minimum:

a. legal history; and _____
b. a preliminary discussion to determine the extent to which the individual's legal situation will influence progress in treatment and the urgency of the legal situation. _____

14.8.1 No part of these standards dealing with legal assistance is intended to contravene any established laws or rules of court or any principle of ethics related to the practice of law. Where a conflict exists between these standards and the laws or rules of court or ethical principles, said laws, rules, or principles shall prevail. _____

Overall compliance: assessment _____

Comments and recommendations
Provide specific documentation for each 2 or 3 rating.

_____

_____

_____

15. TREATMENT PLANS

15.1 Each patient shall have an individualized written treatment plan which is based upon the assessments of that patient's fundamental needs. _____

15.1.1 The treatment plan shall be developed as soon after the patient's admission as possible. _____

15.1.2 Appropriate therapeutic efforts may begin before finalization of the treatment plan. _____

15.1.3 The treatment plan shall be a reflection of the program's philosophy of treatment and shall reflect appropriate multidisciplinary input by the staff.

15.1.4   The overall responsibility of the treatment plan shall be assigned to a member of the clinical staff.

15.1.5   The plan shall specify services required for meeting the patient's needs.

15.1.6   The plan shall include referral for needed services not provided directly by the program.

15.1.7   Speech, language, academic education, and hearing services shall be available when appropriate either within the program or by written arrangement with a qualified clinician or facility in order to meet the patient's needs.

15.1.8   The treatment plan shall include clinical consideration of the patient's fundamental needs.

15.1.9   Goals necessary for the patient to achieve, maintain, and/or reestablish emotional and/or physical health and maximum growth and adaptive capabilities shall be included in the treatment plan.

> **15.1.9.1**   These goals shall be determined on the basis of the assessment of the patient and/or the patient's family.
>
> **15.1.9.2**   Specific goals with both long-term and short-term objectives and the anticipated time expected to meet these goals shall be established.
>
> **15.1.9.3**   Treatment plan goals shall be written in terms of measurable criteria.

15.1.10 The patient shall participate in the development of the treatment plan, and such participation shall be documented.

15.1.11 The treatment plan shall describe services, activities, programs, and anticipated patient actions and responses, as well as specify the staff assigned to work with the patient.

15.1.12 The treatment plan shall delineate the locations and frequency of treatment procedures.

15.1.13 The treatment plan shall designate the means for measuring the progress and/or outcome of treatment efforts.

15.1.14 The treatment plan shall delineate the specific criteria to be met for termination of treatment and aftercare services. Such criteria shall be a part of the initial treatment plan.

15.1.15 A specific plan for the involvement of the family or significant others shall be included in the treatment plan, when indicated.

15.2   Treatment procedures which place the patient at physical risk or in pain shall require special justification.

15.2.1   The rationale for the use of such procedures shall be clearly stated in the treatment plan.

15.2.2   Evidence in the treatment plan shall verify that such treatment procedures have been specifically reviewed by the head of the clinical staff before implementation.

15.2.3   The plan for such treatment procedures shall be consistent with the patient's rights and with the program's policies governing the procedures' use.

15.2.4 The clinical indications for the use of such procedures shall be documented in the patient's record.

15.2.5 The clinical indications shall outweigh the known contraindications for the individual patient.

15.3 The use of physical restraint or seclusion shall require clinical justification and shall be employed only to protect a patient from self-injury or from injuring others, and shall not be employed as punishment, as a convenience for the staff, or as a mechanism to produce regression.

15.3.1 There shall be observation and examination of the patient prior to the writing of the order for the use of physical restraint or seclusion.

15.3.2 The rationale and authorization for the use of restraint or seclusion shall be clearly set forth in the patient's record by the clinical staff member responsible for the patient.

15.3.3 The written order shall specify the length of time restraint or seclusion is to be used.

15.3.3.1 The written order of a physician, renewable every 24 hours, shall be required for the use of restraint or seclusion for a period longer than one hour.

15.3.4 The staff implementing the written order shall have documented training in the proper application of restraints and the use of seclusion.

15.3.5 All use of physical restraints or seclusion shall be reported to the head of the clinical staff daily.

15.3.6 The written approval of the head of the clinical staff shall be required when physical restraint or seclusion is utilized for the continuing treatment of a patient for longer than a 24-hour period.

15.3.7 The head of the clinical staff shall review the program's use of physical restraint and seclusion daily and investigate unusual or unwarranted patterns of utilization.

15.3.8 Physical restraint or seclusion shall be used in such a manner as not to cause any undue physical discomfort, harm, or pain.

15.3.9 Every 15 minutes, appropriate attention shall be paid to a patient in physical restraint or seclusion, especially with regard to regular meals, bathing, and use of the toilet.

15.3.10 Physical restraint or seclusion may be employed in the event of an emergency without a written order under the following conditions:

15.3.10.1 When restraint or seclusion is employed in an emergency situation, a written order for physical restraint or seclusion shall be given by a member of the clinical staff who is qualified by experience and training in the use and application of physical restraint and seclusion.

15.3.10.2 When restraint or seclusion is employed in an emergency situation, the written order of the psychiatrist or other clinical staff member responsible for the patient's individual treatment plan shall be obtained in less than four hours.

15.4 The program shall have specific written policies and procedures governing the use of electroconvulsive therapy and other forms of convulsive therapy.

15.4.1 Written informed consent of the patient shall be obtained and made a part of the patient's record. The patient may withdraw consent at any time.

15.4.2 In child and adolescent programs, electroconvulsive therapy or other forms of convulsive therapy shall not be administered unless, prior to the initiation of treatment, two qualified psychiatrists with training or experience in the treatment of children and adolescents, who are not affiliated with the treating program, have examined the patient, have consulted with the responsible psychiatrist, and have written and signed reports in the patient's record which show concurrence with the decision to administer such treatment.

15.4.2.1 For patients under the age of 13, documentation that such reviews are carried out only by qualified child psychiatrists shall be included in the patient's record.

15.4.3 In circumstances when the family and/or legal guardian are required to give written informed consent, such person(s) may withdraw consent at any time.

15.5 There shall be written policies and procedures for the initiation of lobotomies or other surgical procedures for the intervention in or alteration of a mental, emotional, or behavioral disorder to be performed on adult patients.

15.5.1 Lobotomies shall not be performed on any adult patient unless, prior to the initiation of such treatment, one qualified psychiatrist who is not affiliated with the treating program has examined the patient, consulted with the responsible psychiatrist, and written and signed a report which shows concurrence with the decision to administer such treatment.

15.5.1.1 Documentation of such consultation shall be in the patient's record.

15.5.2 Policies shall prohibit lobotomies or other surgical procedures for the intervention in or alteration of a mental, emotional, or behavioral disorder in children or adolescents.

15.6 Documentation shall verify that an evaluation of the fundamental needs of the patient has been completed prior to discharge.

15.6.1 Documentation shall confirm that this evaluation is initiated by appropriate clinical staff as early as the clinical condition permits.

15.6.2 Documentation shall confirm that this evaluation is used as the basis for the patient's long-term treatment plan.

15.6.3 Documentation shall confirm that this evaluation is available to other components of the program. _____

15.6.4 Documentation shall confirm that this evaluation is available to other community service agencies that will provide continuous care following discharge. This information shall be made available only with the written consent of the patient, consistent with the program's patients' rights policies governing the release of confidential information. _____

15.7 Progress shall be reviewed regularly at multidisciplinary case conferences that are oriented toward evaluation of the individual patient's treatment plan as well as evaluation of the patient's progress in meeting the stated treatment goals. _____

15.7.1 Results of these reviews shall be entered in the patient's record. _____

15.8 Progress notes shall be entered in the patient's record and include the following items:

a. chronological documentation of the patient's clinical course; _____
b. documentation of all treatment rendered to the patient; _____
c. documentation of the implementation of the treatment plan; _____
d. descriptions of each change in each of the patient's conditions; _____
e. descriptions of responses to and outcomes of treatment; and _____
f. descriptions of the responses of the patient, patient's family, and/ or significant others to significant intercurrent events. _____

15.8.1 Progress notes shall be dated and signed by the individual making the entry. _____

15.8.2 All entries that involve subjective interpretation of the patient's progress should be supplemented with a description of the ac-behavior observed. _____

15.8.3 Efforts should be made to secure written reports of progress and other patient records for patients receiving services from an outside resource. _____

15.8.4 When available, outside resource patient records shall be included in the patient's record. _____

15.9 Reviews of and changes in the treatment plan shall be recorded in the patient's record. _____

15.9.1 Progress and current status in meeting goals outlined in the treatment plan shall be recorded regularly in the patient's record. _____

15.9.2 Efforts by staff members to help the patient achieve stated goals shall be recorded regularly. _____

15.10 The treatment plan shall be reviewed and updated regularly. _____

15.10.1 Programs with an anticipated length of stay of under three months shall review treatment plans no less frequently than within the first 72 hours, after one week, and every two weeks thereafter for the duration of active treatment. _____

15.10.2 Programs with an anticipated length of stay of three to twelve months shall review treatment plans no less frequently than required by the schedule outlined in Section 15.10.1 for the first three months and every three months thereafter for the duration of active treatment.

15.10.3 Programs with an anticipated length of stay of longer than twelve months shall review treatment plans according to the schedules outlined in Sections 15.10.1 and 15.10.2 and every six months thereafter for the duration of active treatment.

15.10.4 In an outpatient situation, treatment plans shall be reviewed no later than after the sixth outpatient session of assessment and treatment and once a month for the first three months thereafter. Subsequent treatment plan reviews shall be held at least once every three months for the first twelve months of treatment and no less frequently than every six months following the first twelve months of treatment.

15.11 A discharge note shall be completed within 15 days after discharge and shall be in accordance with the "Patient records" section of these *Standards*.

15.12 There shall be a written aftercare plan developed, with the participation of the patient, prior to the completion of treatment.

15.12.1 The individual aftercare plan shall be designed to establish continued contact for the support of the patient.

15.12.2 The aftercare plan shall include, but not be limited to, the methods and procedures whereby the needs of the individual are met by the aftercare personnel through direct contact and/ or assistance from other community human service resources.

15.12.3 Documentation shall verify that the aftercare plan is jointly formulated by prior treatment providers, aftercare personnel, the patient, and the patient's family.

15.12.4 Documentation shall verify that the patient has a specific point of contact to facilitate obtaining needed services.

15.12.5 A periodic review and updating of the aftercare plan shall be carried out.

15.12.5.1 The frequency of review and update of the aftercare plan shall be determined jointly by the treatment providers and the patient.

15.12.6 The aftercare plan shall include criteria for reentry into primary treatment and for termination of aftercare services.

15.12.7 As a means of ensuring contact if the patient intends to relocate, the aftercare plan may include provisions for referral to another aftercare agency.

Overall compliance: treatment plans _____

Comments and recommendations
Provide specific documentation for each 2 or 3 rating.

E. National Institute on Drug Abuse Model Records Manual

F. Psychohistory Form

Patient's Maiden Name: _____ INITIAL INTERVIEW

Name (Last, first, middle initial):	Client Number:

Address:

	Month	Day	Year
Street Apartment	Date of Interview:		
City County State ZIP Code	Date of Birth:		

Telephone Number:	Length of Time at Present Address:	Place of Birth:	Sex: ☐ Male ☐ Female

Social Security Number: ☐☐☐-☐☐-☐☐☐☐   Mother's Maiden Name (Last, first, middle initial):

Wife's Maiden Name (Last, first, middle initial):
or Husband's Name   Father's first name:

In Case of Emergency, Notify:

Name (Last, first, middle initial):	Relationship:
Address:	Telephone Number:

If client is a minor, do we have permission to contact parents/guardian? ☐ Yes ☐ No--Why?

What other people can be contacted? _____

● Race/Ethnic
Background:
☐ White (Not Hispanic origin)   ☐ Hispanic--Mexican   ☐ American Indian
☐ Black (Not Hispanic origin)   ☐ Hispanic--Cuban   ☐ Asian or Pacific-Islander
☐ Hispanic--Puerto Rican   ☐ Hispanic--Other   ☐ Alaskan Native

● Marital
Status:
☐ Never married   ☐ Separated   ☐ Widowed
☐ Married   ☐ Divorced

● Living Arrangements: ☐ Alone ☐ With spouse
☐ With parents ☐ With others

● Home-
maker:
Maintains a household with one or more dependents? ☐ Yes ☐ No
Number of dependents: ☐☐   Ages of dependents: _____
Creed: ☐ Catholic   ☐ Protestant
☐ Islamic   ☐ Other
☐ Jewish   ☐ None

EDUCATION

● Highest School Grade
Completed:
☐ None
☐ Elementary through grade ___
☐ High school through grade ___
☐ College--number of years completed ___

Training Schools Attended:
☐ None
☐ Vocational
☐ Business
☐ Technical
☐ Other

● Presently Attending School
● Type of program: ☐ Education ☐ Training
Date of enrollment: _____
Area of study: _____
☐ Not Attending School

HEALTH

Have you ever had psychiatric treatment? ☐ No ☐ Yes--Explain: _____

How would you rate your present state of health? ☐ Good ☐ Fair ☐ Poor

Do you have any of these communicable diseases? ☐ Tuberculosis ☐ Hepatitis ☐ Venereal disease ☐ None of these
☐ Other (specify): _____

Do you feel you have any other medical problem? ☐ No ☐ Yes--Indicate nature of problem: _____

Are you pregnant? ☐ No ☐ Yes ☐ Don't know

Additional Comments

Number of prior admissions to any drug treatment program.   Date Disch: _____
Number of prior admissions to any Clinic this area: _____   Where? _____

Mil Svc: _____   Weight: _____   Height: _____
Type of Discharge: _____

Initial Interview--Page Two	Client Name:		Client Number:

DRUG USE HISTORY

Frequency:
0 - No use during past month
1 - Once per month
2 - Once per week
3 - Two to three times per week
4 - More than three times per week
5 - Once daily
6 - Two to three times daily
7 - More than three times daily

How Taken:
1 - Oral
2 - Smoking
3 - Inhalation
4 - Intramuscular
5 - Intravenous

Severity:
0 - Not a problem at time of admission
1 - Primary
2 - Secondary
3 - Tertiary

Types of Drugs Used	Past History			Current Use (During One Month Prior to Admission)				
	Year and Age of First Use (Year / Age)	Year of First Regular Use	Maximum Use/Dose and Frequency	Current Use (Yes or No)	Frequency of Use (Use Code)	Usual Dosage	Usual Route of Administration (Use Code)	Degree of Severity (Use Code)
Heroin								
Non-Rx Methadone								
Other Opiates or Synthetics								
Alcohol								
Barbiturates								
Other Sedatives, Hypnotics, Methaqualone								
Amphetamines								
Cocaine								
Marihuana/Hashish								
Hallucinogens (Specify, if Possible)								
Inhalants								
Over-the-Counter Drugs								
Tranquilizers								
Other(s) (Specify):								

Current Drugs of Preference: Primary: _____
                                Secondary: _____

Current Cost of Drugs Per Day: $_____

Initial Interview--Page Three	Client Name:		Client Number:

DRUG USE TREATMENT HISTORY

● Number of Prior Treatment Experiences: _____

Date of Admission	Voluntary	Involuntary	Name and Address of Treatment Facility	Type of Program Modality/ Environment	Discharge Date	Completed	Not Completed	Reason Not Completed (Use Code)

Longest Period Drug Free:

Length of Time Continuously on Drugs Since Last Withdrawal or Use:

● Number of Months Since Last Treatment Experience:

Type of Program Abbreviations:
Modality:
  Detoxification = Detox
  Methadone Maintenance = MM
  Drug Free = DF
  Other = Oth

Environment:
  Residential = Res
  Day Care = DC
  Hospitalized = In-Pt
  Prison = Pris
  Outpatient = OP

Reason for Leaving Codes:
1 = Completed Treatment--Goals fully achieved
2 = Completed Treatment--Goals partially achieved
3 = Left with facility advice
4 = Left against facility advice
5 = Noncompliance with facility rules
6 = Jailed
7 = Transferred
8 = Referred
9 = Other

Additional Comments

| Initial Interview--Page Four | Client Name: | | Client Number: |

ALCOHOL USE AND TREATMENT HISTORY

Frequency of Alcohol Consumption: (In any amount or kind)

- [ ] Every day
- [ ] 2-3 times per week
- [ ] Weekends only
- [ ] 1-2 times per month
- [ ] Binges (Specify frequency): _____

Indicate Kind and Amount Consumed on Above Occasions:

- [ ] Wine: _____
- [ ] Liquor: _____
- [ ] Beer: _____
- [ ] Combination (Specify): _____

Usual Type of Drinking:
- [ ] Always with others
- [ ] Usually with others
- [ ] Sometimes with others
- [ ] With others and alone equally
- [ ] Sometimes alone
- [ ] Usually alone
- [ ] Always alone

Longest Dry Period During Last Three Months: _____

Hospitalized/Detoxified for Alcohol Use? [ ] No [ ] Yes--How many times? _____

Additional Notes

_____
_____
_____
_____
_____
_____

LEGAL

Have you ever been arrested?   [ ] No [ ] Yes   ● Arrests During Last 24 Months: [ ]

Do you have any current legal involvement?   [ ] No [ ] Yes [ ] Probation [ ] Parole

(If client has either current or past legal involvement, please complete full Legal History as part of Initial Interview.)

If Client Is a Minor:

Have you ever been officially declared a juvenile delinquent or in need of supervision from the juvenile court?
[ ] No [ ] Yes--When: _____ Under what circumstances: _____
_____

Have you ever been committed to an institution for juvenile delinquency or a place for supervision by a juvenile court?
[ ] No [ ] Yes--How old were you at your first arrest? _____

Additional Notes

_____
_____
_____
_____
_____
_____
_____
_____
_____

Initial Interview--Page Five	Client Name:	Client Number:

EMPLOYMENT

● Current Status:
- [ ] Employed:
  - [ ] Full-time (35 or more hours per week)
  - [ ] Part-time (less than 35 hours per week)
- [ ] Unemployed:
  - [ ] Looking--has sought employment in last 30 days
  - [ ] Not Looking--has not sought employment in last 30 days
- [ ] Retired
- [ ] Leave of absence
- [ ] Other (specify): _____

Number of Months Employed in Last Two Years: _____

Usual Occupation When Employed:
- [ ] Professional, technical, managerial
- [ ] Office, clerical, sales
- [ ] Craftsman
- [ ] Entertainer, musician
- [ ] Operative
- [ ] Service worker
- [ ] Laborer
- [ ] Other
- [ ] No work experience
- [ ] Student
- [ ] Housewife

Source of Income: (Check all that apply and indicate amount)

	Client's Income	Spouse's Income	Family Income
[ ] None			
[ ] Monthly salary, if employed	$_____	$_____	$_____
[ ] Unemployment Insurance--Number of weeks remaining: _____			
[ ] Workmen's Compensation--Number of weeks remaining: _____			
[ ] Veterans benefits			
[ ] General assistance			
[ ] Social Security Insurance			
[ ] Social Security Disability			
[ ] Supplemental Security Income			
[ ] Family/friends			
[ ] Illegal activities			
[ ] Savings			
[ ] Aid to Families with Dependent Children (AFDC)			
[ ] Child support/alimony			
[ ] Other (specify): _____			
Total Monthly Income	$_____	$_____	$_____

● Do you have health insurance? [ ] None [ ] Medicaid: #_____ [ ] Medicare: #_____ [ ] CHAMPUS
[ ] Blue Cross/Blue Shield #_____ [ ] Other private insurance, specify name of company: _____
Name of subscriber, if other than   Policy #_____ Name of subscriber, if other than applicant:
applicant: _____

[ ] Health Maintenance Organization or Prepaid Group Plan--Name: _____ Number: _____
[ ] Other public funds for health care, specify: _____

Have you ever been declared eligible to receive benefits from:

	Yes	No	Receiving Benefits		Yes	No	Receiving Benefits
[ ] None							
General Relief	[ ]	[ ]	[ ]	SSI-State Suppl.	[ ]	[ ]	[ ]
Medicaid	[ ]	[ ]	[ ]	Food Stamps	[ ]	[ ]	[ ]
ADC	[ ]	[ ]	[ ]	State Title XX	[ ]	[ ]	[ ]
SSI	[ ]	[ ]	[ ]				

Are you the surviving dependent (spouse or child) of a veteran who was killed during a war?
[ ] No [ ] Yes--Deceased veteran's name: _____

MILITARY HISTORY

Were you ever a member of the armed forces? [ ] No [ ] Yes--Indicate: Rank/rating: _____
Length of service: _____ Date of discharge: _____ Type of discharge: _____
Duties performed: _____
Were you ever overseas? [ ] No [ ] Yes--Where? _____
Were you ever incarcerated while in the military? [ ] No [ ] Yes--Reasons: _____

Initial Interview--Page Six	Client Name:		Client Number:

SOURCE OF REFERRAL

- [ ] Self-referral
- [ ] General hospital
- [ ] Mental hospital
- [ ] Community Mental Health Center
- [ ] Social/community services agency
- [ ] Private physician or mental health professional
- [ ] C. I. U. or another drug treatment program

- [ ] Family or relative
- [ ] Friend
- [ ] Employer
- [ ] School
- [ ] NARA I
- [ ] NARA II
- [ ] TASC

- [ ] County/state probation
- [ ] County/state parole
- [ ] Federal probation
- [ ] Federal parole
- [ ] Police
- [ ] Other (Specify): _____

If accepted for treatment, do you have adequate transportation to this clinic? [ ] No [ ] Yes--What type? _____

Driver's License: [ ] None [ ] Currently valid [ ] Suspended until _____
[ ] Revoked [ ] Expired Why? (Explain): _____

DISPOSITION

- [ ] Accepted--Date of next appointment: _____
- [ ] Rejected--Reasons: _____

- [ ] Referred to: _____ Date of appointment: _____
- [ ] Refused treatment--Reasons: _____

Note: When an applicant is found to be ineligible or inappropriate for admission (i. e., rejected or referred), the reason and the course of action taken must be recorded.

Admission Type:
- [ ] First admission
- [ ] Readmission
- [ ] Transfer admission from: [ ] CODAP [ ] Non-CODAP

Modality Admitted to:
- [ ] Detoxification
- [ ] Methadone Maintenance
- [ ] Drug free
- [ ] Other

Environment Admitted to:
- [ ] Prison
- [ ] Residential
- [ ] Day care
- [ ] Outpatient
- [ ] Hospital

INITIAL ASSESSMENT

1. Truthfulness and Accuracy of Client's Responses During Interview:

_____
_____
_____
_____
_____
_____
_____
_____

2. Client Characteristics Requiring Consideration In Developing Treatment Plan:

_____
_____
_____
_____
_____
_____
_____
_____

Initial Interview--Page Seven	Client Name:	Client Number:

3. Apparent Areas of Client Strength:

_____

_____

_____

_____

_____

_____

4. Apparent Areas of Client Weakness:

_____

_____

_____

_____

_____

_____

_____

5. Other Significant Observations: (Note: Must include any prior history of mental illness)

_____

_____

_____

_____

_____

_____

6. List Apparent Problems and Current Priority of Each: (Note--Use these problems to initiate Treatment Plan)

_____

_____

_____

_____

_____

7. Staff Member Responsible for Monitoring Treatment (Primary Counselor):

_____

_____

_____

Date:	Signature:
Date Reviewed:	Signature of Physician (Required for Methadone Program):

PSYCHOSOCIAL HISTORY Page One	Client Name:	Client Number:

Relationships:

1. Childhood Family Structure:

Name/Relationship	Your Relationship with Them: Good	Fair	Poor	Aware of Your Habit: Yes	No	Drug User: Yes	No
____	☐	☐	☐	☐	☐	☐	☐
____	☐	☐	☐	☐	☐	☐	☐
____	☐	☐	☐	☐	☐	☐	☐
____	☐	☐	☐	☐	☐	☐	☐
____	☐	☐	☐	☐	☐	☐	☐
____	☐	☐	☐	☐	☐	☐	☐
____	☐	☐	☐	☐	☐	☐	☐

2. Present Family Structure:

____	☐	☐	☐	☐	☐	☐	☐
____	☐	☐	☐	☐	☐	☐	☐
____	☐	☐	☐	☐	☐	☐	☐
____	☐	☐	☐	☐	☐	☐	☐
____	☐	☐	☐	☐	☐	☐	☐
____	☐	☐	☐	☐	☐	☐	☐
____	☐	☐	☐	☐	☐	☐	☐

3. Significant Others:

____	☐	☐	☐	☐	☐	☐	☐
____	☐	☐	☐	☐	☐	☐	☐
____	☐	☐	☐	☐	☐	☐	☐

4. At present, which of the individuals designated in questions 1, 2, and 3 do you consider to be most significant in your life, and why? ____

5. What are your reasons for designating "good" relationships in answer to 1,2, and 3? ____

6. What are your reasons for designating "poor" relationships in answer to 1,2, and 3? ____

7. How do the people listed in 1, 2, and 3 perceive your problem? ____

8. Are any of the people listed aware that you are receiving treatment? ☐ No ☐ Yes--What are their expectations? ____

9. Are any of the people listed willing to become involved in your treatment? ☐ No ☐ Yes--Specify: ____

10. How do you perceive problems that are presently faced by family members in areas such as education, employment, legal involvement, health, drug usage, etc.? ____

(Note to Counselor: Can these be verified? ☐ Yes ☐ No)

Psychosocial History--Page Two	Client Name:		Client Number:

11. How would you rate your relationships with the following: **Males:** Good Fair Poor **Females:** Good Fair Poor
    Friends/peers ☐ ☐ ☐   ☐ ☐ ☐
    Authority figures ☐ ☐ ☐   ☐ ☐ ☐

12. What are your reasons for designating "good" relationships in question 11? _____
_____

13. What are your reasons for designating "poor" relationships in question 11? _____
_____

14. Past Living Arrangements (Including Childhood)
    (1) How many places did you live? _____

    (2) If you lived in more than one place, what were the reasons for moving? _____

    (3) What was the longest period that you lived in any one place? _____

    (4) With whom did you live during this longest period? _____

    (5) If at any time you did not live with your natural family, with whom did you live? _____
    _____

15. Living Arrangements--During the 12-month period prior to entering this treatment program:
    (1) How many places did you live? _____
    (2) What was the longest period that you lived at any one place? _____
    (3) With whom did you live during this longest period? _____

    (4) With whom are you living now? _____

16. Sexual Orientation
    (1) What were your impressions of sex during your early life? _____
    _____
    (2) From whom did you learn about sex? _____
    (3) Have your impressions about sex changed? _____ In what way? _____
    _____ Why? _____

    (4) How would you classify yourself sexually? ☐ Heterosexual ☐ Homosexual ☐ Bisexual ☐ Other
    (5) How would you rate your degree of satisfaction with your sex life? ☐ Satisfied ☐ Dissatisfied
    (6) Do you believe that drugs interfere with your sexual activity? ☐ No ☐ Yes--Explain: _____
    _____

17. Money Management
    (1) How do you generally handle money when you have it? Specify: _____
    _____

    (2) Do you presently owe money? ☐ No ☐ Yes--To whom? _____ How much: _____
    _____   _____
    _____   _____
    _____   _____
    _____   _____

Psychosocial History--Page Three	Client Name:		Client Number:

18. Recreational Activities:

(1) In the past year have you engaged in any of the following activities? (Check all that apply)

Frequency

	Daily	Weekly	Less than Weekly
Parties	☐	☐	☐
Dancing	☐	☐	☐
Watching television	☐	☐	☐
Writing	☐	☐	☐
Painting or sculpting	☐	☐	☐
Theatre	☐	☐	☐
Listening to music	☐	☐	☐
Playing musical instrument	☐	☐	☐
Movies	☐	☐	☐
Reading	☐	☐	☐
Museums or art galleries	☐	☐	☐

Frequency

	Daily	Weekly	Less than Weekly
Spectator sports events	☐	☐	☐
Sports activities--Specify: ___			
Camping	☐	☐	☐
Physical conditioning	☐	☐	☐
Hobbies--Specify:___	☐	☐	☐
Other--Specify: ___	☐	☐	☐
___	☐	☐	☐
___	☐	☐	☐

(2) How do you currently spend your leisure time? ___

19. Abuse History:

(1) Were you an abused child? ☐ No ☐ Yes--How: ☐ Mentally ☐ Physically ☐ Emotionally ☐ Sexually
By whom? ___

(2) Have you been abused since you have been an adult? ☐ No ☐ Yes--How: ☐ Mentally ☐ Physically
☐ Emotionally ☐ Sexually   By whom? ___

(3) Do you think you have the potential for abusing others? ☐ No ☐ Yes--Explain: ___

20. Interest in Recovery:

(1) Do you believe you have any serious problems? ☐ No ☐ Yes ☐ Maybe
If Yes or Maybe, specify: ___

If Yes or Maybe, do you believe that you need help for these problems? ☐ No ☐ Yes ☐ Maybe

(2) Do you believe that other people (family, parole officer, etc.) feel that you have any serious problems?
☐ No ☐ Yes   Maybe
If Yes or Maybe, specify: ___

(3) Do you believe that other people feel that you need help for these problems? ☐ No ☐ Yes ☐ Maybe

(4) In the past, have you received treatment for psychological problems somewhere other than a drug program?
☐ No ☐ Yes--Indicate:
Where: ___
By whom: ___
Dates of attendance--From ___ to ___   Nature of problem: ___

(5) Are you presently receiving treatment for psychological problems somewhere other than a drug program?
☐ No ☐ Yes--Indicate:
Where: ___
By whom: ___
Dates of attendance--From ___ to ___   Nature of problem: ___

21. Is there anything about which we haven't asked you that you think we should know? ___

Psychosocial History--Page Four	Client Name:	Client Number:

22. <u>Note to Counselor</u>: Review responses to questions regarding client's military history (Initial Interview, page five) for psychosocial follow-up.

PSYCHOSOCIAL ASSESSMENT

Include client's strengths and weaknesses. Evaluate current status and priorities. List all problems in Treatment Plan.

Signature of Interviewer:

Name Index

Subject Index

Abstinence, 4
Acting-out behavior, 23
Addiction, 9, 35
    Jaffee definition, 37
    WHO definition, 36
Addiction, heroin, 15
    characteristics of, 25
    as chronic problem, 23, 114, 167
    etiological factors, 25
    secondary gains, 25
    sociocultural factors, 25
Addict Rehabilitation Center, 6
Addiction system, 27
Aftercare treatment, 4
    see also Community houses; Day-
        care centers; Halfway houses;
        Multimodality approaches to
        treatment.
Alcohol, 3
Alcoholics Anonymous, 22, 25
Alcoholism:
    conjoint treatment with drug abuse
        16–17, 30
    cultural variations in incidence, 38

similarities to drug abuse, 136
Simmel typology, 22
synergism with barbiturates,
    42–43
withdrawal from, 42–43
Amphetamines, 3
    active–reactive phases, 44
    adaptive users, 42–43
    "crash," 42
    escapist users, 42–43
    NIDA treatment study, 18–19
    physical effects, 42
    psychic effects, 42
    treatment of narcolepsy and
        hyperactivity, 51–42
    withdrawal, 42
    withdrawal syndrome, 42
"Angel dust," 16
    see also Phencycladine (PCP); "Roc-
        ket fuel"
Antagonists, see Narcotic antagonists
Antidepressants, 26, 30
    see also Tranquilizers
Authority: see civil commitment; Coer-